What Others Say About #yourmoney

"#yourmoney is a tremendous resource to support our work in Scottish Schools. It's full of relevant details and is highly readable – a must read for young people who want to manage their money effectively. Always keep this in a safe place...like your money."
The Stewart Ivory Financial Education Trust

***

"#yourmoney will help you take control of your finances, guide you in making some of the most important financial decisions of your life and help you understand the basics of banking so it works for rather than against you. It is an accessible read and one that you can keep referring to over time."
– Lily LaPenna, founder and CEO of MyBnk

***

"Today's students are entering a world of record tuition fees and rising unemployment and a slew of money management books have hit the shelves in response. Jeannette A Lichner's *#yourmoney* takes a pared-down approach to some of the most tedious but inevitable financial issues facing young people today. The result is a veritable survival guide to the scary world of finance: from HMRC, to student loans, to achievable savings goals.

There are a few very basic money-saving tips, such as 'avoid getting mugged', but the accessible language, personal anecdotes and inspirational quotes make it one of the more manageable additions to the financial books marketplace.

For veterans of the financial crisis, and financially astute young adults, there will be no huge revelations here. But for young people setting out on the road to financial independence, *#yourmoney* will be a must-read."
– Regional newspaper book review

***

"This is a personal finance book for real people in the real world – two hundred and thirty pages jammed full of common sense, wisdom, and practical information that everyone needs to know."
– Isaac T Tabner CFA, DipPfs, personal finance lecturer

***

"I found #yourmoney to be bite-size, relevant and engaging. Though aimed at the 16–25 age bracket, I think its teachings are very worthwhile for people of older ages too."
– James, 28

***

The advice and information I gained from reading #yourmoney was invaluable. The clarity and detail which Jeanette provides help in explaining how important it is to be on top of one's personal finances. In the same way a tourist might take a Lonely Planet abroad, I think everyone should take this book with them through senior school, university, and the start of a career."
– Piers, graduate student starting his first job

***

"We will recommend this book to the sixth form for extra reading because it is an excellent resource, very useful and clearly set out."
– Senior school headmistress

***

"This excellent and much-needed book fills a gap for parents and for their offspring, and for once the publisher's blurb and the strap line are WYSIWYG: it really does answer all the important questions about earning, spending and saving for the teenager, for the university student, and for others. Jeannette Lichner puts across her lessons in a clear prose style, which commands attention without – as it could easily be – being bossy, and there is a bright idea, clever note or vital tip on nearly every page. #yourmoney kept my undergraduate daughter absorbed in the back of the car, and once she had reached university, started her budgeting and saving. This is an essential life-style book which every parent should read and give a copy to each of their children."
– Peter, parent of a 20-year-old

***

"#yourmoney: a book which explains all the basic fundamentals of finance and much more! All the information you wished you had been taught at school when you first earned money of your own or received it is contained in the various chapters. An excellent read!"
– Hannah, university graduate in first job

***

"An accessible book aimed at young adults starting out in the world, *#yourmoney* is a comprehensive guide to getting to grips with your bank balance, but also offers a refreshing take on personal finance for both young and old. Dealing with the practicalities of everyday money as well as obstructive jargon, this book will be a trusted companion."
– Moneywise magazine

***

"I was surprised by how much I enjoyed this book – who would have thought that a book about money would be so easy to read! I liked the way it was set out in digestible chapters that dealt with specific topics, and I learned lots of things I had not known or understood before. I found the section on what to do with your savings particularly enlightening, and the section on spending really made me think about some of the decisions that I make every day (both good and bad!). The short stories and quotes brought the concepts to life and encouraged me to consider how these matters might apply to me. A great introduction to making the most of your money."
– Nick, aged 25

#yourmoney

Everything You Need to Know About
Earning, Spending and Saving

Jeannette A Lichner

CISI

CHARTERED INSTITUTE FOR
SECURITIES & INVESTMENT

First published in Great Britain in 2012 by the
Chartered Institute for Securities & Investment,
20 Fenchurch Street, London, EC3M 3BY

© Jeannette A Lichner, 2016

This edition revised July 2016

10 9 8 7 6

ISBN: 978-1-910590-66-9

Printed and bound in Great
Britain by Allander Print Ltd

Acknowledgements

A heartfelt thank you to all of those people who were so generous with their time and encouragement as I created this book.

Thank you to the Chartered Institute for Securities & Investment (CISI) for supporting me in publishing the original edition and each subsequent version. Their commitment and contribution to the campaign for improving the level of financial understanding amongst young people is inspiring.

And a huge thanks to my family: Andrew, Jess and Kit, who sustain me in everything I do.

Foreword

ALMOST FIVE YEARS AGO we produced the first edition of #yourmoney which addressed the pressing need for financial facts, clear definitions and explanations for the sometimes impenetrable jargon of the financial industry. The aim of the book, then and now, is to provide guidance and to offer straightforward, impartial advice on how #yourmoney works and how you can make it go further.

Our 2016 edition has never been more relevant as the financial world evolves quickly with new products and new rules amidst an ever changing global economic world, particularly as the UK works out when, and how, it will disengage from the European Union. Already we are seeing reports of inflation rising significantly which could mean higher interest rates alongside international creditors now regarding the UK as a riskier place to invest – all of which will affect #yourmoney..

This edition has been revised to reflect the major changes during the year, amongst which are new tax rates, saving initiatives, pension products and the growth of contactless payments cards – something that didn't exist five years ago.

Within these pages you will find a wealth of information providing answers, solutions and tips relating to many of the simple (and not so simple) questions.

The Chartered Institute for Securities & Investment (CISI) is delighted to continue to support this book and believes this is one of the best resources for young people.

Surprisingly, even today, there is no other book which so succinctly covers the topics an individual needs to understand and manage money – it explains the principles of budgeting, reveals how your tax code works and deciphers the alphabet soup of financial jargon, helping you to understand the difference between AERs, APRs, direct debits and standing orders.

The response from readers has been exceptionally positive. Here is what the Stewart Ivory Financial Education Trust said about the 2015 edition: "It's relevant, it's readable and it's realistic. #yourmoney is really helpful to us in reinforcing our messages to young people about managing money. Always keep this in a safe place, like your money."

It is encouraging that financial literacy was added to the core curriculum in schools from 2014 and this book provides a useful accompanying practical guide both for students and their teachers.

#yourmoney is a book that provides real value to the reader and should be essential reading for anyone starting out in the world on their own and having to manage their own money. It is equally relevant for the 16 year old who has a first job and to those going to University.

The CISI already works closely with many schools and colleges whose students take its professional qualifications, some of which attract UCAS points and are also the first rung on the ladder in the financial services industry.

The CISI believes so strongly in financial education and in the relevance of this book that, through its Education Charity, it has donated copies to schools up and down the country whose pupils are enrolled on the CISI qualification programme.

I hope you will want to invest time in reading it, either in bite-sized chunks or all the way through. In return, you will have a much greater understanding of how to make the most of #yourmoney.

Simon Culhane, Chartered FCSI
Chief Executive, Chartered Institute for Securities & Investment
July 2016

The CISI is the professional body for the investment industry in the UK and many global financial centres. We have 40,000 members worldwide, most of whom have sat CISI qualifications to become competent in their chosen job role.

Through our unique schools and colleges programme, which comprises relevant industry examinations and practitioner engagement, we provide clear pathways to employment for those aspiring to a career in finance, whether this is directly from school or from university.

Contact Richard Bennett, Assistant Director for Education, at richard.bennett@ cisi.org to discover how your school can get involved.

cisi.org/education
+44 20 7645 0714

Contents

THIS BOOK DOES exactly what it says on the cover – in it you will find clear explanations of everything you need to know about money. I wrote it because I wanted to make sure you, and others like you, have what you need to control your financial destiny – to make every money decision one that you will be happy with in hindsight. I also wanted to help you avoid making some of the same small and large money mistakes that so many people make at your stage of life, just because they don't understand how things work. The book has been updated to reflect changes in taxes and other areas of money that will matter to you, and I have also incorporated feedback from first edition readers.

The book is written primarily, but not only, for 16–25-year-olds because that is when most people become financially independent and start making money-related decisions that have long-term implications. That is a critical time to lay down good money management practices. Having said that, we will discuss attitudes to money and you need to be aware that your attitude to money was most likely formed by the age of 7! It is written in a straightforward, pragmatic style, so I hope that you will also say, "I understand that now." I wanted the book to be entertaining, so I have included relevant quotations, newspaper references, tips and personal anecdotes to keep you interested and make the explanations and topics "real".

You can read this book a few different ways: you may like to read it page by page, from the beginning to the end; you may want to skim the table of contents and read chapters about issues you are currently facing; or you may prefer to flip through the whole book, scanning what is there, and then put it on your book pile for "sometime later" when you need it. Whatever your approach, I suggest you have a pen (real or virtual) in hand, so you can actively engage in the question sections, make notes of things you want to research further and mark things that you want to come back to later.

The first few chapters explore values and attitudes to money. These are important in helping you understand what influences the money decisions you make, consciously or not. That way, you will be able to figure out why you make the earning, spending and saving choices you do, and decide if you want to change anything about your approach. You can then read about specific money topics like budgeting, getting paid, banking and insurance, before turning your attention to big money decisions like buying cars and renting or buying where you live. Next comes information about credit scores, economics and financial pitfalls to avoid. The final chapter includes "Relevant Readings" that I couldn't fit in elsewhere but wanted to include because they are rich in useful information. In case you are wondering why I felt qualified to write this book, let me give you the three main reasons. First, the majority of my 30-plus-year working career has been in banking, so I understand this stuff. Secondly, I have a daughter and son and have seen just how difficult it is to learn about these things and the money they lost along the way. And finally I have been told I have an ability to explain complicated things in a way that people can understand them. I hope you agree with that last point!

I hope you enjoy reading this book as much as I enjoyed writing it.

Jeannette

Chapter One

Money Habits

I N THIS CHAPTER you will explore your money habits. To do that, I ask you to look at two things. First, think about what you do on a day-to-day basis that involves money in some way. Secondly, consider the values and attitudes you bring to money decisions and how those influences have come to be. The reason for doing this is because, armed with this information, you will be able to make better decisions about how you want to manage your money going forward – making the right decisions for yourself about earning, spending and saving.

Let's start by considering the number of money decisions you make on an average day. How many would you say that is? You might think "not many", or "a few", or "lots". When I started gathering information I was surprised by just how many conversations that I eavesdropped on had a money angle to them. I repeatedly heard comments like the ones below (fill in the XXXs to make the comment reflect your reality). Do they sound familiar?

- "Can I go out tonight?" "Okay, let's go out." "Where can we go?"
- "Can I go on holiday? – to Cornwall? Or Croatia? Or XXX?"
- "Let's go out to eat at XXX." "Let's cook something at my place and then go out."
- "I have to earn some money over the holidays to pay for XXX."
- "The train is a rip-off – £200 return. If I had booked it a month ago it would have been £45. It's cheaper if I travel after 7pm."
- "Where did my money go this month?"
- "How come I have money in my account? What will I do with it?"
- "Where will I get the money for XXX?"

Think about the time you spent with your friends over the last few days and how many of the discussions you had, or things you did together, involved money in some way. Chances are that you are spending money without even thinking about it. You may be surprised at what you find when you focus on this.

It may be that you haven't had to think much about money. Maybe you've been financially supported by your parents and they have replenished your money supply whenever you asked them to. Or maybe you have thought a lot about it. Perhaps you've worked throughout the school year or holidays, earned all your own spending money, saved up for university or to buy something special. Or perhaps your parents did give you money and you've had to manage that money really carefully to get through each month. Your financial situation may be any of those and anything in between. Whatever your situation, now is a good time to start paying more attention to your money, giving more thought to the choices you make, consciously or otherwise, and evaluating whether you want to make changes to what you are currently doing.

EVERYDAY MONEY DECISIONS

If you look more closely at your typical day, what money decisions do you make? The box below contains a list of what your day may involve and a few money choices you may make at the time or beforehand. Go beyond what I have included here to get a full picture of your typical day.

- Get up, shower (what soap? shampoo?), phone/text a friend (landline or mobile?) to meet up before class or work.
- Go online to check your email, Facebook, sports scores, the weather, the news. (Free, charge to access?)
- Meet a friend at a coffee shop, have a takeaway coffee and something to eat. (Or coffee and breakfast at home?)
- Go to classes or work. (Walk, cycle, take the bus, take the tube, drive?)
- Time for lunch. (Eat at uni/college/work? On a self-catering or catered food plan? Have a meal deal from a chemist or shop? Have lunch at a pub or restaurant? Eat what you made at home earlier? Go home to eat?)
- After classes/work (drive, walk?) to the gym (do you have a good deal?) and then to visit a friend. (Spend anything there?)
- Check your emails and maybe buy a few things online that you got emails about. (Needed or wanted what you bought?)
- Settle down to work or study. (Heating on or off? Lights on or off in rooms you passed through on your way to your desk?)
- Meet up with friends for dinner (in halls, at the pub, at home?) and plan a holiday. (Is it really what you want to do? How will you pay for it? What will you have to give up in order to pay for it?)

What did you find? Did you come up with anything surprising? Maybe the total number of money decisions you made surprised you. Or maybe the number of money decisions you made in advance, like your mobile phone contract, your shampoo and your internet access package, was surprising. Maybe you found that you spend much more money in one day, without thinking about it, than you expected. Or maybe you spend less than you expected? You may find it a fun challenge to see how low you can get your one day number – or how high?

> "Where does my money go?" my daughter asked me with a tone of despair a few years ago. She was not amused when I said, "Every time you use your mobile for a call or a text, or hop in the car, you are spending money."

I'm not suggesting that you need to think long and hard about every money decision. What is important is to know when to invest time evaluating options and when not to. As a general rule, if you're spending a big chunk of money or committing to something for a long period of time, it pays to be thoughtful. On the flip side, if it is a small amount of money on a one-off item, just get on with it. Here is an example: debating with yourself every time you pick up your phone is not a good use of your time, but debating with yourself when you are organising a new mobile phone contract is.

How often, if ever, do you and your friends have differing views about doing something because of the money involved? Do you always agree on spending for things like phones, going to the pub, going to sports matches or concerts, shopping for clothes or going out to eat? It would be surprising if you always did! Some of your friends, or you, may "have to have" the latest and greatest of whatever (phone, clothes, sports equipment) and some may not. Some may like to hold onto their money and others may spend it without thinking. Some may love to "flash their cash" and others may be downright miserly. Some of your friends may have what seems like lots of money available to them and others may seem to have little, which may impact their perspective. Have you ever felt uncomfortable for yourself or for a friend because of something to do with money? How did you handle it? How would you handle it next time?

> It isn't unusual to make money decisions without realising what you are thinking. Someone recently pointed out to me that I am always willing to spend money on a meal out but am really hesitant about buying shoes or clothes.

Sometimes it is hard to decide what to do when you face a money decision. A few examples: Should you work all weekend rather than do something with your friends? Should

A survey of students revealed that 70% received pocket money when they were growing up. 70% recall that their early spending was on sweets; Pokemon cards, toys and ice creams also came up as frequent spending choices.

you spend your money on that new phone or going to a concert? Can you recall having a particularly difficult time making a decision or helping a friend make one? The debate always seems to end up being around whether something is "worth it" or not. But how do you figure out if something *is* worth it until "it" is done? Those decisions can be particularly hard if the sums are relatively large, because each of you may be in a different financial situation. Spending £20, if it is all the money you will have for the next week, is a different proposition from when it is all the money you will have for the next month. So, if you and your friends are in different money places, it's totally natural for you to have different views and judgements about what to do with your money. Being aware that those differences exist is useful to avoid falling out about a decision to do or buy something.

As you go about your daily routine, think about the money decisions you make and what may be influencing you. And be in tune with your friends to explore how they make their decisions and what may be influencing them.

EARLY MONEY MEMORIES

Try to think back on when you were little and first became aware of money. Then think about how your thoughts about money have evolved and how your life experiences so far have contributed to shaping your current perspective.

Here are a few questions that may help prompt you as you reflect:

- Do you remember constantly wanting things you saw advertised on TV?

"Nearly 40% of Britons run out of money before pay day. Almost half of families living on more than £70,000 suffer money worries." Kantar Media, May 2015

- What did your parents say when you asked them to get you the same stuff that kids in your class had?

- Do you remember being totally unaware about money? (I was told some lovely stories by parents about their young children marking up Argos and Toys "R" Us catalogues to show everything they wanted.)

- The first time you had your own money to spend, what was the first big spending decision you made?

- When did you start getting pocket money or an allowance?

- When you started earning your own money, what did it feel like? What did you do with it?

Think of your great and not so great personal money stories.

YOUR ATTITUDE TO MONEY – INFLUENCES FROM THE PAST

Thinking about your upbringing, and its influence on your life now, is useful in helping you figure out of why you think about money the way you do and why you do the earning, spending and saving that you do. So take a few minutes to recall what growing up was like for you and how money featured.

> *The first bit of financial responsibility for my kids was when they rode bikes to the village shop to spend the 20 pence we gave them – it was always spent on sweets. They deliberated for ages as to which ones to buy. Those were the days – how much pleasure for only 20 pence! They were so happy because they decided what to buy all on their own.*

Every adult I know can recall what his (I will use "his" to mean his and her throughout this book) family's financial situation was like when he was growing up and the impact that upbringing had on his values and life. When I collected people's stories, which I did from a wide range of backgrounds, the same topics kept coming up as major shapers of current money attitudes. I have posed them as questions to help you with some self-reflection.

- Was your family well off, middling, or struggling financially? What was your family's situation compared with other families around you? When did you become aware of any differences? How did they make you feel?

- Did you grow up in a one-parent household? Or with both parents? Or with other family members?

- What family members did you see going to work on a regular, frequent or infrequent basis? Was your family partially or fully reliant on government benefits?

- What financial choices did your parents, or other adults responsible for you, make? What did they choose to spend money on, if they were able to make choices? What was considered a "luxury" in your home?

- What was the view on education? Holidays? Eating out? Owning a home?

- How were possessions treated? Valued and protected? Disposable?

- What was used to pay for things – cash or credit cards? Were you aware of debts – growing credit card balances, overdrafts, or loans?

> *My three sisters and I have the same overall attitude to money – we are pretty careful, probably because our parents emigrated to the US quite late in life, with very limited financial resources. But we make very different individual earning, spending and saving decisions.*

- Were there open discussions about money – earning, spending and saving it? What were they like?

Your sense of financial independence and responsibility will also have been influenced by your home life. The questions below relate to your attitude emerging from that:

- Did your parents give you spending money? How old were you when you started to receive it?
- Did you have to work for that money by doing things around your home?
- When did you start earning your own money?
- How financially independent do you think you are now?

Do you ever wonder why your brothers and sisters, if you have them, have different attitudes to money, even though you grew up together? It is because your perspective on money will have been influenced not only by your life at home, but also by your own perception of what was going on there and by all of your experiences beyond your home. In other words, your money values are specific to you.

Outside of home, the friends you grew up with will have had the biggest impact on you in all areas of your life. Consider them and their financial backgrounds, as well as what you learned from them, and they from you.

TODAY'S INFLUENCES ON YOUR ATTITUDE

Your attitude towards earning, spending and saving money will continue developing throughout your life, always shaped to some extent by your past but updated for new influences. The primary influences in your life today are likely to include:

Your friends – you, like most people, probably have a desire to be part of a group, to "fit in" with the crowd you spend time with. It isn't therefore surprising that the lifestyles your friends lead, their families' financial situations and how they make money decisions are going to impact you. When I was writing this book, many people shared stories about feeling awkward because they couldn't buy or do things that some of their friends could. I noticed that people only talked about having less than others, never about being the one "with the most". (There is something about human nature there which is not so great.) You and your friends may also have differing views about earning money. Some of your friends may work, or may have worked, during school terms and/or holidays and some may not have. Some of your friends may feel they have to work really hard to earn money and some may have a more casual approach to work. It is useful to notice those differing attitudes, consider what impact they are having on you and make sure you are happy with the attitude you have.

A friend's son provided a relevant anecdote. He told me about his end of 6th form trip to Europe with a group of good friends. What was supposed to be a great trip went a bit flat when some of the group had only a bit of money to spend after paying for their flights and hotel and others had lots of money to spend. Some wanted to go to expensive bars and restaurants and others couldn't. There was tension all around, which was a sad outcome for something they had all looked forward to for so long.

Your friends' money decisions are influenced by their pasts, but you'll find you can't predict the future from the past. You may notice that some friends who grew up surrounded by money are very careful with it to the point of being a bit "tight", and some friends who had very little money growing up are now carefree (even careless) with their money. And vice versa and every possibility in between.

Hobbies and interests – the types of activities you get involved with will impact your perspective on money. For example, if you get involved in expensive things, you will probably need to do some earning and saving. If your interests are low-cost, you may not be driven to do the same. Some hobbies and interests such as cycling or serious photography require big up-front investments. Some are expensive on the day, like going to watch sports matches or concerts. On the other hand, some sports like running and walking are nearly free, so an unlikely source of financial influence. Socialising definitely can be expensive and that does count as a hobby! The amount of money you need to support your interests may influence your choice of hobby, may influence your attitude to earning money, and most definitely will influence your spending of money.

College or university – the environment you are in will shape you. At your college or university you will meet, or will have met, people from a wide range of financial backgrounds. You are likely to meet people who are financially better off and worse off than you. You may also get glimpses into the financial values of your friends' families. Try to avoid leaping to assumptions about people based on what you see, as you will be working with limited information. For example, if your friend lives in a huge house you may assume he is wealthy; if he lives in a small house he isn't; if the family has a Bentley they must be wealthy, and if they drive an old banger they aren't. You never really know. Families make all sorts of choices about spending the money they have, however much that is. Once they have met their basic needs, they spend money on what they value, be it travel, property, cars, education, eating out, or other things. Back to my earlier statements: used Bentleys are not expensive to buy but they are expensive to run. Some people choose to invest all their money in their house and have little excess cash – they are property rich/cash poor. And sometimes people put up a façade that all is financially fine when it isn't. So avoid gauging an individual or family financial situation from how you see people spending their money. Take the opportunity to observe the money values and attitudes of the wide range of people you meet during this phase of your life and think about what influence you want them to have on your attitude.

Work colleagues – whether you work part-time or full-time, chances are this group is one that you may want to "fit in with". If you are working full-time you are likely to spend more time with your colleagues than with anyone else in your life. Be aware of the varying views on money that you come across and once again observe the range of perspectives and financial situations of your colleagues. It is very easy to fall into the same spending patterns as those you work with and you can inadvertently get carried along with the crowd. It can be really hard to say "no thanks, I want to save my money" when everyone is going out after work. It is also hard to say "no" when the group starts planning a weekend away; or when everyone decides to go watch a big rugby match. You may think it would be a real black mark if you don't go along with the crowd. People I spoke with all thought that would be the case for them. But, when I asked them how they would react if someone turned down a suggestion of their own, they said it would be fine. So don't assume you will be harshly judged for opting out of something because it's what you choose to spend your money on.

Alcohol and drugs – when I collected stories about losing or wasting money, I frequently heard stories that involved an element of alcohol or other drugs. These included: "losing" money during nights out; forgetting to take money out of the cash machine that had been withdrawn; and "wasting" money on very long taxi rides home. Your decisions about drink and drugs are yours, but do be aware that, if you are partaking, it is easy to lose track of what you are doing with your money. I heard a few good ideas to help minimise the risk of wastage (no pun intended). The most frequent suggestion was to take only the amount of money you really want to spend with you, when you go out for an evening and don't take your cash machine card. Since you don't want to have to make a dangerous journey home, because you have no money, stick with your friends and have one of you stay sober enough to make sure everyone gets home safely. (Can't help it – I'm a mum!)

HOW WOULD YOU DESCRIBE YOUR MONEY VALUES AND ATTITUDE?

Now that you have explored the past and present influences on your attitude to money, take a moment or two to consolidate your thinking about what your views really are. What money situations have you felt uncomfortable with? Or noticed others feeling uncomfortable with? How would you describe your character? What do you value, e.g. are willing to work or save for? How do you like to spend your money? How do you decide what is "worth it" or not? How do you feel about working and earning money?

When it comes to spending money, people tend to fall into one of four categories. Work through the questions that follow, to see which one best describes you.

What Kind of Money Personality are You?

1. When you earn or receive money, you are most likely to:

   A. Spend it as soon as you see something you like?
   B. Put it into your bank current account as you are likely to spend it soon?
   C. Put it directly into a savings account to fund something expensive you are saving for?

2. When your phone bill arrives at the end of the month, your reaction is likely to be:

   A. Shocked beyond words and thinking, "How did I spend so much?"
   B. Pleased that you are a bit over or under your contract.
   C. Pleased that you are well under your contract again this month and thinking about calling the provider to renegotiate your contract.

3. You and your friends are planning a trip together and it turns into a bigger, more expensive one than you expected and can afford. You will:

   A. Go along with the plans as you don't want to miss out – you'll figure the money out later.
   B. Get the group talking about other options to get to a final plan that is affordable for everyone.
   C. You let the plans proceed but decide not to go along on the trip, unless you are going to have time to save up for it.

4. How often do you put money in your savings account:

   A. Never. You don't have a savings account of any sort.
   B. Occasionally.
   C. All the time. Every time you have excess cash you put it away to avoid the temptation to spend it.

5. How often do you use your overdraft, go overdrawn, or need to borrow money from somewhere?

   A. Most months.
   B. Very rarely, maybe once a year.
   C. Never. You never get even close to that situation.

- Mostly As: you are a spender and you may find that your money seems to just disappear.

- Mostly Bs: you are a fairly balanced saver/spender, confident about what you do and don't want to spend your money on and how much you want to have in savings.

- Mostly Cs: you fall into the saver category and are very careful about how you spend your money, preferring to miss out on something if you don't have the money for it. Do be careful not to turn into a miser (the fourth stereotype), though. You can lose friends by not paying your fair share of things, or not doing even low-cost things, because of money.

Chances are you had a mixture of responses to the questions. If you think more broadly about your own life, you will see that you will fall into a different category depending on the situation. That is just your values, developed by your past and current situations, guiding you towards your decision. Now that you have increased your awareness of money decisions and your underlying knowledge, you will be more likely to make the right decisions every time.

I collected a few stories that help demonstrate just how different people's views can be. Some of these examples show differences between your generation and your parents, which is interesting. Here are a few quotes:

- "Wow, it costs me £2 to have a shirt laundered when I drop it at the shop on my way to work." The parent pointed out that there was a cheaper place around the corner. One parent was surprised that the laundry was being sent out at all.

- "How much do these young women spend on manicures, pedicures and haircutting?" A few parents expressed surprise at the money spent on grooming these days. They wondered why people didn't think about doing these things themselves or just skipping them.

- "I spend about £5 a day on lunch." The cost of lunch was the most frequently mentioned money concern. Some people are really good at scouting out meal deals at shops, using coupons or finding 2 for1 restaurant deals. Relatively few people I met considered making their own lunches, which the previous generation frequently did.

- "The price of petrol is outrageous." This came up frequently although, despite the grumbling, people with cars were pretty much used to using them and didn't spend much time considering other ways to get around.

- "Young people spend much more on eating out than we did at their age." Parents said this often. The fact is that the cost of eating out is much less than it used to be and therefore it isn't perceived as the luxury it once was. That is not the case for everyone, though! Food money is the area where you can probably influence your spending the most, by choosing proactively between eating out, eating prepared meals in, and cooking with raw ingredients. A few people explained they had limited choices because they don't know how to cook – which is definitely fixable. Others pointed out that it takes time to plan, shop, and cook, and time is money. That is an important factor to consider. Sometimes you will find you are just too busy to spend time cooking or that your time is better spent studying, working or doing something else.

- "We save a lot of money by going to happy hours, student discount nights and drinking before we go out." Many interviewees were pretty good at figuring out how to stretch their social spending!

One value that you don't want to have creep into your attitude is the idea that if you have lots of money you will be happy. A fundamental truth that has been proven time and again is that, whilst money can buy most things, it does not buy happiness. Abraham Maslow, a renowned psychologist, defined a hierarchy of needs that humans seek to meet. These needs are, in priority order, having food and water, shelter and safety, love and belonging, and self-esteem. Even in the UK, there are people who do not have the fundamental needs met – childhood hunger and poverty is not something reserved for developing countries. Once basic needs are met, though, what role does money provide in motivating us and enhancing our happiness? Frederick Herzberg, the eminent psychologist, asserts, "The powerful motivator in our lives isn't money; it's the opportunity to learn, grow in responsibilities, contribute to others and be recognised for achievements." Additional studies showed that it is the recognition of our achievements and contributions that matter most to us. We will explore this more fully in the next chapter, but for now just hold the thought that you create your own happiness – it comes from within you, not from the pounds in your bank account or the stuff you own.

"Anybody who thinks money will make you happy, hasn't got money." David Geffen on fool.com, Money Week, June 2015

MY FINANCIAL STORY

I thought it would be helpful to share a little bit of my own story with you, because my lifetime has had quite a bit of money learning embedded in it.

My parents were immigrants to the US from Czechoslovakia and Argentina; both well educated. I remember being pretty poor for much of my time growing up. After university I moved from Virginia to New York City to start my accountancy career and became (i.e. was made to be) totally financially independent. (I had paid for half of my university fees by working summers from the day I finished classes to the day they started up again.) Without sharing all the gory details, this is what I recall as the reality of financial independence at age 22: three of us shared a one-bedroom flat and pizza by the slice was a diet staple, as was boxed macaroni and cheese; I could afford two beers in a bar per weekend; and I allowed myself one coffee a week from the fantastic-smelling coffee-shop in my office building. I had an MSc degree and my starting salary was £11,500 a year. I was paid a company allowance of £20 per day (in cash whether I spent it or not) when I travelled for work and I travelled about 150 days a year for the first two years. I spent as little of that allowance as I could, which I think saved me financially.

Within three years of starting work, I bought my first flat, a studio in the centre of Manhattan. To buy that £37,500 flat, I needed a 50% deposit, which I borrowed from my parents and a friend. I paid both of them monthly instalments, including interest at a market rate. Within a year I moved to the UK for "a year or two" and have been here for 28 years. I have been described as "successful", whatever that means. My friends are starting to talk about retirement, but, to me, that is as odd a thought as being 40 probably is to you. I like work – I like earning money, but more importantly I like working with interesting people and learning new things.

My views towards earning, saving and spending money have definitely been shaped by my early years (I am not good at spending on myself, and will make my own coffee rather than buy one on the way to work every morning), the things I value (friends, family and education), and the company I keep. When I reflect on my experiences and consider key messages I want to share that may be helpful to you, I come up with the following:

- **Financial discipline didn't kill me!** I have always been careful with money, no doubt because of my upbringing, and that has been okay. Of course there were, and sometimes are still, times when I wish I had more money at my disposal, and a few decisions I wish I had made differently, but overall I feel I earned, spent and saved my money well.

- **We have been pretty tough with our own children, who have been financially independent since they finished university, in order** to make sure they understand the value of money and have a good work ethic. Some people (especially them) may say we have been too tough. We have made them work from an early age and manage their allowances with no bail-outs from us. Sometimes this approach has been difficult as they wanted what "everyone else has" and we didn't agree with that. We have treated our son and daughter the same, despite peer pressure from our friends to "give girls more allowance as they need make-up" and "give boys more allowance as they have to pay for dates". We think the money values we think we have developed in them will serve them well and we believe embedding those was a key part of helping them become responsible, independent adults.

- **Life has included a few financial disappointments** such as businesses that we invested money and time in, and a few career moves that didn't turn out quite as planned. And I just plain wasted money on things, wondering still "what was I thinking when I did some of the things I did?" But, on reflection, I do see I learned and got some benefits even from financial missteps. And I got over them...well, most of them!

- **I remain strongly influenced by my parents' financial attitudes** even though they have passed away. I am still frugal – when I go to the grocery store, I am always tempted by bargains and I love BrandAlley, eBay, Groupon and other websites where I can get a great deal. But I am getting better about enjoying the fruits of my labour – maybe that happens when the time left to enjoy them starts shrinking. And, I still value hard work for the fun of learning and recognition.

When I reflect on myself and my observation of others, it's clear to me that financial stress doesn't come from how much money you do or don't have. The stress comes from feeling out of control or having no discipline about your financial situation.

My three simple concepts to help you to live less stressful lives moneywise are:

- **Control your destiny** – be in charge of your own decisions, rather than being overly influenced by others. Have enough confidence in yourself and respect for your values to stick to your convictions.

- **Make decisions you are likely to like with hindsight** – this is easier said than done! Avoid the "wish I hadn't, what a waste of money, why did I buy those?" regrets. Ensure you give yourself time when you are making an important decision – "sleep on it".

- **Think about what is driving your decision** – what is the motivation for it? Are you making the decision based on what is right for you or someone else? Is it a short-term desire that may not really matter tomorrow? Is it about being accepted by others? Is it a decision that sits comfortably with you and your money values?

MONEY NOW AND LATER – CLOSING THOUGHTS

By now, you will be warmed up to the topic of money and will have given some thought to your personal history and your current views about it. You will also understand the impact that your upbringing and current situation have on your attitude to money.

Great monetary successes frequently come from financially adverse circumstances, humble beginnings and unusual career paths. Think of J. K. Rowling, who wrote *Harry Potter* whilst on benefits. Think of Jamie Oliver, the famous chef. Think of David and Victoria Beckham, who have multi-faceted careers that they built from nothing. So don't let your financial past dictate your financial future.

It makes sense on many levels to consider money implications when making decisions about today and your future. For today, it means being thoughtful about each decision that involves money and making sure you take the decision you really want to. Whilst researching, I heard many stories of regret over buying something, of surprise about how much money was actually spent when little daily spends were added up over a year, of a lack of understanding around money matters. Some people were very financially aware and others frankly didn't think about money at all, other than getting from one month's allowance to

> *One 19-year-old was running a successful business whilst at university. He was spending the money he earned on each contract to buy a nice piece of designer clothing or accessories. He felt that having a reward for each project kept him focused. I can see that, but I wondered if he would be wise to save some so when/if the business became less successful he would have something to show for it. Is that thinking old-fashioned or smart?*

"Being in a position where they live such a privileged life, it is important that they appreciate how their parents have worked very hard to create this life for the family, and that they too have a responsibility to work hard, be respectful and never, ever take anything for granted." Victoria Beckham, Money Week, 15 May 2015

the next. In order to set up healthy money patterns, you may need to start thinking, or change your attitude, and establish money management practices that will serve you for life.

As far as the future goes, I mention it with some trepidation. Many adults told me that "young adults aren't interested in the long term". That was not at all what I found when I talked with people. It is hardly surprising that you and your peers are anxious about your long-term financial future and employment prospects in light of the economic uncertainty in the UK and globally. The papers are full of dispiriting news. Interviewees expressed concerns about topics including: deciding whether or not to attend university (particularly in light of the fee increases), not knowing what options were available for vocational training, whether they would find a job, whether or not they would ever be able to buy a home, and whether and how they would ever be able to save any money. These are real, practical concerns.

What I heard very clearly was a desire to learn in advance of making mistakes. Everyone was interested in understanding why they spend money the way they do, what influences their decisions, and how they can manage whatever money they have better and smarter. They also asked me about saving money and asked for help to do that.

At the end of the day, by thinking about how you make your decisions about earning, spending and saving money, you will be able to evaluate whether you want to make any changes to your approach. The information in this book will give you the technical know-how to make specific decisions, armed with facts. Ultimately, the goal is for you to spend your money the way you choose to – today and in the future.

Chapter Two

Earning Money

THIS CHAPTER WILL help you think about your views towards working to earn a living, your earning aspirations and the education and work-experience decisions you are making now that may impact your long-term earnings. This chapter ignores the possibility of your winning the lottery!

PUTTING THINGS IN PERSPECTIVE

When you were young, most of your financial needs were probably met by your parent(s) and you may or may not have been aware of how they managed to do that. The money they gave you may have been supplemented with money from relatives or family friends for birthdays or other celebrations. As you got older, you may have worked to supplement what you were given, or to contribute to your family's income. As your full-time education career moves towards the end, or ended, you are likely to become solely responsible for your finances. Ninety-nine per cent of students I surveyed indicated that they expected to support themselves immediately or soon after leaving formal education. They all hoped to go to university, which has money spending, as well as earnings aspiration, implications. (If university is an important topic for you right now, turn to Chapter 10.) One per cent of the students I surveyed said they planned to live on government benefits. The government's planned benefit reductions may make this increasingly difficult, except for those in the greatest need.

> *When my son was little he thought that the money we were living on came from "the pocket money Daddy had saved up". Imagine!*

WHY WORK?

I want to declare at the outset that I am biased about this. I really do believe that people live more fulfilling lives if they work. I accept there may be reasons why some people cannot work, but those who can usually find benefits beyond money from doing so.

The unemployment rate has been hovering around 5–6% for several years and has decreased from 5.7% to 5.1% in the past year for 16–64-year-olds. The actual rate, however, varies significantly by region. As you know, the UK government is committed to providing basic services to everyone, including education, healthcare and unemployment benefits. Following the 2008 economic crisis and ongoing global aftershocks, governments are rethinking

> *"Too many people spend money they haven't earned, to buy things they don't want, to impress people they don't like." Will Rogers, actor, The Week, July 2015*

what benefits should be provided and to whom. Greece, Cyprus, Portugal and Spain, in particular, have found that decades of providing significant benefits (such as pensions from a young age) without corresponding tax collections (someone has to pay for these things) has left them nearly bankrupt. Several of those countries remain in significant fiscal difficulty, with Greece being the most fragile. The UK faces a lesser problem than those countries, but the government has begun implementing numerous changes to the benefits system, many of which are aimed at getting people who can work into work. A proportion of unemployed people are unable to work for health or other reasons. However, some people have chosen not to work because they receive the same or more money from the government by not working than they would get if they did work. (The calculation a person does may include transportation, child-minding and other costs.) The benefits changes seek to increase the incentives to work, by decreasing the benefits paid to those who choose not to work purely because of the maths. These plans are not supported by everyone, as you will see in the news, and the implementation is time-consuming and complicated.

The transition into work will be a real motivational and emotional challenge for many of those impacted. The government is funding initiatives to assist people in preparing for interviews and jobs, which will also help increase their self-confidence. If you have recently been applying for jobs and been turned down repeatedly, you will have a glimpse into how a lifetime of job application rejection could impact a person's morale. That experience would make it pretty hard to get motivated to start applying again. And, if you were in a family where you didn't see people going to work, it would be even harder and scarier to get going.

The papers continue to report doom and gloom about jobs for young people and the "lost generation" of your age group who won't find jobs. Well, I don't totally buy it. Everyone may not find a job they love, but I believe that by following a few basic guidelines many people who are currently discouraged will be able to find a job. When coaching, I encourage young people to start work early – like as soon as they are legally allowed to do so. It doesn't matter what the job is; just showing that you can be relied upon to turn up for work when you are supposed to, and do a good job at whatever the job is, is a positive start. When you have any free time, use your internet skills to research what types of jobs, industries and work environments you might enjoy, so that you can hone in on jobs you might be interested in and might do well in. Armed with this knowledge, your work track record, and a disciplined approach to searching for a job, you are highly likely to find a job post-education. I also encourage people to search broadly, both in terms of city of choice and companies (we all seem to consider the same most well-known companies in a chosen industry – there a tons of companies to consider where the competition may be less keen). Keep in mind that it is always easier to find a job whilst in a job, no matter how menial the work itself, so start with anything. Remember that you can create your own job by figuring out what you can do that others will pay money for. By the way, don't let people put you off jobs you are interested in because your grades aren't great. I know quite a few people whose grades were pretty awful and they had to work harder than average to land a job. But, once they found their work niche, they blossomed and were successful. Academia doesn't bring out the best in everyone!

There are four main reasons why you will benefit from working, whatever the job:

- **Boosts your self-esteem** – there is something very satisfying about going to work, doing a good job and getting paid for doing it. If you are lucky enough to have a good boss, the praise from a job well done, as well as the learning you get from candid performance feedback, will increase your self-confidence. If you work as part of a larger team, you will also benefit from the boost of teamwork. If you deal with clients and they walk away pleased with what you have done, that too will impact how you feel about yourself. I've noticed that when people stop working, it is hard to start again. Just as working boosts your self-esteem, not working, regardless of the reason, seems to sap self-esteem.

- **One job leads to others** – we all think we are supposed to love our job and some people do from the outset. But for most people, particularly in the early stages of careers, it can be a bit hit and miss. Very few people get the right job, in the right company, with the right people, in the first instance. Data shows that 80% of entry-level job-holders change companies within three years of starting their job. Being in a job that has more things you like than you don't can be good enough for this stage of your career. Entry level jobs are rarely fascinating in every aspect. Because a first job leads to another and another, what is most important is doing each job as if it were the most fascinating ever…that is what gets you the next job!

> "A sense of purpose, higher professional standing and sense of control motivate us as much as a pursuit of ease or balance does: and that's all right. A lot of today's graduates in the midst of an uncertain recovery will have to take jobs they don't want, for wages they think are too low and with shaky futures. I don't envy them that climate but they will learn the lesson that the wellbeing gurus forget. We graft for all sorts of reasons and don't always expect it to make us happy. That's why they call it work."
> Evening Standard, 24 August, 2011.

- **Social interaction** – human beings are social creatures. That doesn't mean we like being with people all the time, but we all recognise that people are by nature more or less outgoing. However, even the most introverted people I know gain some pleasure from being in the company of others. Managers and supervisors at work aim to create a sense of community and team, which you get to be a part of when you are at work. That sense of inclusion, or belonging, is likely to be important to you to some degree – the relative importance varying amongst us.

- **Earning money** – I have yet to meet anyone who doesn't get satisfaction from getting paid. Seeing the fruits of your labour in cash or transferred into your bank account feels pretty good, whatever the amount. The earnings alone won't be enough to sustain your enthusiasm for a job that doesn't have anything else you like about it, but it is likely to dull the pain for a moment. If you find a job you love and you get paid well for it – that is the best!

WHAT ARE YOUR EARNING GOALS AND DREAMS?

In Chapter 1 we explored influences on your attitudes towards money. These influences certainly play a part when it comes to earnings aspirations, but how they show up in attitudes is unpredictable. For example, some people I know who had very little money growing up have been driven to earn a lot of money, and some just can't be bothered with trying to earn a living. On the flip side, some people I know who had lots of money growing up can't be bothered to work as they know they will always be provided for, and some are totally driven to earn money, in some cases to trying to prove they can be better off financially than their parents. There are also some people from both types of backgrounds, who drop out to live fairly bohemian lifestyles, rejecting money and wealth of any sort. But, for the most part, people I've

> "Your money blueprint, ingrained in your subconscious mind since childhood, is the single most important factor in determining your level of wealth" explained T Harv Eker, Chief Executive of Peak Potentials Training, who went from zero to a million by "resetting his financial mindset".
> City AM, 2011.

met in all aspects of my life are just trying to lead financially comfortable and contented lives. Your view of what a comfortable life is, or what you want your life to be, will influence the decisions you are making now about your education, early jobs, and longer-term career.

How would you describe your financial aspirations or goals? A survey I conducted produced the following responses:

- "To earn some income." "To hold down a job." "To be able to work only two jobs to make ends meet."

- "To earn a comfortable living."

- "To be better off than my parents." "To have the same lifestyle as my parents gave me."

- "To be able to send my kids to good schools." "To be able to send my kids to university."

- "To own an Aston Martin DB9." "To own a BMW." "To own a car of any type."

- "To make enough money to live." "To make a lot of money." "To make tons of money." "To be a billionaire."

- "To have two nice holidays a year." "To travel loads." "To see the world."

- "To have more than two pairs of shoes." "To own 20 pairs of Jimmy Choos."

- "To have season tickets to Chelsea."

- "To never have to cook." "To eat out once a year."

That is just a flavour of the wide range of aspirations I found. Take some time to think about what your financial dreams are now and recognise they may change over time, as your life unfolds. It may be hard to imagine, but in a few years' time you will be making life decisions that will impact your earnings and spending. Like what? Further education, a job, a new job, a total career change, a change to the country you live in, marriage, children, other responsibilities. Who knows what is just around the corner? Who knows what possibilities will pop up for you, perhaps when you least expect them?

"Worrying about money isn't a useful way to spend your time. No one ever got more money as a result of worrying." Tim Chaney, life coach

THINKING ABOUT YOUR FUTURE

Did You Know That...

- The average household income in the UK with two adults working is £40,000? For single households in the UK, the average is £16,000; but that belies a high of £35,000 in London and a low of £11,000 in Nottingham.
- People earning £50,000 have consistently tested as "the happiest" in the UK?
- There are 65,000 "homeless" households in the UK?
- 1% of people in the UK earn more than £150,000 per year?

If I collected reactions from you and other readers to the previous statements, I would get a range of reactions. Some people would think £40,000 and £35,000 are big numbers, while others would consider them small. The same goes for the £50,000. And what about the 1% statistic? These three figures are useful markers for you to use, as you set your lifestyle and earnings expectations. Remember that the 99.9% of us in the real world (not "instant" celebrities or zillionaires) will have to earn our money the hard way, by turning up for work every day. So find something you like doing enough to do a lot of it. I am an avid reader of people's life stories and one thing that always strikes me is that people who are really financially successful are always passionate about what they do.

You may be tempted to skip the next section, wondering why you should spend time now on long-term stuff when you are at a busy time of life. I can offer two simple reasons. One – you will find that life is always busy and you can fill your days with all sorts of activities; you will only find those things that will lead you to a more fulfilling life if you make space in your life to find them. Two – in moments of quiet, you will have the greatest insights into what you want to do with your life, so get your subconscious working on these big issues when you are busy doing other things.

Take some personal time to think about:

- What do you want from your life? What do you want to achieve professionally? Personally? What is important to you to have done by the time you are 30?

- How much time do you plan to dedicate to work? What does managing a work/life balance mean to you? If you have a family, will that influence your commitment to your career or the hours you will be willing to dedicate to it? What interests do you want to have time to pursue?

- Try to picture what your life will be like in five or ten years. What will it cost you to "get by"? What extra money will you need for your life's pleasures? Do you hope to raise a family? Where do you plan to live? All of these questions and more (I won't list them as you know them) will influence what you will aim to earn.

- Can you quantify these things? What are your numbers? What is your earnings target for next year? Five years from now? Your lifetime? What will you be willing to sacrifice to achieve those aims? What will you gain?

Working through these questions throughout your life, as you find yourself in the day-to-day work world or when you are making career decisions, will help keep you grounded on what you want from your life.

A few students I surveyed said they hoped to become billionaires, and some said they hoped to win millions in the lottery. I hope that happens for them. but I am reminded of a quote that is appropriate in so many ways: "hope is not a strategy". A strategy for reaching your financial dreams may seem hard to develop. I agree that it is. But I will also tell you that it doesn't get any easier over time without practice. So begin with setting a strategy now and practise adjusting it as you go. Choices you make now will, in some way, either help or hinder the likelihood of you reaching your goals. Luck does come into things but as Sam Goldwyn, the famous film producer said (based on words by US President Thomas Jefferson), "The harder I work, the luckier I get."

Did You Know That...

- 20% of UK citizens are living below the poverty line?
- There are 104 billionaires in the UK – more per head than any other country in the world?

It was only in my 40s that I learned the power of expressing my own goals in a positive way. Up until then my personal goal was "to not be poor" which is not a very useful goal. When would I know if I reached it? I became more contented and successful when I started describing my financial and other

"There is a serious defect in the thinking of someone who wants – more than anything else – to become rich. As long as they don't have the money, it'll seem like a worthwhile goal. Once they do, they'll understand how important other things are – and have always been." Anita Loos, American screenwriter and author.

personal goals in a positive way. Two examples of goals I have held true to are: remain open to learning throughout my life and provide financial stability to my family and a good education to my children. Give it a try – it really does work! Studies prove time and again that we get what we focus on.

A FEW EARNINGS THOUGHTS AND ANECDOTES

In the career coaching I do across all age groups, I frequently hear: "I will do that job I love when I have enough money that I don't have to worry" or "I will earn a lot in that job and then I can do XYZ".

Maybe it has always been the case but it feels to me that in general we are more worried – yes, worried – about how much money we want, and we believe we will not be happy until we have it. Of course, the amount of money you or anyone else reading this will think is a lot will differ, as it is all relative to what you have now. You may be surprised to learn that studies show that, whatever your number is now, it will keep getting bigger as the amount of wealth you have increases. You will never actually get to the number you think you want. So stop stressing about it! Once you understand that, life becomes easier, because it helps you realise it isn't about the money, other things matter more. Think about your happiest moments in life so far. What made them so special? Was it really about the money?

I wanted to share a few, perhaps somewhat random, money-related thoughts that may be useful to you now or later:

- **Is money a motivator or demotivator, satisfier or dissatisfier?** – this is a huge topic, so I will just summarise it here. Many studies have been done aimed at figuring out if money can be used as an incentive to get people to do things. In your case, did your parents offer you money if you earned certain grades at school? Did it work; did you study harder because of it? How did you feel if you didn't get the grades and didn't receive any money; and how did you feel if your brother or sister did?

  Psychologists have found that once a person's basic needs are met, getting more money, on its own, stops being a motivator. They also discovered that if a person finds out that someone else is paid more than them for a reason that is not readily apparent, they get demotivated; the "why bother as it is unfair" syndrome. In other words, even though the pay remains the same, the recipient's satisfaction turns into dissatisfaction. What a bummer, but this happens again and again. I saw it many times during my investment banking career. As a senior banking industry figure said a decade ago, "I have never seen so many unhappy people earning so many millions."

- **Money gives you freedom** – you may think that once you earn lots of money you will have the freedom to choose how you spend your time and life. You may be able to pay other people to do some of the more mundane jobs of your life, like grocery shopping, cleaning, whatever your drudgery is. But it is likely that you had to make sacrifices of your freedom whilst you pursued your money goal and you need to take those into account.

- **Money expands your horizons** – having money can lead to new and interesting experiences if you seek them out. By the same token you can expand your horizons in many ways, spending shedloads of money or very little. Learning is easy – read a book, take a course, go to a museum, go to free concerts. Travel options cut across a huge financial range: accommodation from a 6-star hotel down to a shared room in a youth hostel and everything in between; from Michelin-starred restaurants to market stalls.

- **Money will make you happy** – I don't want to overplay this, but I can't help but point out that, despite what feels like a societal view that more is better, it just cannot be the case. If it were, it would mean that richer people would always be happier than poorer people. We all know that is not the case. Are you happier when you have more money in your pocket or bank account? I don't think so.

Research in the UK shows that the happiest people in the UK are those that earn £50,000 a year. That puts them well above the poverty line and above the average UK family income of £40,000 for two workers. That figure may seem unattainable to you, particularly at the moment, and perhaps ever. My point is though that the number is not millions or even hundreds of thousands! Happiness research shows that, once your basic living needs are met, how you react to luxuries differs based on the frequency of those luxuries. If you get them infrequently, you will get a

> "Fall in love with what you are going to do for a living. It's very important. To be able to get out of bed and do what you love for the rest of the day is beyond words. It's just great. It'll keep you around for a long time." George Burns, American comedian, actor and writer.

bigger emotional uplift from them than if you get them all the time. Put another way, the more luxuries you get, the more you need to maintain your satisfaction level.

And, on the flip side, there is plenty of evidence that shows that lots of money doesn't lead to happiness. Think of the celebrities, talented musicians and other famous people whose lives ended early. Money didn't help them be happy, did it? One thing we know for sure – money doesn't protect you from the possibility of unhappy events. Those things are just part of life. You are always in control of your own state of happiness; more money and more stuff on its own won't do it for you.

- **Charitable acts are a winner** – not everyone gives much thought to this, but studies show that the most uplifting thing we can each do to gain short- and long-term satisfaction is to do something to help others. Think about how you feel when you perform a simple act of kindness – even just a smile, holding the door open for someone, putting a small bit of money into a collection tin.

  Spending time on a charitable cause is recommended for people who have lost their jobs, lost loved ones, or are suffering from depression. If you can combine your personal interests with a charitable cause you are really onto a winner. Time and money focused in one place is impactful – take a look at what Bill Gates and Warren Buffet have managed to do. They are extremely wealthy, but each of us can spend a bit of time and money to make a difference.

Lots of food for thought here. I hope the message comes through that, at the end of the day, it is all about you. Set your financial targets within a greater context of your life – money is only one element so avoid making it overly important. Research shows you won't be disappointed with that approach.

DECISIONS YOU ARE MAKING NOW WITH LONG-TERM EARNINGS IMPACT

At your age you will have made, and will continue making, decisions that are likely to impact your potential lifetime earnings. The two biggest and somewhat interrelated decisions that will have that impact, are what you decide on post-sixth form education and how you start off your working life and career.

Post-Sixth Form Education

Wherever you are in your academic career, I encourage you to apply yourself – learning to learn is a great thing, so don't let the ongoing testing wear you down! In general, a strong academic record, in whatever formal education you complete, will open more doors than a poor academic record. I am not saying that is fair, but that is the way it is. Some people really struggle with academia, due to dyslexia or other disadvantages, but then find their niche and have fantastic careers; it is just harder work. Successful dyslexics include Richard Branson of Virgin fame, Florence Welch of Florence and the Machine, and Orlando Bloom, the famous actor. If, like them, academia is not your thing, my advice is to get out and get working as soon as you can. I say that, having seen young people in that sort of situation feel pressured by parents and friends to go on to further study, and then drop out without completing their course as it was just too hard and frustrating. That did little for their self-esteem but they each have bounced back and flourished in jobs!

Things are changing quite quickly around further education in the UK for two reasons: the increase in university tuition costs in recent years, and the related increase in interest in vocational colleges and careers. The annual tuition cost for most university students is now £9,000 a year, and students incur living costs on top of that. As a result, the maths of the cost of university versus potential incremental earnings is getting harder to make work.

Some companies that have been doing most of their recruiting at universities are now rethinking that strategy and offering apprenticeships for post-GCSE and post-sixth form students, and other entry-level positions. (The government is encouraging, meaning giving financial incentives, to firms offering apprenticeships.) These opportunities are expanding and firms are offering training across a wide range of careers, including plumbing, accountancy, beauty and banking. I encourage you to take a look. Speaking of plumbing – look up the career story of the owner of Pimlico Plumbers – he has built a fantastic and profitable business!

At the same time, vocational colleges are increasing their marketing efforts. Read the Sunday papers in particular and search the internet to learn more. The colleges are building strong relationships with employers, so they offer a great opportunity to get real-world experience – something employers are keen on! If you do well at your college course and at your work experience gained through that, your career will be off to a great start!

So, Yes To University?

University was fully funded by the government across the UK until 1998. In Britain and Wales, some universities started charging £1,000 a year for tuition and, in 2004, a flat annual tuition fee of £3,000 was imposed across all British and Welsh universities. By 2012, they could charge up to £9,000 for annual tuition. In Scotland, for Scottish students, the government continues to fully fund the university – in other words, students do not pay tuition fees. Living expenses, if you don't live at home, are also substantial, although some of those may be covered by a grant. It will be difficult for most families to cover these expenses, so the level of student debt by the time of graduation is expected to increase. You do the maths – it will be a lot of money and, pre-2012, took graduates an average of eleven years to pay off their debts. Take a look at Chapter 10 to learn more about university student loans.

In addition to the cost of university, students have banks offering them lots of "free" credit and/or overdrafts. At some point after graduation they will start charging interest on those amounts, so those debts are also likely to increase, unless, of course, you planned for the change and have the money to pay the debts back once interest is charged. I hear quite a lot from people in their late 20s who regret their spending and build-up of debts.

> When asked why they took on loans and overdrafts when they were offered, most people say "because they were offered and it was free". Followed quickly by "I wish I had thought more about it at the time but it was easy not to".

The message now is that university is a significant investment of time and, across much of the UK, money. There is value in learning for the sake of learning, but chances are that, if you are considering university, you will have to factor finances into your thinking. There are careers that will continue to require a university education and frequently provide higher income-levels. If you do decide to go to university, make sure you make your investment count. Picking the right university and course is important.

Working hard once you get to university is important. Whatever you hear from others, you need to know that the results for your first year do matter. If you want to apply for internships during the summers after your first and second years (which I recommend) you will be asked what your grades are so far. Anything below a 2:1 is unlikely to be good enough. I'm not saying you won't find something; what I am saying is that you are making it much harder for yourself as a result. Similarly, finishing your course with anything less than a 2:1 will make finding a job difficult, as most firms won't let you access their online application system without that result.

When you are applying it is appropriate to ask the university questions such as "what percentage of your graduates get graduate-level jobs?"; "what percentage of students have those lined up before graduation day?"; and "what does the university do to help students get jobs?" Beginning in 2013, universities have been required to publish the percentage of students, by course, that have secured jobs upon graduation.

Always remember, if you decide you don't want to go to university straight after sixth form, or if you decide to opt out of education after GCSEs (or the Scottish equivalent), you can always go to university later on in life.

There are plenty of stories of 80-year-olds earning university degrees, and a new record of the oldest person to earn a degree was earned recently by a 98-year-old at Utah State University.

Alternative Career and Earnings Paths

There are many people who took what are described by those biased towards university as non-traditional paths to financial success. Sometimes I wonder what traditional means when I read people's biographies. A few stories spring to mind: Helen Mirren's acting career took off in her 50s but she had worked hard at her career since her 20s. Julie Walters' parents despaired when she gave up her nursing career for acting. Dick King Smith was a failed farmer twice over before he became a successful children's book author. David and Victoria Beckham earned no A-levels, but they have established varied careers and are now "ambassadors" for Britain.

"Behind every overnight success lies years of hard work and sweat." Often quoted, never attributed.

I recently read the results of a study into excellence and what drove it. The study demonstrated that what lies behind excellence, being viewed by others as being great at something, is directly correlated to hard work. Yes, talent is important, but many people have that to some degree. It is the dedication to relentless practice and the commitment to learning to do better that make the difference.

So who is luckier, the person who finds their calling early or the late bloomer? Even in the darkest moments of your future career, take heart – for many people, the first time they are fired or made redundant is the making of them. During a recent City of London downturn, numerous people were being made redundant and starting new careers in all sorts of businesses – I just read about a bespoke tailor and a jewellery designer! Maybe they are finally following their passions!

The point I am making is that you never know what will happen in your career and related earnings. Lifetimes of work can take many twists and turns. Some people are driven by potential earnings when they make their work choices, and some purely by a passion. For most it is a combination of things, in which education may feature. And some earnings paths are straightforward upward climbs and some are all over the place. There is no right or wrong answer – every career is unique, so maybe they are all alternative?

Career/Job Choice

For most people, a career is what you see when you are middle-aged and you look back at all the jobs you have held and how they somehow tell a story. There are a minority of people who know (or think they know) what they want to do workwise, for a lifetime, when they are deciding on GCSE or A-level subjects. And maybe a few more people are clear when the time comes to apply for university. But in my experience very few are clear – I can say that from working alongside many people who were drafting UCAS forms and trying to convince the reader of their passion for a subject. So don't feel pressured into making a lifetime decision about what you are going to do. There are many opportunities that will present themselves that haven't even crossed your mind yet; the key is to do great things at every job you take on and keep open-minded.

When you are thinking about your first job and where it could lead in terms of earnings, it's pretty easy to find out. You can go online, look at job advertisements or look through career books. As you do your digging, consider entry-level jobs and longer-term jobs in that area of interest, so you can get a feel for the long-term earnings potential. Some jobs are higher paid than others, but be careful to consider the average, or expected, rate of pay, not the pay for superstars! Typically, professions that require a big investment in education will pay more – think lawyers, investment bankers, doctors. If you are a star in any of those, you may make really serious money. Sadly, some professions are not as well paid, such as teachers, but teachers do have the benefit of long holidays which the first professions I mentioned do not. Nursing is another career that, despite its impact on society, does not generally pay terribly well. People in trades such as plumbers, builders and electricians seem to make a good living and have the flexibility (and risks) of probably running their own business. In a nutshell, every career path has good stuff and bad stuff. What is important is to find something that you are interested in doing a lot of, as you will perform better at a role that interests you than in one that doesn't.

As you consider careers and first jobs, I think it is most important to think about the environment you will be working in. I advise young people to think through some basic questions about their likes and dislikes, along the lines of those included in the following box.

Work Environment Preference Questions

Do you…

- Want to work inside a building or outside?

- Prefer working with other people or on your own?

- Prefer working with computers or people?

- Like a routine where you go to the same place at the same time most days, or do you like to have a changing or unpredictable schedule?

- Have a preference for the ages of the people you work with?

- Like working with numbers or words?

There are many sources for advice if you search the internet. My advice? Just get going with the working and earning money and see where it leads you. If you have to stack shelves or pick vegetables, just do it! Once you are eligible to work, get a job working summers and/or evenings rather than hanging out at home. Be a "mucker-inner" once you get a job – a positive "do whatever I can to help" attitude goes a long way.

KEEPING PACE WITH THE CHANGING WORLD

As you develop your career and financial aspirations, take into account what is going on in the world around you. The general economic situation in your country is important, but so is the situation more broadly. Keeping apprised of the geopolitical and economic changes around the world and what they may mean to you is important and challenging. The current UK basic income tax rate of 20% may seem reasonable but, when you add in National Insurance, quite a lot of money gets deducted from your pay. If you multiply that by the years you will work, the number is significant. It is not surprising, even if it is a bit disappointing, that some UK citizens are moving to other countries. There is much movement to the East, as countries there provide the double attraction of low taxes and huge economic growth. That is just one example where keeping an open and global mind can help you identify career and financial opportunities.

The world as you see it has changed dramatically and will continue to do so. A few countries/regions with "big events" during the last 30 years, which have manifested in visible changes in the UK, include:

- **Russia** – the iron curtain was removed in 1989 and before then you would have heard little about any of the countries behind it, let alone travelled there. You would have thought of communism, not capitalism. Well, who owns Chelsea football club? Where did he make his money? He took a few risks, didn't he?

- **China** – there is an iconic press photograph of US President Richard Nixon and Chairman Mao Zedong, leader of the People's Republic of China, shaking hands in front of the Great Wall in the 1970s. Until then, China hadn't had a great deal of press coverage in the western world for some time. Closer to home, 20 years ago you wouldn't have seen many Chinese nationals working in London or coming as tourists. They didn't have the financial ability to travel. China now has 213 billionaires, second in number to the US. The enrolment rate of Chinese nationals in US and UK universities is accelerating exponentially. Numerous Chinese banks have opened offices in the City of London, and one has even taken over a building vacated by the Bank of England. How did that change happen in such a short time?

- **The Middle East** – familial political regimes have ruled countries such as Libya, Egypt, Syria and Bahrain for generations. People within these regimes increased their personal wealth at the expense of the common citizens. At the same time, the unemployment rates for the under-30s in those countries increased alarmingly, to levels in excess of 40%. The Arab Spring of 2011 was punctuated by uprisings, violence and ultimately regime change in many of those countries. The governments of EU nations with high youth unemployment rates recognise the similarity of situations – although there are clear differences as well.

- **Africa** – this is a huge continent, full of natural resources, yet facing many environmental and economic issues. Many economists and business people believe there are great opportunities there which would also improve the lives of Africa's inhabitants, but progress comes in fits and starts. Chinese businesses are investing heavily in these nations. If you are interested in learning more about this continent, and the job opportunities that are emerging there, do explore them through the internet.

- **South America** – this is another huge continent, rich in minerals and natural resources, with lots of business opportunities that are now being pursued, as many of the countries have addressed their fundamental economic issues. The quality of life is improving and the cost of living and taxes are now reasonable compared with the past 30 years. Some footballers, well known in England, are choosing to return to their home countries as their economies have improved. The first Olympic games ever to be held in South America will be held in Rio de Janeiro, Brazil in the summer of 2016.

Each of the above – and these are just a few examples – has had an impact on real people like you and your families. As you decide your career and financial aspirations and work to achieve them, it is a good idea to engage proactively in world events and consider what the implications may be for you and your dreams. There are downside risks and huge opportunities when significant changes occur in the world.

"Pennies don't fall from heaven, they have to be earned here on Earth." Margaret Thatcher, December 1979

TAKE CONTROL OF YOUR EARNINGS DESTINY

"Three out of five Premier League footballers go broke within five years of retirement; one in three get divorced within a year of retiring." The Times, March, 2013

We have covered a lot of ground here. The thing is, unless you are planning to be supported by the government, you are going to have to support yourself. And that will mean making decisions about education and finding a job that will morph into a career. You may or may not be one of the few who has a passion and career path planned already. The decisions you make now about university and jobs will have an impact on your long-term and lifetime earnings potential. Consider your financial aspirations as you make those decisions, bearing in mind the aspects of happiness, freedom and personal interests.

And remember that you never know what is just around the corner. If your dream is to win the lottery, as some people told me theirs was, take a look at the stories of previous winners. It is disappointing to see how often they squandered their money and a few years after their win had nothing to show for it. Along the same lines, it is shocking to learn that many homeless people living on the streets were at one time financially well off, held professional jobs and were well educated. Thankfully there are plenty of other stories of incredible success and impact achieved by people who appeared unlikely to do so.

The skills you are learning now about managing your money will put you in a good position to reach your goals and be prepared for whatever your life holds in terms of career and financial situations. So, give yourself time to think about these things, set your aspirations and go for it! Planning now will help make sure you don't have any regrets later.

Chapter Three
Spending Money

Small Spends Add Up

Immediate Gratification

"Good" And "Not So Good" Spending

Pause And Reflect

Escape Routes

Missed Opportunities

A S WE SAW in Chapter 1, most of the time you may not give too much thought to money decisions you are making. As you go about your day-to-day stuff, you just do what you do. You will now know that you actually make quite a few money decisions on any given day. We are going to look more closely at your spending.

The purpose of this chapter is to increase your awareness about your spending decisions. That will help you make smarter money choices – decisions that ensure you spend your money on what you really want, not what you want right now, just because the moment grabs you. By that, I don't mean a ten-year view but just a pause to think, "If I do this with my money now, what might I be giving up tomorrow or next week?" It's just another way of thinking about "Is this really what I want to spend my money on or is something else driving my spending decision?" That way, when you are down to your last few pounds at the end of month you can think, "Yes, I made the right decisions."

The reality of spending is that it is very easy for money to trickle out. How much time and effort do you put into making your spending decisions? I found that quite a bit of thought went into one-off, relatively big expenditures. But I also found that people didn't think explicitly about cutting out one expense to fund another. Chances are you do think at least a bit before you spend. A common theme I heard during my research was that young people really started thinking about their spending once they started earning their own money to support themselves. Do you ever think, "one beer is two hours of work" or "a pair of shoes is two days' work"? That can get a bit obsessive, though there are people who do just that all the time because they have to.

> What would you do if you won £1 million on the lottery? £5 million? What would you spend it on? What does that tell you about your spending and life values?

SMALL SPENDS ADD UP

If you concentrate on your daily small spends, you can see how they add up to a lot of money. Here are a few examples that might be relevant to you:

- **Daily coffee** – £2.10 twice a day, 300 days per year, costs you £1,260 a year (probably after tax). Could you bring the cost down by going to a local shop rather than one of the big brands? How much would it cost you if you made your own coffee?

- **Mobile phone** – you "have to have" the latest handset, or you upgrade regularly, and remember that each time you use it you are spending money. How much do you spend a year?

- **Newspapers** – at £1 daily and 365 days a year you'll be spending about £365 a year if you buy a newspaper. Is it less expensive to read it online? What about reading it in the library? What about agreeing with your friends who will buy what and sharing?

- **Cinema visits** – how often do you go? At £10 to watch the film plus popcorn and a drink, how much does each trip cost you?

- **Sporting events** – with tickets going up in price (now £35–60 for a Premier League match), plus transport, plus food and drinks it can be a pretty expensive afternoon out. Is it worth it, when you take the full cost into account?

- **Pubs and restaurants** – you may be surprised at how much you spend every month or week at these. What do you think you spend? Are you okay with that figure?

- **Grabbing lunches** – at £5 a day for a meal deal or other lunch, you will spend roughly £1,800 a year if you buy it seven days a week. What else could you do for lunch?

- **Travel expenses** – do you run a car? What does it cost you each year? What is the cost difference between driving and taking the train, taking a bus, or sharing a car? If you plan long trips in advance, you can reduce the train costs for sure. Do you think about what you spend a year on getting around the country?

What do you think you spend your money on? Any idea what that looks like if you look at a year? Or per month? Do you think it changes much from month to month? What portion of your spending is fixed – rent, utilities, education – and what varies – gifts, clothes, meals out, drinks? This is all useful information for you to get to grips with.

"Women are buying four times as much clothing as 30 years ago. They also throw out more. It is estimated that they buy 62 pounds of clothing a year, half their body weight. All due to the 'fast fashion trend'."
The Times, May 2011.

IMMEDIATE GRATIFICATION

Between your generation and the previous one, the speed with which you can get things you want has increased dramatically. You can watch any film you want at any moment; you can talk to anyone in the world from anywhere in the world at any time; you can access your email at any time from anywhere; your smartphone (once the domain of senior business executives) means you are in touch all the time. Everything is instantaneous! How great is that?

Well, you may have already learned that there can be downsides to everything being instant and to making instant decisions, because with hindsight they may not seem so great. Have you ever heard of something called the marshmallow test? It was an interesting study done many years ago where five year-old kids were given the option of getting one marshmallow immediately or getting two marshmallows if they waited "a bit". Of course they had no idea what "a bit" meant. Most of them took the one even though they could have twice as much for a little wait. Ring any bells for you in relation to spending?

Quite often if you slow down, pause and think, you may make a better decision or get something even better. "Better" here means more in line with what you really want.

"GOOD" AND "NOT SO GOOD" SPENDING

I collected stories of spending decisions that people of your age were happy and unhappy about. I also did quite a bit of eavesdropping on conversations. Here are a few of my findings:

- Frequent first memories of money, which we touched on earlier, included: having money to spend on sweets, being limited on how many Pokemon cards could be bought, getting pocket money for being good.
- Nearly everyone had a story about saving money for something and they explained that it felt great to have whatever it was they bought. They tended to really enjoy that special something.
- Everyone had "wasted money" stories about shoes, clothes, CDs, mobile phones and other stuff they bought in haste and regretted later.
- Only a few had funny stories – paying for a fairly expensive item with one pence coins, paying someone to do something bizarre like eat a slug.
- Nearly all (99%) indicated they expected to be financially independent shortly after completing their formal education (A-levels or university); 20% said they hoped to win the lottery.

> *My biggest mistake is to buy clothes on sale. If something is a good brand and a good colour and 70% reduced in price I just have to have it. My present-giving cupboard is supplied by many of those mistakes.*

This leads me to think that you and your peers want to be financially responsible and probably are already moving in that direction. It also tells me that an easy way for you to make even better financial decisions than you do now is for you to increase your spending awareness and slow down your spending process. Spending hindsight, when it has an element of regret, is not much fun. Perhaps you have stories of your own along these lines:

• My daughter "had" to have a Furby (an electronic robotic toy which was a "must-have" a few years ago) so we traipsed all over London trying to find one as they were in huge demand. We finally found one and she spent all the money she had saved up from multiple birthdays. Once she got Furby home, it was so annoying that it was banished to the cupboard within a month. It turned up ten years later when we cleaned out the cupboard and was quickly banned to the attic. Have you ever spent money you saved for ages on something you then didn't even like?

• Maybe you bought a car – a good one at a really good price. But you found you didn't use it often and, when you did, there always seemed to be something wrong with it – a flat tyre, a slipping clutch. And parking it was a nightmare. In the end you may have regretted buying it in the first place.

• You splashed out on a really nice pair of shoes, a dress or a shirt for some special event. Afterwards you thought about the fact that no one said anything about it, the event was cancelled, it rained and your item got ruined, or you decided not to wear it as it "didn't go with other things".

• You bought something at a fabulous discount on sale. A great bargain. You didn't bother trying it on. Then, when you got it home, it was a poor fit, or you decided you just didn't feel comfortable in it so, in actual fact, you wasted money when you started off thinking you were saving it.

• You got roped into a holiday plan that was well beyond what you planned to spend. Maybe it was because the group you were going with had more money than you, or they were just that bit older and earning more than you. Maybe you managed to cobble the money together to go on the holiday, but every time you did something during it, you were stressed as it was one more thing you "couldn't really afford".

• You went out for a meal with your friends. You didn't talk about how to split the bill, but you assumed you'd each pay for what you ordered (roughly).

When the bill came someone suggested an even split. You didn't want to raise a fuss, even though you had chosen what to eat with your wallet in mind and knew it was going to financially stretch you to make up for it somehow. And on top of it you left the restaurant hungry!

Maybe a few of these sound familiar or maybe you have your own stories. The purpose is to point out that we all have one or two spending decisions that are tinged with regret. And we can figure out how to avoid them in the future which is what we will do here. The spending goal is to have "no regrets" or better yet, the flip side – "conscious, in-control spending" all the time.

PAUSE AND REFLECT

Making conscious, in-control spending decisions requires just one thing. It requires you to avoid making snap decisions in the heat of a potential spending moment, choosing instead to pause and reflect on what you are doing. I have taken suggestions made by interviewees and summarised them as questions below for you to work through.

- What spending decisions can you remember that, with hindsight, you wish you hadn't made? Take the time to jot a list of them down (now, not later). Then, go back to the list and think about how you could have handled those situations differently. You may want to talk them through with friends to see if they have other ideas.

- What are you spending your money on at the moment that surprises you? Look at the list at the beginning of this chapter. What is your own list of small spends that turn big?

- What do you think you can do to make your money go a little further? Think back to the days leading up to the last time you were stuck at home, because you had no cash for a few days.

- Where could planning ahead have saved you money? Fertile ground for this one is travel arrangements, grocery shopping, cinema visits, coupons including Groupon and vouchercloud.

- How often do you lose track of your spending when you are out partying? The best advice people have suggested to deal with that is to set a money limit for the night, including your transport home, and don't take your credit card out with you.

Give yourself some time to reflect on these and come up with your own questions to add to the list. The test will be, does the list help you next time you are making a spend decision? Keep testing it out and adjusting it as you go along. You may find that you get it down to just one or two questions which make it easy to use every time you are deciding whether or not to spend your money.

ESCAPE ROUTES

Inevitably you will get stuck in awkward money situations, and the more financially diverse the group of people you spend time with, the more likely it is these will happen. That is totally fine, as long as you have a few coping mechanisms to help you. Here are a few ideas:

- By far the easiest thing to do is be non-committal. When you feel pressured into spending on something you aren't sure about, or are already sure you don't want to but don't know how to say so, find a way to buy yourself some time. Do this by simply saying something like "I want to think about that" or "Can I come back tomorrow on that?" Then think about: Is this something you really want to do or spend your money on? What is motivating you to spend – you or other people? Are you trying to please someone else for some reason? How can you say "no thanks" without causing a fuss?

- Another approach is to consider what will happen if you don't spend on whatever it is. How will you feel about it? Is it really that important? Is it worth it? Will a moment of awkwardness now make things easier in the future? What do you want to spend your money on instead? What pleasure will that give you?

- Try to anticipate and avoid tricky situations. Peer pressure is very hard to deal with and something that will continue throughout your life. How often do you hear "you have to come" and "you don't want to miss out" type statements? How can you get yourself out of those jams (when you want to) without feeling you look pathetic, or cheap, or different? Well, frankly we are all different. What is surprising is that despite the angst of standing up for oneself in these situations, they pass very quickly and friends don't tend to hold it against you. It is very unusual for people to push someone hard into doing something once they have had the courage to firmly say "no, thanks" or "can't afford it".

- Consider alternative ways to get the same result and suggest one of them. Think about how you can get the same outcomes for less. For example, have your beers in your room rather than the pub, or buy Pizza Express pizzas at the supermarket and cook them at home rather than going out to eat, or watch a sports match on tv rather than attend in person.

Think too about how you handle situations when you are the one trying to get people to spend money on something. How do you react when people hesitate to go along with your suggestion? Have you considered that maybe they are hesitating because they can't afford it? Do you make it easy for them to adjust your idea or say no? Chances are your friends treat you the same way as you treat them. Good friends are unlikely to dump you because you don't want to spend money on something.

There are lots of ways to enjoy life without spending much money. The Internet is a real blessing when it comes to this. But you do have to break what may be old habits. Rather than thinking about going to an expensive club or out for a film, search the web for "what's free in your city?" and "things under £10".

MISSED OPPORTUNITIES

A lot of this chapter has been about managing your spending more carefully, and that implies spending less. Whilst that was my bias, as so many of the young adults I spoke with wanted help with that, there is another side to controlling your spending. That is when you give lots of thought to something and decide not to spend your money on it. Maybe it is a good deal on a car, or tickets to a World Cup match of some sport, or a holiday with friends. There is a chance that you will regret the decision to not spend the money. One young man explained it really well when he said, "My personal philosophy is that I take care and think hard about money decisions but try every possible way not to let opportunities pass me by because of money."

In a nutshell, you are in control of your spending, no one else, so take that control with gusto. Find ways to slow your spending decision-making so you make each decision within a bigger context. Setting spending targets will help you with that and is covered in the next chapter. And remember the goal is no regrets, whether you decide to spend or not!!

Chapter Four

Managing Money Coming In And Going Out

What's A Budget?

Budget Step One: Collect Detailed Money Information

Budget Step Two: Fill In Your Money Spreadsheet

Budget Step Three: Begin Exploring And
Understanding Your Money Reality

Budget Step Four: Create Your Monthly Budget
Analysis Spreadsheet – Setting Budget Targets

Managing Your Money The Way You Want

Keep Your Tracking And Targeting Going...Forever

Managing Your Money

I N MANY CASES, once we understand something, we have some level of control over it. By the time you are done with this book, you will have the understanding and tools you need to manage your money the way you want to – so that every money decision you make lines up with your goals.

Absolutely key to managing your money is having the knowledge of what money is actually coming in and going out and then being able to compare these actual amounts to what you had planned (or maybe "hoped" would be a more appropriate word at the beginning of this chapter). To achieve this, you need to collect detailed information about everything you spend money on and every bit of money that comes in to you. You will then be able to summarise that information into categories and set a target figure for each category. And with that you will have a budget. Simple!

The critical factor to this process, and the usefulness of the output, is your diligence in collecting data. We will spend more time on this but it is such a critical concept that it is worth being really firm about it up-front. If you track every single pound that goes out and comes in, your budget will be meaningful and useful. If you don't, it won't be. With practice, the discipline of collecting receipts and other tasks will become second nature and it is a skill that will serve you well for life. When you first start out, though, it will be a pain. There are many technology solutions that can help you with the data collection and analysis – useable on laptops and smartphones – but they all rely on your consistent human intervention.

Reasons given for not wanting to "waste time" preparing a budget and why you may want to reconsider:

- "I don't know what I've spent my money on." Exactly why you need a budget. You can't manage what you can't see.

- "I don't have enough money to worry about budgeting." Another good reason to have a budget. With one, you may find you have more money choices than you think.

- "My parents control what I spend because they fund me and will top me up if I need it!" This may sound great, but at some point it may end in tears as parents won't fund you forever. Learning to manage your money is an important life skill that, like many things, is easiest if learnt early, and it gets easier with practice.

- "I don't have the time." Which really means "it's not important enough". And it may not be, until you face a financial crisis or really want something that you could have had if only you had managed your money better.
- "I can't be bothered." Well, there is something to be said for honesty.

When you read the comments above, they may or may not sound rational, but they definitely aren't consistent with controlling your money destiny, which is the reason you are reading this book. If you think about other times when you learned something new (say, writing a poem or mastering a maths concept) it may have seemed like hard work at first and you may have avoided it, hoping it would go away. But, once you learned it, the thing was easy. You may recall feeling pretty good about conquering whatever the "it" was. Well, budgeting will be like that too. You can wait to learn how to do it until you absolutely have to, when your current way of managing your money stops working or when some external event forces you to plan your finances more thoughtfully than in the past. Rather than wait until then, with the risk of looking back and thinking you may have wasted your money, you can learn how to budget now.

In this chapter I will take you through a step-by-step process to collect information, analyse it, set budget targets and monitor how you are performing against them. I have tried it out on many people and it worked for them so it will work for you. You can use technology, but I will do it here assuming you only have a spreadsheet capability, so that you know how to do it at the most basic level. I promise that once you set it up and then have a bit of practice, it really is quite easy to maintain.

There are many technology applications that will help you with tracking and analysing information. It is very helpful if your bank transaction information can be automatically uploaded to whatever application you use, although you will still need to classify each item. Top smartphone applications include IReconcile, Expenditure, MoneyBook, and Mint. Top laptop applications are Quicken and Microsoft Money.

Many high street banks are offering budget analysis apps to their clients at no cost. They actually provide summary statements of incoming and outgoing monies, categorised into predefined headings. This won't eliminate all the work outlined here, but may get you a good way towards what you need.

WHAT'S A BUDGET?

A budget is a plan. It shows you what money you plan/expect/hope (you choose the word that works for you) to get in. And it shows you what money you plan/expect/hope (again, your choice of word) to spend.

On the money coming IN side, a budget helps you answer questions like: where will your money come from and when? Did the money you actually receive match what you expected to receive? If you are on an annual salary, which becomes a monthly amount of pay, it is pretty easy to figure out what will come in. However, in the early days of your job, the amount of cash you receive is likely to fluctuate as your tax code gets sorted out (see Chapter 7). If you aren't on a fixed salary, the incoming money may fluctuate significantly. Look out for changes in the number of hours worked and the impact of not working as many hours as you expected, especially if overtime is paid at a higher rate than regular hours. And remember that you won't be paid for time taken away from work for holiday, doctor and dentist visits, and being off sick.

When you get money in you have two choices – save it or spend it. In this chapter we will focus mostly on the "spend it" option. That is, understanding what you spend your money on and how to make sure that what you are actually spending it on is what you want to be spending it on. On the money OUT side a budget helps you understand: Did you spend your money the way you planned to? What would you like to spend your money on? What spending decisions do you make up front and what do you decide at the time of purchase? What took you off course and by how much?

Budgeting will also help you be better able to fund non-standard financial events from your ongoing cash flow like holidays, presents and big nights out, and will help you avoid getting into debt for those. Your budget may even help you start to save money. Well, let's not get too carried away.

Before we get started, please go to my website and look at the tools I have included there to help you with this. They are:

- **Money IN and OUT Categories** – *a list of suggested categories for you to choose from to use in your own spreadsheet. You can create your own categories to meet your money management needs.*

- **Your Money Spreadsheet** – *a sample spreadsheet which shows how you can capture and categorise your money transactions.*
- **Your Monthly Budget Analysis** – *a sample monthly budget analysis, which brings together your actual and budgeted numbers by category and will enable you to review what has happened in the month, or over a few months, and identify what, if anything, you want to explore further or change.*

(You may also want to skim through Chapters 7 and 8 covering payroll, bank accounts, credit cards, debit cards and store cards.)

BUDGET STEP ONE: COLLECT DETAILED MONEY INFORMATION

The starting point is to track your money coming in and going out in detail. To collect this information, you will rely on some data provided by others, including bank statements, payslips and credit card statements. You will also need to track money ins and outs that aren't captured by those. This means you will need to focus in particular on tracking cash transactions, which we will spend quite a bit of time on. If you are relying on your bank app for detailed information, remember that it won't provide details of where 'cash withdrawal' money goes. All of the information collected from source documents mentioned below will be used for inputting into your money spreadsheet.

I will explain how to do that, but keep in mind that you need to track everything that comes in and everything that goes out. (Like dieting or quitting smoking or exercising, if you aren't totally disciplined about it you won't get the results you want.)

Keep a money diary or list somewhere in whatever way works for you. Every item needs to have a date, an amount, what type of transaction it was (cash, credit card, debit card, store card) and an explanation of what the payment or receipt of money was for. You may want to record everything in a notebook, or you might like to track things on scrap papers or receipts or you may want to log the data directly onto a spreadsheet as you go. (I prefer the scrap paper and receipt approach.)

Tracking Money Coming IN is usually relatively easy. These INs include any allowance you receive, earnings from a job, birthday money, government money, and maybe other things. Include everything so you get the full picture.

When you get paid for work (monthly or weekly) your payslip will be your money spreadsheet source document. If your parents deposit money into your bank account, your bank statement will be your spreadsheet source document. If you are paid cash for work, you need to make a note straight away, including any tips you receive. If your pay has deductions for income tax and other things, you must use the details included on the payslip to reflect the total you earned as money coming IN and the monies deducted for tax and other things in the appropriate OUT sub-category.

Your bank account statement, as described in more detail below, is a key source document as it will list every payment into your account. You should be able to recognise every item that appears on it.

Keep your payslips filed securely. And keep any documentation of other incoming money filed separately.

Tracking money going OUT is harder than tracking your INs, because there are many more OUTs. Ongoing spending means you'll need quite a bit of discipline to make sure you capture every outflow. The key is to capture the

Employee No.		Employee Name			Process Date	National Insurance Number
11		Mr. Angus Smith			24/06/2016	BA4321C

Payments	Units	Rate	Amount	Deductions	Amount
Salary	1.00	2,416.0000	2,416.00	PAYE Tax	292.60
				National Insurance	205.01
				Student Loan	83.00
				Work Pension	36.25

Tax Code: 1100L	Tax Period: 3	Dept: Marketing Payment Method: BACS	Net Pay	1,799.14

information as the event occurs. If you pause for even a moment and think "I'll deal with that later", stop yourself and write it down there and then! Recreating spending records after the fact is impossible, so don't be tempted to try it. You will find it useful to keep separate envelopes or files for your marked-up cash machine withdrawal slips, credit card slips, and debit card slips.

There are several source documents that will be the basis for entries onto your money spreadsheet. Here is some information about them with a few tips for each:

• **Cash machine withdrawal slips** – every time you get cash out, get a receipt and write on it what you spent the money on. You may have to carry that receipt around for a bit as you may not spend the money immediately. Keep the receipts in a place where you can find them when you go to record your money outflows.

One of the biggest gaps in spending records is when you go out for a night and get £20 out of the ATM on the way out, forgetting your process. It's also easy to forget to record money you withdraw during your night out. I can't tell you how many times I have heard someone complain that "someone took their money" or they "lost their money" on those sorts of nights. So get the slip, stick it in your pocket or wallet so you remember you got money out, and mark it up the next day.

• **Bank account statement** – bank accounts, including what is processed through your current account (e.g. debit card transactions which include 'contactless' payments) is explained in Chapter 8, so you may want to read through that section now.

```
THANK YOU FOR YOUR CUSTOM
11 08 16  8:19  AF493096
*************3230
                        *005
MOORGATE E1
                        1596
RECORD NO.        £50.00
CASH WITHDRAWAL
FROM   71974
```

11th August
Petrol £30
Food £20

Because nearly all of your money-related activities will sooner or later flow through your bank account, it is a great source of information. Every time you get cash from a money machine, check your account balance to make sure is in line with what you expect. Then every week, or at a minimum once a month, you need to go through your bank statement item by item. To do this, print the statement out, mark it up and from there load the information into your money spreadsheet. Or, if you have an app that facilitates this, you may be able to classify each item directly into a budget Money OUT category automatically. If there is an entry you don't recognise, you need to investigate it urgently.

BUILDING SOCIETY

A/C No 330419133
Sort Code 08-60-82
CLASSIC ACCOUNT

Date 01 SEP to 30 JUN 2016
Previous Statement 31 MAY 2016
Page 2 of 3

STATEMENT

DB signifies overdrawn balance

DATE	DESCRIPTION	MONEY OUT [£]	MONEY IN [£]	BALANCE [£]
2016				
3 JUN	BALANCE B/FORWARD			615.57
7 JUN	LNK 39 THE STREET CD 0176 13/06/16	CPT 10.00	✓	605.57
9 JUN	VISA PURCHASE TESCO STORES 2812 LEATHERHEAD ON 08/06/16	DEB 25.00	✓	580.57
13 JUN	CASH DISPENSER Gatwick N Teardrop London ON 13/06/16	CPT 40.00	?	540.57
14 JUN	VISA PURCHASE Amazon Digital Dwnlds 866-321-8851 ON 13/06/16	DEB 5.00	✓	535.57
21 JUN	ARCHFIELD RENTAL SERVICES	DD 550.00	_RENT!!_	- 14.43 DB
24 JUN	Iandi ELECTRICAL Ltd	_WAGES_	1750.00 CR	1735.57

The balance in your bank account decreases with debits and increases with credits. Debits include direct debits, standing orders and transactions you made with your bank debit card, including cash machine withdrawals. Credits include deposits into your account, the most frequent being payments received from your employer, money deposited by your parents and any cheques you deposited.

- **Credit card statement** – every month, each credit card provider will send you a monthly statement via the post and/or email. Credit cards are covered in detail in Chapter 8, so either read that now or just focus on tracking spending. The monthly statement will include the beginning balance, every transaction, and the ending balance. What you need to do for money outgoing tracking purposes is analyse every entry and allocate each to a budget category.

I recommend that every time you use the card you get a receipt, immediately write on it what you bought, and put it in an envelope somewhere. You may think you don't need to do this because you will remember what you spent your money on, but it is very hard to remember after the fact. To add to the difficulty, sometimes the name of the shop you bought the thing from is not the same as the one that appears on the credit card receipt. When your credit card statement comes, take out your envelope of receipts and tick them off against the statement, marking on the statement the budget category that each amount relates to. If you have used a contactless card, you may or may not have had the option to receive a receipt. If not, make a note somewhere of the spend, what it was for and the date.

Feel free to use whatever categories make sense for you. The list I have suggested is just a proposal. You will see that there is an "other" category

---

account information

Rates of interest
Cash withdrawals - annual rate 12.44% p.a. (variable)
All other amounts payable under this agreement - annual rate 12.44% p.a. (variable)

Your monthly minimum payment must be 2% of your statement balance (min £5, or full balance if less than £5); or, if more, an amount equal to the total of interest, late payment, over limit or returned payment charges, the PPI premium on your statement and 0.5% of your statement balance.

New transactions and charges	£429.49
New balance	£367.49
Minimum payment due	£7.34
To reach your account by	04 Sep 2016
Estimated interest £5.37	

Minimum payments
If you make only the minimum payment each month, it will take you longer and cost you more to clear your balance.

date of transaction	date entered	reference	description		amount £
			BALANCE FROM PREVIOUS STATEMENT		187.85
28 JUNE	28 JUNE	MT122410500000760	PAYMENT RECEIVED - THANK YOU		187.85CR
08 JUNE	09 JUNE	MT122220298000010	THE COFFEE HOUSE	BANBURY	6.50
13 JUNE	15 JUNE	MT122280293000010	THE SANDWICH STATION	NOTTINGHAM	6.00
15 JUNE	16 JUNE	MT122290175000010	JC CLOTHING UK	NOTTINGHAM	104.00
18 JUNE	21 JUNE	MT122340302000010	EXPRESS CHEMIST	MAIDSTONE	30.09
21 JUNE	22 JUNE	MT122350301000010	FINEST SUPERMARKET	MAIDSTONE	110.00
22 JUNE	23 JUNE	MT122360318000010	TOM'S WINE BAR	NOTTINGHAM	50.00
29 JUNE	30 JUNE	MT122430298000010	MOBILE COMMUNICATIONS LTD	0845 6000789	10.00
30 JUNE	31 JUNE	MT122490369000270	ANGELINOS ITALIANO	BASINGSTOKE	50.90

New balance	£367.49

Sandwich + Coffee £12.50
Clothes £104
Chemist £30.09
Food shopping £110
Social £100.90
Phone £10.00

£367.49 ✓

Page 1 of 2

which you can use for things that don't fit anywhere else. If the balance in that category gets sizeable, you will need to break it down into other categories – it means you didn't realise that you would have significant outgoings of that type.

Make sure you account for every item, even very small ones. Fraudsters make a lot of money from people by charging small amounts to lots of people regularly. If you don't think you should have been charged for something, ring the credit card company immediately. They will have a process to follow which will include reversing the entry out of your account quickly.

Once you have accounted for every item on the statement, calculate the total amount of money that has gone out for each budget category of your spreadsheet. Make sure that the grand total of your individual category totals is the same figure as the total monthly credits shown on the credit card statement. Were you charged interest? If so, this will show up on the statement and needs to be captured on your summary. These spend totals will be entered onto your spreadsheet as described below.

- **Debit card statement** – there is no such thing as a debit card statement. Every time you use your debit card, the transaction will immediately impact your bank account and the transaction will appear on the bank account statement. What's important is to keep and mark up your cash machine advice slip and debit card machine slip every time you use the card.

- **Store card statement** – this is the same as when you use a credit card. You will receive a slip that shows the amount and date, so mark it to show what it bought you and retain it for later use.

BUDGET STEP TWO: FILL IN YOUR MONEY SPREADSHEET

I will describe this assuming you use a spreadsheet application. Using a specifically designed technology application may automatically load payment information from your bank account, which means all you will have to do is allocate each item to a budget category.

- Take all the source documents you have collected for Money IN and OUT transactions and populate the spreadsheet. See the sample spreadsheet and replicate it, putting in the budget categories that are right for you. I find it easiest to start with any payslips and other work-related documents, followed by bank-account-related receipts (cash machine and direct debit advice slips and receipts), then my bank statement and then my credit card statements.

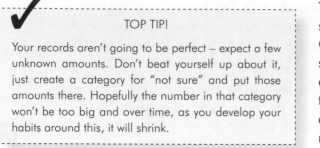

TOP TIP!

Your records aren't going to be perfect – expect a few unknown amounts. Don't beat yourself up about it, just create a category for "not sure" and put those amounts there. Hopefully the number in that category won't be too big and over time, as you develop your habits around this, it will shrink.

The process is fundamentally the same for each source document. Going from left to right on the spreadsheet columns: put in the date, then the amount into either the Money IN or Money OUT column, the event type (e.g. cash machine, direct debit), and an explanation of what the entry is for. Some people find it easiest to complete the line for each item as they go along, i.e. put the amount into the correct IN or OUT category column. Others find it easiest to get every IN and OUT item listed in the left-hand columns and then go through the classification process. Do whatever works best for you, but my process explanation will assume you do the categorisation as you populate the spreadsheet with each item.

- Turn to your bank account statement. The process there is to tick items on the statement for which you have already made entries onto the Spreadsheet (e.g. debit card entries will already have been entered, based on the advice slip and receipts, but which also appear on the bank statement). Next, look at what entries on the bank statement have not been ticked off and enter them onto the spreadsheet, completing all of the columns with the information required. Enter the amounts in the budget category columns as well.

- Then turn to your credit card (and store card) statements. Put the total amount in the OUT column and, having ticked off every receipt to the

	A	B	C	D	E
1	**MONEY SPREADSHEET**				
2	**Money Coming IN and Going OUT**				
3					
4	Date	**Amount IN**	**Amount OUT**	**Type: Cash, Credit, Debit, Other**	**Explanation**
5	01-Jan		20.00	Cash machine	Out for dinner/pub
6	01-Jan	400.00		Direct Credit	Allowance
7	03-Jan		211.00		Rent
8	05-Jan	12.00		Cash	Work tips
9	06-Jan	120.00		Pay slip/Debit	Weekly pay
10	09-Jan		5.72	Cash	Lunch
11	12-Jan		10.00	Debit Card Cash	
12	12-Jan		100.00	Cheque	Paid rent
13	13-Jan		12.35		Lunch out
14	14-Jan		15.20		Cinema

statement entry (as described in Chapter 8), enter the amounts you have summarised by category into the right hand columns.

- Next, total the entries – create a total for Money IN and also for Money OUT. Deduct the money out from the money in for the period of time you are analysing to see what you have leftover. Then do totals for every column in the spreadsheet.

- As you prepare the category totals, consider if it would be useful to break any of the categories down further (e.g. car cost can be broken down into repairs, taxes, petrol) and pay particular attention to the "other" category for each group.

- It is useful to include control figures (which are on the sample spreadsheet) so that you are always sure that the totals for summed columns are the same as the totals for the INs and OUTs columns. The spreadsheet has summary figures that result from equations in bold green to help you see where they are.

So, that is your data collected and entered into the spreadsheet. It is likely to take quite a bit of time to do this for the first few months, but it gets easy quickly.

> **TOP TIP!** ✔
>
> Add a line item for "Savings" and deduct that from the "Leftover" figure. Start to fool yourself into thinking that a little bit you are tucking away is already committed! If you try a bit, you will be amazed to find that it is remarkably easy to put aside, say, £5 a week, which is £260 in a year. You can even instruct the bank to make a monthly standing order transferring money out of your current account and into your savings account. It's like me setting my watch five minutes ahead of time so I don't miss my train. I don't know why but it works.

BUDGET STEP THREE: BEGIN EXPLORING AND UNDERSTANDING YOUR MONEY REALITY

Now you can start the interesting part of looking at the information you collected and asking yourself a bunch of questions. Just a few to start:

- What is this spreadsheet telling you overall?
    - Are you happy with the general story of what is coming IN and going OUT?
    - Does it show what you expected? What do you see that is surprising (good and bad news on this one)?
    - Do you wish you had spent differently? What was worth it and not worth it in hindsight?
    - What is your leftover figure? What could that figure have been?

- What do you think of the IN and OUT category totals?
  - Is there anything you want to do differently on the INs?
  - Where could you reduce the OUTs? Pick out a few items that you want to change or want to think about changing.
- Thinking about making changes going forward? Which of these will be a challenge to change? Which will be easy?
- What would it take to get the total IN and OUT numbers to match? Or to have money leftover?

BUDGET STEP FOUR: CREATE YOUR MONTHLY BUDGET ANALYSIS SPREADSHEET – SETTING BUDGET TARGETS

A target is a number you set for each IN and OUT category (and overall) that is what you would like the number to be. It's the figure you are going to work towards, not necessarily your first month's result.

So far so good? Congratulations for sticking with it – it does get easier! Now take the monthly figures from your money spreadsheet and populate (put the figures into) the budget analysis spreadsheet. You can now set targets for your Money IN and OUT categories. Go to each category and insert a number. You may have to have a few goes at this to get to the numbers you want and get the INs and OUTs to balance, at least as best you can. Use the first month as a guide, if that is helpful, but you may decide to ignore it as you don't like what you see. Remember, this is about you being in control of your money, so deciding what you want your money situation to look like is what you are aiming for. Take another look at your numbers, this time with an eye to target setting.

Money IN – How do the actual figures look? In total and by each component? How much of it is certain to come in and how much is hopeful? Where is that money coming from? Is it from your parents, from work or somewhere else? Is it from student loans or other educational subsidies? Or from a "free" overdraft? (Remember, money is never lent for "free".)

You can add notes on the far right of the spreadsheet for anything you want to remember about how you decided on a number. For example, you may want to make a note that in a specific month when you can work full-time, the number will be bigger.

Chances are that, at this stage of life, the Money IN part of your budget will be fairly straightforward, but it is still worth focusing on. If you increase your Money IN number because you are planning to work more, remember to factor in the income tax that may be withheld at source. That will reduce your immediate cash inflow, although you may get it back from the Inland Revenue later – almost like a forced savings plan. If you are paid cash you need to track that as well and assess whether you have earned more than the Personal Allowance and therefore need to pay money to Her Majesty's Revenue and Customs (HMRC). (To learn more about income tax, see Chapter 7.)

If you consider working more, remember to consider what impact that may have on your long-term aspirations. If you are already busy with lots going on in your life, including your studies, what will be the impact of taking on more work? It can sometimes be easier to reduce your spending than boost your earnings in order not to jeopardise your ambitions.

Make a decision on what you think is a reasonable target for each line and put that figure in each of the Money IN categories. Then summarise them as a total Money IN figure on the spreadsheet.

Money OUT – Follow the same process for these figures as you did for Money IN. It is probably going to be harder to do than the IN was. Ask yourself some questions about what you see so far and what you would like to see. What do your actual figures look like? What is surprising about them – which are you happy with and which do you want to change? What do you want to spend your money on going forward?

> **TOP TIP!**
>
> Only use cash machines that give free withdrawals. Don't be tempted to use one in a bar – incurring a £2 fee on a £20 withdrawal is not financially savvy. Note that some high street banks are limiting who can withdraw cash out of their machines for free, sometimes driven by the type of account holder you are, so be careful and check you won't be charged before you take money out.

What's Your Number?

- How many pub trips or drinks a week is reasonable?
- How much per week on eating out or socialising is reasonable?
- What do you think you need to spend on transport?
- What is reasonable to spend on clothes in a month?
- How much do you really want to spend on watching or doing sport?
- Do you really need to buy those magazines every week?

Think about the little things you could do to reduce your spending in ways that wouldn't be huge inconveniences. A few things others have suggested include:

- Surprised by London or other public transport costs? Don't buy a tube or bus ticket for a trip. Get an Oyster card or use a contactless card. A single trip within Zone 1 on the tube is £4.90 if you buy a ticket, but £2.40 with an Oyster or contactless card.

- How much do you have to spend on your car or motorcycle? How can you reduce that figure? What about driving more slowly? And revving the engine less? (Annoyingly, this has been pointed out to me!)

- Plan ahead when you are going to make a trip by train and do the same for flights.

- When you do eat out, go somewhere where you can use a coupon or they have a special deal.

- Make your own lunch to take to university, work, or school.

- Invite friends around for drinks and ask them to bring their own. That's always less costly than drinks out – over £3 for a pint compared with about £1 for a bottle of beer at home.

- Do the same for meals. Don't go out, get everyone to share or take turns cooking.

- Cut clothes purchases to zero. Only buy when you really really need it, not just because it is on sale, is easy to buy off the net, or is cheap. The most frequently cited waste of money I heard about was spending money on unneeded clothes.

Think too about where you need to put in a figure that is larger than your current month's analysis shows. Are there any categories that were unusually low and don't reflect reality? Perhaps you were busy studying for exams so you didn't have much time to spend money. Perhaps you had no big birthday parties to go to – no travel, no presents – but a few are coming up. As you set targets, take what you know is happening in the next month and typical months into account. Set realistic targets so you avoid getting fed up with the whole thing – you want to give yourself the chance to have a few easy wins with this rather than have it all be painful and impossible.

Enter the targets by category into your spreadsheet and summarise the amounts into a total Money OUT figure on the spreadsheet. Keep adjusting the figures until you are satisfied with your result.

Money IN less Money OUT

As you went through the process described above, you probably kept an eye on the IN minus OUT figure at the bottom of the spreadsheet. Now take a closer look at that.

Did you get a positive number? Great! Is that what you expected? Maybe you are already putting money aside for something big coming up or you are a saver. Or was it just a lucky month where you worked extra hours and earned more than usual or you spent less than usual?

Did you get a negative number? Possibly not a good outcome. Take a look at why. Were your INs unusually low for the month or your OUTs unusually high? Or was it a typical month, which would not be great? Look again at the INs and OUTs to see what you can do to adjust them further, but remember to keep them realistic.

Obviously if the total OUTs are bigger than the total INs every month, you are going to get into a big hole. That obviously isn't what you want, so go back again and look at what you can do to change the outcome. How are you going to fund that shortfall? Are you expecting something dramatic to change? Soon?

Once you have made any adjustments, take a last look at your results. How confident are you that you will be able to deliver on those commitments? Are you satisfied with the overall outcome? Are you living within your means or not? Are you able to save for expenditures which you know are coming up soon? And for the longer term? If you see a continual shortfall, what are you going to do about it? Keep asking yourself those questions and revising your targets until you are happy with your budget and your personal plans to meet your numbers.

A Savings Target?

Most of the people I spoke with were just trying to make ends meet, so not even thinking about saving money. I understand that situation for people still in education or not earning much money. What I couldn't understand was people earning quite a bit of money and still spending everything that came in, as if it would just keep arriving. Some of the jobs they were doing did not guarantee that steady stream of income for the longer term. What did the higher earners spend it on? Fancy restaurants, pricey holidays and expensive clothes. They explained this at the same time that they were telling me that they were worried about saving money to buy a car or a home. They hadn't thought about this saving thing. Of course I gave them a few ideas!

So can you now think about saving? It is a possibility – really! Chapter 6 covers savings in detail but a few relatively painless ideas to save a bit are included here as well.

Simple Saving Ideas

- Collect £1 coins in a jar – put your coins in daily.
- Collect copper coins in a jar – slower than pounds but an easier start.
- Set up a standing order with your bank to transfer £5 weekly or monthly from your current account to your savings account.
- Cash wage earner? Put 10% of your pay aside, storing it somewhere. (Keep in mind you may have to pay potential income taxes.)
- Earn tips as well as salary? Put 25% of tips aside after each shift. (Some of this may have to be paid over for income taxes.)
- Birthday presents? If you get cash, put it directly into a savings account so it doesn't get spent as general cash.

You can start saving as soon as you want to. In practice you will most likely start saving when you need to. I bet that you have probably already done this without thinking of it as saving. Maybe you wanted to have money for an end-of-term holiday, to travel during a pre/post university gap year, or you wanted to buy a piece of equipment for a hobby, or you wanted to buy a bike or a car, or you had a bunch of 21st birthday parties coming up. Those types of events probably made you save money, at least for a bit.

> The most frequent response I got when I asked for a "good" money story was one about saving hard to buy something (most frequent – MP3 players or games) and loving having it afterwards. Every person who told me their story conveyed a real sense of satisfaction.

You may find it useful to talk with your friends about how much money they get in and what they spend. You may be surprised to find that the numbers are all over the place. It is interesting how some people can make their money stretch really far and save; while others, who have the same amount of money coming in, or even more, are always short. How does that happen? I've found it is the little spending and saving that adds up to give a different overall result.

Research shows that nearly 40% of Britons run out of money before payday. Of the people that did have money left at the end of the month, 56% put the money into savings, 11% blew the lot on socialising and the rest left it in their current accounts. A Citizens Advice study revealed that almost half of families living on more than £70,000 suffer money worries, while even families on six figures have concerns every day over making ends meet. Precise report, May 2015

MANAGING YOUR MONEY THE WAY YOU WANT

Well, you are there! You now have a budget. Remember, the purpose of this is to help you manage your money, so get the system to work for you, adjusting the sample documents as you want. The amount of effort you will have to put into meeting your IN, OUT and SAVE targets will depend on how much you want to change what you currently do. You may have decided to change things radically or opted to just tinker around the edges, depending on past and current financial situation. At this stage of life, chances are that the changes you are trying to make are focused on the OUT categories. If those changes you are trying to make are really hard, try some simple tricks to help you.

> Stop/Slow Your Spending – HELP!
>
> * Ask your friends to help you. Let them know you are serious and want them to be firm with you.
> * Keep a crib sheet in your wallet of the categories with tough targets and keep a note of what you spend as you go along, so you always know where you are in relation to that target.

> • Put a note to yourself to slow down in front of the note section of your wallet.
>
> • Put a post-it note on your credit and debit cards saying "Do I need it?"

Changing money habits, like any habit, can be really hard at first. But changing a money habit you have chosen to change can be really satisfying. It is just like meeting other challenges you set for yourself – in sport and in your studies. I really encourage you to stick with it. If you focus on short-term money management and your long-term financial aspirations, your chance of success is really high. Why? In actuality there really is nothing mysterious or complicated about this!

KEEP YOUR TRACKING AND TARGETING GOING...FOREVER

Having done all this work, you now need to keep feeding this beast. That means continually tracking what money is coming IN and going OUT. I recommend you keep doing the detailed tracking that was outlined at the start of this chapter. So keep at it!

Collecting the Money IN and OUT data on an ongoing basis is critical. The frequency of reviewing how you are doing, relative to the targets you set for yourself, is not a daily activity. You will need to figure out the right frequency for you. Early on, or if your money is tight, you may want to do your review fairly frequently. If money isn't so tight and once you get the hang of your "normal" money patterns you may not feel the need to do it too often. Having said that, it won't be of much help to you if you do it less than every couple of months.

We have done this tracking for years and I still notice two things: there is always something that surprises me when we do a periodic review; and when things are tight it really helps us figure out where we can cut our spending, even if we need to do it just for a month or two.

What does this periodic review involve? As you review the numbers, the fundamental decision you need to make is: if there is a gap between the actual and target figures, is it due to an inappropriate target that should be adjusted, or is it due to behaviour inconsistent (good or bad) with your plans when you set the target? If the actual and target numbers are the same, consider them too and think if you want to change any of them. Some sample questions to kick-start your review are included in the following box.

Sample Questions for Your Periodic Money Reviews

• Where do the target and actual numbers differ?

• Have you managed to achieve your Money IN and Money OUT targets?

• How do the savings figures look?

• As you go through each category, what do you think? Were you on the money or did you have a one-off target miss that needed adjusting?

• Are your targets too optimistic? Or did you go off track a bit but think the target numbers are good and want to keep them?

Give the INs and OUTs a thorough review and examine what your see. Then decide on what targets you want to set for yourself going forward. Input those into the spreadsheet, retaining your target history, so you can reflect back on your successes over time. I have included a year-to-date figure on the far right of the spreadsheet. You can use that and do all sorts of other analyses of averages, trends and whatever else you want.

If you keep doing this you will find that you pretty much know how you are doing versus your budget at any time. Your efforts at increasing awareness of what you do with your money will pay off, and by the time you get to the end of each month you will be pretty sure if you are near your targets or not before you prepare your analysis. Having a nil balance in your bank account, being overdrawn or having cash in hand to move to a savings account won't come as a surprise. You'll know without having to look if your back account is healthy or sickly.

MANAGING YOUR MONEY

You now have what eventually will feel like an easy way to know what is going on with your money. That puts you in a position of control. You will know how much you can earn and spend and each time you make a money decision you will be able to do it based on facts. As you do this tracking, you may conclude that you can't match your INs and OUTs every month – and that is okay. There are a lot of variables, particularly around spending. It is hard for example to absorb big spends like holidays and parties into the monthly targets. This is where saving will help you – putting a bit aside regularly is an easy way to be ready for those bigger events. That isn't the way to fund the buying of a house or a car, but it is the easiest way to even out some of the smaller money needs you will have. The other way to meet short-term money needs is to go overdrawn, use your credit card or borrow money from somewhere. Each of those has costs attached, which are explained in the next chapter.

You may find that repaying borrowed money and the costs of borrowing that money never feels great. That is probably because the fun from the money you spent is already a distant memory. Have you ever been a bit fed up in that situation? You start thinking, "Why did I splash out so much on that party?" "Why did I buy those shoes?" "That concert wasn't that much fun." You get the picture? If, on the other hand, you can absorb those special events through money, you have already saved up, so you have done the hard work of saving you might find that you enjoy the event even more due to the satisfaction of having earned it.

I am confident that, by incorporating the ideas included here into your daily life, you will begin to increase your control over your financial decisions and destiny. And that is likely to feel pretty good. This discipline will help you prepare for future, bigger financial decisions you will make, but in the short term it is likely to boost your confidence in you.

Chapter Five

Handling A Money Shortfall

N THE PREVIOUS chapter you learned how to budget, which will help you manage your money effectively. In particular, your budget will help you keep an eye on your spending so you can adjust it (as in spend less) as you go along. It will also help you see exactly how much money you are bringing in. You can even use your budgeting tools to see what you are borrowing and what it is costing you.

So, if you do everything right you shouldn't ever have a shortfall? Well, that would be unrealistic. Chances are that there will be times when you will find yourself short of money – either you got in less, or you spent more, than you expected. It's difficult to keep the money incomings and outgoings perfectly balanced. A small shortfall here and there can be met by drawing money out of your savings account, using credit cards or accessing authorised overdrafts. But what if you find yourself really short for a month or two? What if you don't have any savings to rely on?

I was surprised by the number of stories I heard about people getting way into debt and what they did to get themselves out of it. These stories were from people in their mid- to late-20s who had fallen into big debts without realising what they were doing. The debts crept up, slowly at first and then they accelerated. This is what you want to avoid. Therefore, when you have a shortfall, you need to think about how to find the funds to cover it at the lowest cost to you.

> *Young people are having more money problems than ever before. The number of 17 to 24-year-olds seeking help for debt problems has risen 20% in a year. They have an average debt to income ratio of nearly 70%, which is nearly double the 34% of 25 to 29-year-olds. The amount is roughly £12,000.*

The cost of borrowing from banks and other institutions (e.g. credit cards, store cards) is covered in Chapter 8. We will tackle big borrowing decisions later – those are generally ones you plan for: what you might call "good debt". For now, let's focus on short-term money shortfalls.

YOUR MONEY HABITS

The habits you establish now, around avoiding money shortfalls and handling them well, are an important component of your ability to manage your money the way you want. Some people only suffer temporary cash shortfalls. They are careful, sticking to budgets, putting money aside for later, so they can draw on their savings account if they need money. It is only in the last 15 years or so that credit cards, overdrafts and store cards have been so widely offered, even to those with relatively low incomes, like students. Before that we all existed with cash and cheques. If we went overdrawn, the penalties were large, so we worked hard to avoid running short of money.

It is still possible to manage your money that way. Whilst researching, I found that some young adults who were given credit by their banks, and others, hardly ever used it. On the other hand, some borrowed as much as they could, maxing out on overdrafts and cards. The latter group was sometimes surprised when they had to pay the money back plus interest. University students often get caught out as banks will offer them free overdrafts that become interest-bearing once they graduate. Apparently, more than half of all UK university students do not understand that they will be charged interest on bank loans! (They need to read this book!)

Your approach to managing money is yours to develop. Some people, and this can be at any age, seem to always live beyond their means. That means they are spending more than they have coming in, month after month. You may have read stories like this in the paper – some people even go bankrupt to clear their debts and start again. And some even go bankrupt again. You may wonder how in the world people get themselves into these sorts of situations. Generally people don't aim to end up bankrupt, or homeless which sometimes follows. It is one of those things that starts small and grows when the person isn't paying attention. But you can choose to avoid that situation. Other people seem to be totally in control of their finances, never needing a loan from anywhere. The really cautious ones need to be pushed to get credit cards – which you need to start building a credit history (see Chapter 9 to learn about credit scores).

Here are a few questions to get you thinking about your view towards managing cash flow and debt:

- How would you feel if you were getting further and further into debt?
- How would you know it was happening? Would it matter to you?
- Would it matter enough that you would want to do something about it, or is it something you'd think about "later on", if it does happen?
- Would you have the discipline to change whatever behaviour was the cause of the growing debt?

If you are at university at the moment, here are a few additional questions to consider. Do you have plans for paying off your student debt in total? Or to pay it monthly as a payroll deduction? Which option is economically better for you? What are you doing about that "free" overdraft that won't be "free" forever?

Depending on when you graduate, think carefully before rushing to pay off your student loan, beyond what is mandatory. This is because, for those taking out a loan before September 2012, the rate of interest is low (currently 0.9% until 31 August 2016), relative to other borrowing options, and the cash you use to pay off the loan today is cash you may want to use in the coming years for something else. Let me give you an example: a relative gives you money to pay your loan off in full when you graduate (but doesn't say you must pay off the loan with it). You plan to buy a property in the next five years and you will need a deposit for that. So why not keep your loan outstanding, put the cash in the bank (maybe even tie it up for a few years so you earn a higher rate of interest as explained in Chapter 6), and then use the cash for your home deposit? However, for those who started to borrow from September 2012, the interest rate is 3.9% and much closer to the market, so is less advantageous.

I am not suggesting you should never borrow money, but I encourage you to keep things under your control so you can see the need before you are in a crisis. That means always knowing what your money situation is and making conscious decisions about borrowing money (or buying on credit, which is the same thing, but, for simplicity, bear in mind that when I say borrowing I mean both). It is also about thinking through where and how you borrow money. And making the time to think up-front about how you will pay the interest and loan off. Most importantly, you want to make sure you don't end up in an upward debt cycle where you keep throwing money away on debt interest payments.

FAMILY MATTERS

Earlier on we touched on your experiences with money whilst growing up and the impact they may have on how you manage your money today. This concept also applies to your approach to debt. Families manage their debt levels in lots of different ways. Very few live the "cash only" way, though I do know some who do. Many live fairly prudently – reasonable mortgages for their home, maybe a car loan and credit cards they pay off most of the time and that sort of thing. Others take more risks – big mortgages relative to home value, sizeable personal loans, carrying large credit and store card balances. I like to think that, by and large, people are pretty responsible and the number of people who spend as if they will never have to pay for what they buy is pretty small.

Generally, people get into a financial muddle little by little. They spend assuming they will get pay increases or think they can cut spending in some areas but it doesn't work out that way. And then what feels like a sudden event materialises and they are in deep debt they can't manage their way out of. The last event may not be large; it is just the thing that pushes their financial situation over the edge. How does it happen? People use their credit cards or store cards and get to the point where they can't clear the end of month balance. Those debts get bigger and bigger each month when they are not paid off. At the percentage rates applied, the account balances can get big fast, and so being able to pay the balance gets harder and harder.

Take a moment to think about the finances in your family. In particular, think about the views towards debt – how were overdrafts, loans from friends, credit card and store card debts viewed and managed? What impact do you think you family background has had on your approach to taking on and managing debt? This is another moment for self-reflection.

WHERE TO GO TO BORROW MONEY

So, what do you do, or what will you do, when you run short of cash? Each option described in this chapter will vary in terms of your ability to access funds and the cost you will be charged for those funds. The actual cost to you will be impacted by how much you need, how long you need it, and how risky the lender thinks you are (based on your credit score).

Before you proceed, have answers to four questions:

- How much do I need to borrow?
- How long do I need to borrow it for?
- How much will it cost me in total (what you borrow plus interest)?
- How and when will I be able to pay it back?

When you are making any decision, you identify options, evaluate the pros and cons of each and then make a choice. The decision on what to do if you need money is no different except for two extra elements. The first is who is willing to lend you money and at what cost? The risk/reward trade-off concept mentioned earlier features – the higher the risk you are perceived to be, the more you will have to pay to borrow the money. And the second is speed. Chances are that, when you need money, you need it fast, and speed costs money.

So, places to turn to when you are in need:

Family
There may be many reasons why this is not where you want to go when you need money. Perhaps you have already exhausted this option. Perhaps no one in your family has money to lend you, even if you were willing to ask. Maybe you don't want to ask your family because you don't want them to know you are in a muddle. But, if your shortage is legitimate and one-off and you think someone in your family has the money to lend you, it is worth starting here. A key reason is the risk/reward trade off. The lender knows you and your creditworthiness, so it is likely to cost less than other borrowing routes. As long as they do think you will pay the money back!

The most effective approach to a family member is a respectful one. Explain your situation, how it came about, and how you plan to work your way out of it. This will help your relative understand that you "get it". Offering to borrow money on commercial terms is a very useful tactic. Show the person you mean business by offering to pay a fair rate of interest and suggesting a realistic repayment date. Paying interest monthly rather than at the end of the loan will give ongoing confidence about your payback commitment. Borrowing from a relative can be a win-win because if they have cash in the bank earning a low interest rate and you offer them a higher rate, which is still lower than you would have to pay elsewhere, you will both be happy.

As a parent, I can say that most of us, if we have the resources, are willing to support our families through a muddle or two. When it becomes a chronic problem, we get a bit grumpy. To be honest, I have yet to see a person well served through continual financial mess family bail-outs. Eventually, we all have to stand on our own two feet, so, the earlier we start practising, the better.

The first flat I bought in New York cost £37,500 and I had to pay a 50% deposit. Needless to say, I didn't have the money, so I borrowed from my parents and a good friend who had inherited money. I did proper written loan agreements for both and paid monthly interest. The commercial loan strategy worked really well within my family as I had three siblings and we didn't want each other to get preferential treatment.

Friends

This is also an option for borrowing funds, as long as they are small amounts and you know you can pay them back quickly. On a day-to-day basis, when you are short of cash, this is the most likely place to turn. Your friends will figure out if they can trust you to pay them back and you will do the same about lending to them.

I have seen more than a few awkward situations around this, though. It is easy to forget who lent who what, so, as soon as you lend or borrow money, write it down. Whatever you do, don't forget to pay your friends back as soon as possible and ensure you are similarly paid back when you lend money. This advice may seem silly, but people simply forget. Having to ask a friend for repayment can be uncomfortable. I have seen good friendships go bad when the borrower was poorly organised and the lender had to ask repeatedly for repayment. No one likes a friendship to be taken for granted in any way, let alone financially. If you have a friend who you don't want to lend money to because of payback issues, try to help him sort out his finances including finding other ways for him to borrow what he needs.

Banks

This is a natural place to turn as they are in the business of lending money, though it may be that the lending they have provided is what landed you in trouble in the first place. (Chapter 8 includes a lot of information about banks and explains terminology used below, so flip to that chapter if anything is unclear as you read it.) Always remember that banks are in the business of making money from you. They will always charge more to lend you money than they will give you on money you have deposited with them. The short-term loans you get from the banks, through overdraft facilities and credit cards, may be free to you now, but they will not be free forever, so consider carefully how dependent you want to get on those. Going overdrawn without agreement, meaning there is no money in your bank account, which can happen if you have no overdraft agreement or if you exceed your authorised overdraft limit, is expensive. If you do go overdrawn, check your bank statement carefully for how your cash receipts and payments were processed. Banks are now required to process all direct credits to your account (things that increase your balance, such as payslips) before they process debits.

If your account balance goes below zero, your bank will charge you money as it is, in effect, providing you with a loan. You will be charged interest at the rate disclosed in their terms and conditions AND the bank will charge you a fee/penalty for using the overdraft facility. The government is putting pressure on banks to revise their charging methods – typically a charge to access the overdraft, and then a daily charge. Some banks allow a few days grace for small overdrafts. The key is to read your bank's terms and conditions VERY carefully and notice early if you are likely to go overdrawn.

Don't draw the cash you need by using your credit card, as it will be treated by the card provider as a loan at a very high rate of interest. If you are going to do this, read the terms and conditions for the credit card to make sure you understand the cost that you will incur.

Always read the fine print on the terms and conditions provided by a bank for any product. And if something happens and you feel hard done by, do complain to the bank, clearly explaining the situation and suggesting how they could remedy your situation. This is typically done by calling a complaints number provided in the terms and conditions the bank gave you when you opened your account or set up your overdraft. Be aware that you will probably be ringing into a call centre, manned by people who handle frustrated customers all day, so make it easy for them to help you. If, after dealing with the bank you are still not satisfied, you should contact the Financial Ombudsman Service via www.financial-ombudsman.org.uk.

Banks will also offer you loans for car purchases, personal finance needs and home purchases (mortgages). The amount they lend you, the length (term) of the loan and the interest rate will be impacted by the bank's perceived risk of lending you money. If you take out a bank loan and at some point during the term of the loan you find you are struggling to meet your payments, get in touch with the bank as soon as you see you have a potential problem. Don't think to yourself, "Well, things will get better." They usually don't get better without a change in your money management strategy, which may take a bit of time. If you talk with your bank early, the bank may let you have a payment holiday to give you time to sort yourself out. If anything good came out of the

> I had a shock once, because, whilst I paid all my credit cards off monthly, I didn't realise that if I withdrew money using my credit card they charged me interest on the full month's balance, even though I paid the full balance off that month!

2008 financial crisis, it was the increase in most banks' willingness to work with customers to figure out how to restructure their loans. The banks have learned that they are better off for their payments, maybe absorbing a few months of unpaid interest, but helping the borrower ultimately pay off the money borrowed. If they push the borrower to pay as originally agreed at all costs, the bank may lose all of its money, as the borrower is more likely to go bankrupt and never pay the loan, leaving the lender with nothing. If the loan is secured on a home or a car, the bank may take these to pay off the loan. Banks can be quite patient, actually, but you have to be upfront with them. So if your short- or long-term debts are getting big and messy, talk to your bank.

It is a huge mistake to make a payment on a long-term loan, like a mortgage, with a credit card. Doing that will increase the speed with which your financial situation will deteriorate, because long-term borrowing rates are lower (call it 4%) than short-term ones (currently around 19% on bank credit cards). By paying your mortgage with the card you are turning the cost of borrowing money from 4% to 19% – obviously not a good thing to do.

The Internet

If you need money quickly and short term you can turn to the internet. If you search on "borrow money", "payday lenders" or "short-term money loans", a list of lenders will come up. Many of these lenders have closed down since the UK regulator put restrictions on their fee charging arrangements. Their fees used to be unrestricted but, since late 2014, you can only be charged 0.8% of the loan amount per day, £15 for defaulting on your loan and total costs of borrowing of 100% of the original amount borrowed. There has been a great deal of press coverage about these lenders, most of it negative. However, if one is objective about the costs, these can be the most cost-effective way to borrow money. The BIG "but" here is that whenever you borrow money, you MUST know how you are going to repay it. By that I mean have a really clear plan for how to meet the payment due date with 100% certainty. I am not recommending any of them. If you are going to investigate this route for raising cash, it is probably worth taking a look at moneysupermarket.com, as it has a cost comparison facility, and outlines the risks of these loans in great detail.

I know people who have successfully and unsuccessfully used some of these firms. It is always best to avoid having to borrow money, particularly at a high interest rate. If you must, make sure you are totally sure you will be able to pay it back on the initial day you agree to. Read the small print, particularly regarding repayment procedures, as they are very detailed and it is easy to trip up on them. A few people provided some bad stories about these.

The important issue here is to compare the ways you can borrow money and the actual cost of borrowing. The payday loan providers argue that the annualised percentage rate they provide is not meaningful, as the loan is very short-term in nature. They also argue that banks report misleading costs of borrowing, as the costs they report include interest charges only, not the other fees charged for that borrowing. Which brings us back to the key point – which is, do your sums carefully!

"Ban payday lenders and the vulnerable will be forced to use loan sharks. Restricting payday lending will likely harm the very people it intends to help – the poor. Most attacks on payday loans cite truly eye-watering rates of interest...these are misleading. They are annualised percentage rates which are only a useful means of comparison if a loan is repaid over a longer period. Payday loan rates aren't really interest rates at all. The administration costs of these payday loans are included in the quoted rate...the loans are almost always paid over a shorter period so the actual amount of interest paid is nothing like that suggested by the annualised rate."
City AM, 7 March, 2011.

What the payday loan firms are very good at is processing customer requests quickly, which adds to their risk of lending. They will turn loan applications around in hours, not the days or weeks a bank may take. They will do a basic check of credit information including your credit, employment, and any borrowing repayment history. They in effect do their own credit scoring to put you in a high-, medium- or low-risk category which they use to set the rate of interest they will charge you. If you do take this route, look at the details provided on the website carefully. And most importantly make sure you are going to be able to pay the loan back at the end of the term.

Are payday loan providers really that expensive? Let's assume you borrow £200 from a high street bank for a month under an unplanned overdraft arrangement. That £200 will cost you £80 in overdraft fees, not to mention any charges for returned items and interest on the outstanding balance. To borrow £200 from Wonga will cost you around £66. A few articles in the press have included this calculation to show that payday loans are not inherently a bad thing.

Pawnbrokers

You may not have heard of a pawnbroker, though they have been in the press, as their businesses have increased significantly since the financial crisis. These companies can be used to raise cash quickly through short-term loans. The rates charged will be less than the internet loans described above. Why? Because the loans are lower-risk, as they are secured on whatever you are going to give the pawnbroker to hold until you pay the loan and interest off. Take a look at borro.com.

The way pawnbrokers work is that you take something valuable (this is a limitation as they only accept luxury items such as expensive jewellery, watches and antiques) and they lend you money for a period of time, based on a fraction of the value of what you leave with them. In the past you had to go to a shop, but now you can go online and post your goods to them. Using the online facility you can find out how much the shop will lend you and at what rate before you send your goods to them. You will have to pay the loan back in regular instalments, as well as the related interest. If you pay the interest and loan in accordance with your agreement, you get your possession back. If you don't, they take possession of your valuable item. They in turn will sell that item to get their money back.

Unauthorised Lenders

I mention these with some trepidation, as I don't want to give this group airtime, but you need to be aware of them. These are some not very nice people who take advantage of people in financial distress, particularly those who are desperate for money and can't get it anywhere else. The reasons may include, among other things, being an illegal immigrant, having no credit rating, not knowing how banks or other means of fund-raising work, and being illiterate. When people need money, say to put food on the table for their children, they will turn wherever they have to. Unauthorised lenders (sometimes referred to as loan sharks) provide money at huge interest rates and, if they aren't paid, the situation can deteriorate to one of physical danger. Avoid these at all costs.

GETTING AND STAYING OUT OF A MESS

Whatever approach you take to borrowing money to get you through a short-term challenge (a gentle reminder that if you manage your money effectively, this will be a one-off short-term blip) you will need to find a way to pay the interest and loan back. In other words, having gotten yourself into this, you need to find a way out. And this is where that budget will really help you.

Keep in mind that if you really are in a jam, there may be no time to analyse anything. Take a fast decision and cut back your spending to the absolute bare minimum. Be draconian if you have to be!

Look at your budget analysis spreadsheet to see what caused the shortfall. Was it a problem with the incoming or the outgoing money? Take a look at each category. What do you see? And what can you learn from that? Maybe you were doing just fine with your money and then something unexpected came up and you had nothing saved to fall back on. Maybe you were overly optimistic in the spending cutback targets you set in a previous month. Chances are your money shortfall was caused by the OUT side of the money equation. Consider what happened, and what could happen in the future, to create an overspend in any of the categories. A few things that may have cropped up include major birthday parties, weddings, holidays you didn't want to miss, bike repairs and car services. But it could have been the IN side as suggested in the box below. Review that too for possibilities of what to do for the future.

Possible reasons for less money coming in than expected:

- You were ill and couldn't work.
- Tax withheld from your pay increased because your tax code changed (see Chapter 7).
- Your parents forgot to send your allowance and aren't reachable or don't have the money.
- Your student loan money didn't come through.

Now turn to the practicalities. How big is the shortfall and what timeframe do you want to set for paying it back? Figure out the total amount of money you will have to repay – the loan and interest and when you will have to make those payments. Look at the budget categories and figure out if you can increase the money coming in or reduce the money going out. Consider if you want those changes to be temporary or permanent adjustments to your budget.

> Be realistic about how much you need to borrow and for how long. This is not the time to be overly optimistic. You don't want to miscalculate and fall short on your loan repayment commitments, so don't make it too tight.

If you can't figure out how to make the maths work, try harder and think creatively. You can figure this out, as many people before you have. They also thought it was an unfixable disaster at the time. And, once the trauma subsides, think about setting up a savings category in your budget and figure out ways to start saving that money, so that next time a money crunch arises, as it likely will, you have something to fall back on.

A LEARNING OPPORTUNITY

As I mentioned before, don't sweat the one-off money lapses, just learn to see them early and recover quickly. You would have to be extremely disciplined to never run short of cash. Recovery is manageable as long as the money hole is not too big and it hasn't existed for long, so watch your money carefully throughout the month and during your monthly budget review.

> One of the best techniques to help you stay within your spending budget is to slow down your spending decisions. Stop to think:
>
> • Do I really want that?
> • Do I really need that?
> • Is it worth going off budget or overdrawn for?
> • How will I feel about this tomorrow?
> • Whatever it is, can I get it cheaper?

There will be times in your life when you decide to take a big leap financially. Like when you buy a car or a home or go on a long blow-out holiday or give up your job because you hate it. These may be life-defining moments in many ways. They can turn out to be some of the greatest life and money opportunities despite what they feel like at the time. The work you are doing now to manage your money, learn about financial options, and save a bit will all serve you well. Yes, even digging yourself out of a self-inflicted money black hole is going to be useful. So go easy on yourself, get sorted and move on.

Some money learning opportunities are missed out on due to well-intentioned parents. It can seem easy for parents, if they have the money, to bail their offspring out of financial problems. It starts with little amounts and slowly creeps up to bigger amounts. I have seen families that are always there to top up allowance overspends, provide cars and insurance, and provide housing. I have even watched some "lucky" beneficiaries roll through several major inheritances with nothing to show for them. But when that flow stops, for whatever reason, those same people find themselves financially clueless and seemingly unable to cope with managing their finances. I have seen the same struggle on a smaller scale when allowances are suddenly stopped.

Learning and practising now to set and remain within budgets, as well as learning about borrowing, will save you lots of headaches in the future – promise!

Chapter Six

Excess Money

I F YOU WERE just about to turn the page – STOP! It may not feel like it right now, but this really is a possibility. The goal is to turn saving money into a habit, and the best way to do that is to start small. Small savings, put aside regularly, can turn into sizeable stashes of cash. Small and big savings also come out of not spending; so take all the messages in this chapter to heart, and think before you spend. Mostly, though, start small and think big! In this chapter we will review a few ways to start saving and then explore what to do with it to turn those small savings into bigger money pots.

Saving money is being encouraged by the government through the establishment of a personal savings allowance. The result is that a basic rate taxpayer will be able to earn £1,000 of interest from savings without paying tax. Higher rate tax payers will be able to earn £500 tax-free. Additional rate taxpayers will not be entitled to the personal savings allowance.

One guy told me that at the end of each week he took whatever money he had, converted it into pound coins and put them in a glass jar. Being able to actually see the jar filling up kept him motivated to keep saving. He did say that the tactic took a bit of time to work, as the jar was really big, but it had to be big to meet his high savings hopes. (I now have my own money jar in my kitchen.) How might this work for you? Are you willing to give it a try? Maybe you want to start with a small jar? Maybe just use it to save up for presents for big birthdays coming up or a holiday?

Ideas To Help You Save Money

- Use a glass money jar for general savings – for all coins or selected ones like pound coins.
- Save for a specific need and track your savings progress towards that goal – e.g. a holiday, a pair shoes, or a deposit on car.
- Make a graph of the amount of money in your savings account and put it on your wall.
- Make the graph more complicated to show your income versus savings.

Of course, you can spend every last bit of money you get in. I have seen quite a few people, used to spending all the money they have, keep spending it all even when the money coming in gets large. It seems to me that when your pay increases, it is a great moment to start saving. When I suggested that I got one of two responses: "Why should I? I'm enjoying myself" and "I wouldn't know what to do with the savings; I won't earn anything if I deposit it in a bank account." This chapter will help with the second response.

The first response is a difficult one to address. The thing is, over the course of your working life, you are likely to have financial ups and downs. The ups may be great but, when your income decreases or plateaus at the same time as your expenses increase, you may get uncomfortable. If you want to see what happens take a read through recent articles about the financial services industry where thousands of people have been made redundant – some of those people are creating new businesses, but some are really struggling. The redundancies in the public sector did wreak financial havoc for many families – ones who thought that by working for the government they were guaranteed their jobs for life. I have seen people who were really well off get into difficulties and vice versa. You never know what is around the corner. So, when you find yourself on a money roll, enjoy the ride, but realise that it may not last forever. With that in mind, why not keep some money back? By thinking about it as it happens you are less likely to look back with regret, thinking, "Where did all that money go?"

As you get older you will face bigger financial decisions, like buying cars or property, and non-financial decisions with financial implications, like living with someone, getting married, or having children. Those may all seem like a long time away from where you sit, but add 10 or 15 years to your current age and think again. Setting aside a bit of money each time you get paid, or saving birthday money, or collecting coins, can generate quite a bit of money in a fairly painless way. Just do the maths and you will see how a little bit can become a lot. For example, £10 per month for ten years would give you £1,200. Add in maybe some birthday or graduation money, a few months where you put aside more than the £10, and throw in some interest – and you can see the possibility! The point here is that "little but often" works better for most of us than trying to set big amounts aside. I encourage you to use your budgeting review processes to push yourself to carve out a little more savings every month.

WHAT TO DO WITH SAVINGS –
KEY CONCEPTS AND TERMINOLOGY

Once you have saved up some money, you will start to think about how to make that money make more money for you. As gratifying as it is to see the jar filling up by putting money in, it would be even better if it increased beyond what you put in. You might move your money from the jar to a savings account in your current bank, but then you might wonder if you are getting rewarded enough for leaving your money there. We will explore several options for what you can do with your savings. Before we look at specific options, let's consider the key concepts that apply across the board. As you will see there is quite a bit of "lingo" around investment opportunities so I'll explain that as well.

Rate of return – the fundamental concept of saving is that you want to earn a reasonable rate of return. Bear this in mind as you explore options. The higher the rate of return, the sooner you will reach your financial goal. If you earn a rate that is greater than the rate of inflation you are making economic headway. (Take a look at Chapter 12 to make sense of that comment.) But keep an eye on the level of risk you are taking on and your ability to get your money when you need it (see "Liquidity" overleaf).

Annual equivalent rate (AER) (explained in Chapter 8). This number tells you the rate of interest you will earn if you leave your money in an account/savings vehicle for a full year. Financial institutions are required to calculate AERs by following a set formula which makes it easy for you to

TOP TIP!

Put a small amount of money aside regularly and keep it in a separate bank account from your spending money. Some university students put their student loan funds in one account and all cash in another, transferring an amount from the loan account to the cash account monthly.

compare offerings. The percentage rate is the interest you will receive divided by the money you have invested, annualised. You may be paid interest monthly or annually, with annually being slightly better, although for small amounts it doesn't make much difference. It does matter for large sums. Unlike some other investments we will explore, with these you will know when you will be paid interest and how much it will be. You may be wondering why there are different AERs on offer by different banks and for different products. We will explore the reasons for that soon.

If the rate of return looks too good to be true…it probably is!

Risk/reward principle – this comes up time and again in relation to any money decision. (It is covered more thoroughly in Chapters 8 and 12.) You want to keep this principle top of your mind when you are investing. If an investment opportunity has a return that looks great, you need to look at it carefully. Chances are it poses a high risk, which is fine as long as you understand the potential upside and downside. You will see that any advertising or document related to an investment will have a prominent disclosure that states "the value of this investment may go down as well as up".

Liquidity – this is another critical concept when it comes to investing. What liquidity describes is how quickly you can turn your investment into cash. One of the reasons many bank savings accounts provide such a low rate of interest is that you can withdraw your money at any time without giving the bank any notice that you plan to do it. The longer the period you commit to someone having your money, the more they will pay you for it. So whilst you may be happy with a high rate of return, you won't be so happy if you can't access your money when you want it.

In many cases you will be able to access your money even if you have committed to leaving it for a set period, but you will be charged a penalty fee. In my experience that can easily wipe out any income previously received. Let me demonstrate what I mean by liquidity. You think that investing money in a home is an attractive investment option for many reasons. What is not attractive is the fact that it can take time to sell it and that if you need the money you have invested in it, you can't turn it into cash quickly. A house is an illiquid asset. Follow the guideline that, if you think you may need the money you've saved at short notice, keep it somewhere where you can easily get to it.

> 67% of consumers find choosing suitable financial products too complicated.

Investment-related taxes – whenever you think about investment options, you need to consider the impact of taxes. Chapter 7 covers all things pay-related including taxes on your earned income (meaning from your job). Income from savings and related investments also attracts tax. As a general rule, ongoing investment income earned from money invested, in the form of interest and dividends (see below, under Equities) will be taxed at the same rates as your work-related earned income. As noted above, for the 2016/17 tax year, the first £1,000 or £500 of savings income will be tax-free for basic rate and higher rate taxpayers respectively. The amount earned will need to be included in your tax return if you are required to file one, and if your investment earnings exceed a set amount it may cause you have to file a tax return at the end of the tax year. You may also earn gains from investment transactions, e.g. you sell a share/stock for more than you paid for it. That increase in value is called a capital gain and will be taxed at a lower rate than earned income. Currently (2016/17) you only have to pay tax on these if you make capital gains in excess of £11,100 during the tax year. (The sale of your car, the sale of an asset for less than £6,000 and the sale of your home are exempt from this tax.) In general terms, capital gains that exceed the allowance will be taxed at a rate of 10% for basic rate taxpayers and 20% for higher rate taxpayers.

Tax treatments, rates and exemptions will change over time and are too complex to cover in detail here, though I will alert you to the issues throughout the chapter. Just keep the concepts in mind and when you are investing think: are the earnings generated subject to income tax? Is the transaction subject to capital gains tax? Is the investment of money tax-effective? If it is subject to tax, when does the tax have to be paid? Under the "time value of money" concept, that is explained in Chapter 8, if you can delay paying tax, that is a good thing.

Fixed-term deposit – you are quite likely to hold the money you save with a bank. If it is held in an ordinary savings account, where you can get to it whenever you want, you won't get much interest. The next step up in terms of return and commitment is to put the money on fixed-term deposit, which is exactly what it sounds like: you commit to leaving a certain amount of money on deposit with your bank, or another financial institution, for a specified amount of time. In return for that commitment you will be paid a higher rate of interest. The reason the institution is giving you a higher rate is that it can lend out your money to people who want to borrow money, and those borrowers will have to pay a higher rate of interest than the bank is paying you. If you withdraw your money before the agreed time, you will be subject to a sizeable penalty. Note: you will frequently see these deposit offerings described as fixed-term bonds. (To avoid confusion we will separate these from what I call "real bonds" that are described later. The reason for the distinction is twofold: these are shorter-term than real bonds, and you cannot buy and sell these investments to others.)

Equities (also described as shares or stocks) – this is one of the two fundamental investment types. Equity describes ownership in a company; when you buy a share or stock you are buying ownership. Through this ownership you are entitled to two things: a periodic dividend payment (generally paid annually, or for larger companies semi-annually) and participation in the increase or decrease in the overall value of the company. Many people start by investing their money in these because you can buy shares across a full price spectrum, from pence to thousands of pounds. Shares can be traded through an account you set up with a broker (which can be executed via the internet). If you are interested in investing in equities, consider diversifying your risk by investing through unit trusts, funds, or collectives. These are managed by professional investment managers, whose investment materials will be given to you to review, so that you can see what they are investing in. Rather than buying shares yourself in individual companies, you will be buying shares in pools of investment they manage.

Bonds (debt) – bonds are issued by a government or company to raise money. When you invest in these, you are investing in what is in effect an IOU from the issuer. The issuer commits to pay you interest at a specified rate on specified dates, and to pay the principal amount of the bond when it reaches maturity (the agreed end of the loan period). The rate of interest the borrower commits to paying depends on the perceived level of risk investors have of the borrower. If investors think the borrower is absolutely certain to make the payments as they fall due, the interest rate will be lower (because they are lower risk) than if they think the issuer is less likely to make the specified payments. This holds true for companies as well as governments. Think Greece and Spain versus Germany – who has to pay more in interest?

Bonds are "negotiable", meaning they can be traded on secondary markets. That means you can buy and sell them in the same way as equities. Historically, bonds were issued in large denominations, tens of thousands of pounds, which made them inaccessible to the majority of private investors. The only way to do so was to invest through unit trusts, funds or collectives that operate as described in the preceding paragraph. That changed in 2010 when the London Stock Exchange launched a retail bond platform, enabling direct access to this market, in addition to the previous ways.

One other way to invest in bonds is to invest in UK gilts, which are IOUs issued by the UK government. They are typically issued in denominations of £100, but you can invest any amount you like in them – even just one pence.

As explained earlier, the term "bond" is also used to describe fixed-term deposits held in a bank or building society, but I think it is better to think of them separately to these.

General economic environment – this is a description of what is going on in the environment around you, i.e. what government is in power, what are UK interest rates doing, how is the EU and the euro doing, how is manufacturing doing, what is the rate of unemployment, what is the rate of inflation? This overall environment will have a huge impact on your investments. I hear lots of complaints at the moment about the low returns on investments – "What is the point of saving if I get so little interest?" Well, the flip side of earning a low interest rate on deposits is that the interest rate on any money you borrow will also be low. (Read more about economics in Chapter 12.)

SAVINGS ACCOUNTS

Whilst the money jars mentioned at the start of this chapter are useful, they don't earn you any interest. Once you have a bit of money, you want to find ways to make it make more money for you. Your starting point is likely to be deposit/savings accounts at a bank or somewhere else. We will explore options around this now. You will always want to achieve this outcome: your money is safe, you can get to it when you need it within agreed time constraints, and you want to get paid for letting someone else use your money.

Your Bank

The easiest place to save money is with the bank where you have your current account. Setting up a savings account is as easy as filling in a form, because your bank knows who you are. By having your current and savings account in one bank, you will be able to easily move money between accounts. You don't need to go into the bank, just do it online, and the money will be moved in real time, i.e. effective immediately. You can also set up a standing order with the bank, instructing them to move a specific amount of money from your current account to your deposit account on a regular basis. This self-inflicted savings plan was cited by several people as a good way to keep them from spending all the money they earned.

The downside of keeping your savings invested in a deposit account, whether it is where you have your current account or another bank, is that the bank won't pay you much for leaving your money there. This is because the bank is low risk to you and you can get hold of your money at a moment's notice. The UK government will guarantee that the money on deposit with a bank will be protected, i.e. returned to you even if the bank goes bankrupt, up to a total of £75,000. The bank will express the return you earn as a percentage AER, which you have probably seen on display in banks and in adverts.

Interest earned: If you have £1,000 on deposit in a bank account all month and the AER is 1%, you will earn £0.83 interest in a month (£1,000 times 0.01 divided by 12). And if you leave £1,000 in the account all year you will earn £10 interest (if you are on an annual interest payment scheme) and about 0.05% more if you are paid interest monthly. The latter is because you will earn interest on the interest you have been paid because that interest will be added to your account balance, as well as to the figure used to do the interest earned calculation. This is called "compound interest"). However, banks often offer a slightly lower rate of interest on monthly payment accounts, thus removing that advantage.

If you want to earn a higher interest rate but want to keep your money at a bank, you will need to commit to leaving your money with the bank for a set period of time. Banks are always designing new products with different twists but they all come down to some permutation of a fixed-term deposit. The bigger the amount you invest and the longer it is tied up, the higher the rate of interest you will earn. Banks are keen to get money on deposit, and the keener they are to get your money, the higher the interest rate they will pay. All of these products have to show an AER when they are advertised, which helps you compare products and institutions easily. Always remember that leaving money on deposit is a commitment, and, whilst you will be able to get your money out if you need it, the financial penalties for early withdrawal will be substantial. So, whilst you want to get the highest rate of return you can, what you don't want to do is tie up so much money that when you need cash you either have to pay a penalty or borrow money elsewhere at a higher rate than what you are earning on the deposit.

Other Banks
The bank you have your current account with was probably chosen by your parents or by you without too much thought. When it comes to current accounts there isn't much difference between them in any case. Once you move onto

savings and other products, though it is well worth looking at other banks to see what they are offering. There are online firms like moneysupermarket.com that provide product comparisons, and the money sections of the Sunday papers include lists of rates provided by many banks on many of their products. They at least include what the paper considers the best deals at the moment.

You can have a current account in one bank and a deposit account in another and more investment products across a range of banks – though keep a list of all of them somewhere so you don't lose track. Historically it has been difficult to move cash and investments between banks and new clients were frequently treated better than existing clients, but the UK government is increasing the pressure on banks to change their practices to make things fairer. What happens now is that banks may offer incentives to get people to join their bank, to save money with them or to get a loan with them and those new clients receive a better deal than existing clients. It's a bit like mobile phone companies, where your friend gets the same phone as you but at a better rate because he is a new client. How annoying is that? You may also be offered incentives as a new saver, like gifts of a lump sum of money, or bonus schemes for keeping cash on deposit for a set amount of time.

To be clear, you can have current accounts, savings accounts and other investments at any bank you want – they are not tied together.

For 2016/17, as a basic rate taxpayer (in the 20% range), you can earn up to £1,000 of savings interest without paying tax. This is a result of the £1,000 personal savings allowance. If you are a higher rate taxpayer, you are given a personal savings allowance of £500 and, if you pay taxes above that rate, you have no allowance. Any interest earned in excess of the allowance will be taxed at the same rate as for your earned income, meaning the money you earn from your job. (See Chapter 7 to read more about taxes on your pay.)

It pays to shop around but don't get too clever, as the difference in what your money earns may not be worth your time or the hassle. Whether or not it is depends on two things – the amount of money you are looking to invest and the interest rate you can earn. Let's say you are planning to put £1,000 in a bank for a year and your bank offers you 1% interest and the other offers you 1.5% interest. The difference in what you will earn (before tax) over that year is £5. Your bank will pay you £10 (£1,000 times 0.01) and another bank would pay you £15 (£1,000 times 0.015). You have to question whether it is worth your taking the time to open a new account. However, if the amount you put into the bank were £100,000, the difference would be £500, so it would probably be worth it.

The other variable that impacts your AER is the time you are committing to having your money tied up. The thought process here is the same as it was for your own bank.

National Savings and Investments

National Savings and Investments (NS&I) offers most, if not all, of the same savings/investment opportunities as banks do. The difference is that all of your money held with the NS&I is guaranteed by the UK government (NS&I is an Executive Agency of the Chancellor of the Exchequer) as compared with only the first £75,000 that you have at a bank. You will find that, as the risk to you is lower, so too will be the reward. 26 million people across the UK use NS&I services, which are provided only via the post, phone or online (in the past they used to also be provided in post offices). You may notice that some of the products themselves are provided by other banks, with NS&I as the umbrella provider. (You will see the same when you look at insurance offerings at some of the supermarkets.) You will find NS&I products listed alongside other investment providers in cost comparison websites and newspaper tables so you can easily compare products.

INDIVIDUAL SAVINGS ACCOUNTS (ISAs)

A 25 year-old I met recently challenged me by saying, "If you can explain ISAs to me, you'd be a great writer," so here is my chance. It is simply a tax effective investment; you pay no tax on what you earn on it. If you have any savings at all that you don't think you will need in the near term, then putting it in a tax free ISA is almost a no-brainer. That is, if you invest it in a cash vehicle where there is no chance of a loss in value. The only downside on a cash ISA is that the interest rate paid is quite low. It is therefore critical to shop around to find the best rate and move your money between accounts often. So keep alert!

Key ISA Facts

- An ISA is a tax-free savings account – you pay no tax on earnings or capital gains ever.
- You can put money in an ISA account of your choosing. From the start of the 2016/17 tax year, the government has opened up investment possibilities which mean you can invest in a wide range of ISAs – cash, stocks & shares

("equities"), innovative finance (peer-to-peer lending offerings once the individual offerings are approved by the regulator) and a Help to Buy ISA.

- Unlike other earnings on investments/deposit accounts, any income you earn from the investments is always free of any tax. This means that dividends earned and capital gains made on equity investments, or interest earned on cash deposited, does not get taxed. In contrast, other interest and dividends you earn will be taxable, subject to minimum earnings limits, and this is explained in Chapter 7.

- The government introduced ISAs in 1999 to encourage people to save money.

- You can invest in any type of ISA and any mixture of types – i.e. no restrictions on the investment types. For the 2016/17 tax year, you can invest up to £15,240 in ISAs.

- If you don't invest the full allowance in a given year, you cannot carry forward the unused portion and invest more in a subsequent tax year.

- Beginning in 2016/17, you are allowed to take money out of your ISA and put it back in during the tax year, but the total amount invested in the end must remain within the £15,240 ISA allowance.

- You can move money between ISAs at different banks/investment firms. It is a good idea to keep an eye on what you are earning and switch if you aren't satisfied with what you are earning. It is easy to see how various ISAs are performing on the internet and in newspapers.

- In the 2016/17 Budget, the government announced the Help to Buy ISA. This requires you to save at least £1,600 in a designated ISA and, when you withdraw your money to purchase a home, the government will give you an additional 25% of what you have on account. The amount is capped at £3,000, or 25% of savings of £12,000. You must be a first-time buyer and purchase a property before 2030. The property value must be less than £450,000 in London and £250,000 outside of London. Doing this is a no brainer if you have any money to invest. It is better than just taking advantage of your personal savings allowance.

- In the 2016 Budget, the Chancellor also announced a plan to offer a lifetime ISA. The details are still being finalised, but the plan is to allow people to put up to £4,000 per year in an ISA and they will receive a 25% bonus tax-free at the end of the year. It will be open to people between the ages of 18 and 40 in 2017. With this ISA, the government is encouraging people to save for retirement.

- Many companies offer ISAs – banks, insurance companies, investment firms. If your ISA is with a bank, it is included in the UK government guarantee scheme mentioned earlier.

An ISA is simply a tax-free savings account. You can save cash, invest in stocks and shares or invest in alternative lending arrangements without having to pay any (or limited) tax on resultant earnings; that includes interest, dividends and gains on sale.

Investments in Cash

As mentioned above, plenty of firms offer these, with the rate of interest varying mostly based on the time period you are willing to commit to leaving the money in the firm. In a nutshell, you deposit cash and you get interest at a rate consistent with the advertised AER on specified dates. You can arrange for that interest to be added to the ISA or paid out to you. The bonus here is that you don't pay tax on the interest. Okay, it may not feel like a ton of money to you, or it may, but it is a start, and you will get a higher rate of interest than you would get from a bank savings account. (Currently around 2.5% to 3% compared with 0% on a basic bank savings account.)

It is worth shopping around when deciding where to invest your ISA money. The types of deals you can get have the same variables as deposit accounts. The longer the fixed term you agree to, the higher the interest rate. Similarly, you will find you can withdraw money even if you committed to keeping it locked in, but you will incur a sizeable penalty. You will find that some cash ISAs have a minimum investment amount and the higher that amount, the higher the rate of interest you will get paid.

Investments in Equities (Stocks/Shares)

You can invest your ISA money in a cash account or you can invest in equities. There are two basic ways to invest in these. The first is to invest in individual companies through a self-select ISA, which is usually managed by a stockbroker that you choose. The other is to invest through collective funds such as unit and investment trusts. As mentioned before, these are pooled investments managed by an investment manager who will spread the investment risk across a range of individual companies or industry groups.

The second approach is more commonly used, and if you decide to invest in share ISAs you will find a wide variety of fund managers and funds to choose from. The returns on these ISAs are less certain than with cash ISAs.

With these ISAs you are hoping for increases in the value of the underlying shares or fund, and that the overall return will therefore be greater than what you would earn on a cash ISA. And your hopes may well materialise. But you have to remember that the value of what you invest in may or may not increase in value. The documentation you receive prior to making your investment will make it very clear that your investment may go down and could decrease below the value of your initial investment. That same old risk/return trade off!

> It used to be the case that the stock market always outperformed cash holdings over a 20-year period. Is that still the case?

There are complications around what is tax effective and for some of these ISAs there are only tax benefits to higher rate taxpayers. Therefore, when you consider these, make sure you read the materials carefully. When you make an investment in a share ISA, you will do it through a third party advisor who will charge you a fee for making the arrangements for you.

Any decision to invest in stocks and shares is a complicated one and this is no exception. The subject is too broad for this book. I strongly suggest that when you get to thinking of doing this, you invest time in researching the tax implications and investment options. I want to encourage you to pursue this opportunity as there are few ways to earn tax-free income, but do so thoughtfully and seek advice from several quarters.

OTHER INVESTMENT OPPORTUNITIES

When you consider how you move up the money ladder it can go a bit like this: meet your basic needs like housing, food, socialising; then start saving a bit maybe in an ISA or company pension; then you invest in a home or have some other big event like having children (which cost lots of money!). And then, when all those needs are met, you may have money left over. If you do, or if you don't want to wait that long but are interested in investing your money, hoping to make it grow faster than it would otherwise, there are lots of different types of investment opportunities. Before you start investing, do think about your cash flow, how much money you can afford to lose and how much money you hope to gain. And get a good accountant and tax advisor.

Two things that I have learned from experience are: you must have a strategy around what you are doing – indiscriminately investing in stuff that catches

TOP TIP!

Always remember that the value of a share may go up or down, so, as I have heard many times, only invest what you can afford to lose.

your eye is random! You may as well buy lottery tickets. You also need to think long-term; don't expect to turn a quick profit.

Before we move on, I need to be very clear that I am not giving you advice – the intention here is to expose you to some ideas that you may want to explore further. There are whole books written about investments. Let's take a look at some of the more typical investment opportunities that you may come across at your stage of life.

National Savings and Investment Premium Bonds

As I mentioned earlier, you can buy financial products from the NS&I which operates under the Chancellor of the Exchequer. You can invest a minimum of £100 and a maximum of £50,000. You won't receive interest on your investment but you will be included in a monthly draw for prize money. Those prizes can be up to £1 million and all winnings are tax-free. The other benefits to you are that any money you invest is 100% guaranteed by the UK government and you can take your money out whenever you want. The total pool of prize money is set, based on the relative risk of the investment which, since it is government guaranteed, is pretty low. As of 1 June 2016, the rate has dropped to 1.25%. The odds of winning a monthly prize have decreased from 1 in 26,000 to 1 in 30,000 of the value of outstanding bonds which means that the overall return for all bondholders is what you would expect. The chances of winning a monthly prize are 30,000 to 1. On the one hand you may win no prizes but, on the other hand, you could get lucky!

Equities (Shares, Stocks)

Equities are described earlier in this chapter so I won't repeat the information. However, I do want to mention again that it is likely that you will invest through collective unit trusts to spread your investment risk more broadly than if you picked individual shares. Those trusts may invest in shares listed on the London Stock Exchange or AIM (the Alternative Investment Market). The former has all the major companies listed, and AIM is for start-ups that are big enough for people to be interested in buying shares in.

If you are thinking about getting directly involved in the equity markets, keep in mind that buying and selling shares sounds easy, but making money is not. To get involved you will need to get an account through a stockbroker. It is easy to set up and once it is set up you don't need to talk with the broker again if you don't want to. You can do all your buying and selling online. The broker will charge you a fee for each trade so you need to factor that into your financial planning. On the other hand, if you want someone to advise you on what stocks to buy and sell or if you want someone to do all the work of buying and selling shares, you can hire a stockbroker, who will charge you for his advice.

If you sell a share for more than it originally cost you, you will have a capital gain. Capital gains currently attract tax at a lower rate than income does. If you lose money you will have a capital loss that you may be able to offset against future gains. You need to keep good records of your investment activities to help you complete your annual tax return.

Bonds (Debt)

Bonds (excluding fixed-term deposits) were described earlier in this chapter so take a look there for basic information. When you invest in a bond you are buying the debt of an entity or government. Like equities, the value can go up or down based upon the market perception of the risk that the issuer will be unable to pay the interest payments or principal when it is supposed to. The price of the bond at any given time will take into account (sort of compensate for) the two fixed payment commitments of principal and interest rate and what that means for the investor at a given point in time.

An example of what I mean by that: say the bond you are buying has a stated interest rate of 5% but the current rate of interest the issuer would incur if it borrowed new money is 2%. In order to make up for that disparity in rates, the bond will be traded above the principal amount. That means, that over the course of the bond's existence, its purchase and sale price may go up and down based on interest rates and market sentiment. However, at maturity, whoever holds the bond gets the full amount of principal. This can be a bit confusing, so if you want to invest in this way you do need to take the time to understand it. (You can read more about potential investments which will make this all clearer at the-right-side.co.uk.) Many corporate bonds are traded on the London Stock Exchange. Government bonds are not. Many investors choose to invest in these bonds via funds and collective trusts, managed by experienced fund managers who diversify risk by investing across a range of bonds.

You can also invest in UK gilts and by doing so you are lending money to the UK government. These are issued and traded in denominations of £100 and can be traded in lots of any size, which makes them an appealing place to start if you want to try out bonds. If you want to invest in gilts you will need to go through a broker just like with shares. You may also be able to invest in new gilt issues which are often sold directly to the public at dates disclosed at the Debt Management Office website (dmo.gov.uk).

Commodities

Investing in commodities is the same as investing in stocks and bonds, but what you or a fund manager are doing is investing in goods rather than companies (things like coffee, gold, silver, pork bellies and oil). It isn't possible to buy and sell the majority of commodities directly as an individual and so you have to do it via a broker, although this is changing with the increased interest in commodities such as gold and silver. A few firms have been established to facilitate individuals who are interested in dealing directly in commodities, e.g. therealassetco.com. You are also able to buy gold from a machine at the Westfield shopping centre in London, with more dispensers planned in other locations!

Start-Up Companies

Bill Gates of Microsoft made a lot of his friends, family members and early employees rich by letting them invest in and giving them shares in his fledgling company. You may have read the story about the guy who painted the mural in Facebook's offices and was paid in shares.

It may not happen for a bit, or ever, but you may have the chance to invest directly in businesses being set up by friends, relatives or business colleagues. There are other ways of investing in starts-ups as well – crowdfunding is becoming increasingly popular, e.g. crowdcube, kickstarter. Angel investors (private individual investors), venture capital firms and private equity firms focus on start-up businesses. Angel investors may be willing to participate in the very first round of funding for a company and will therefore be taking the greatest risks. They will expect to be compensated for that. Think Dragon's Den. Venture capital and private equity firms, which are investing on behalf of others, will be more cautious. They are less likely to invest at the very beginning of a company, preferring to wait until it has a track record of success. You can see how the risk/return trade off comes into its own. The higher the risk you take, the higher the potential reward, but also the higher the risk of losing what you invested.

In any given year a private equity firm will receive an average of 200 business ideas, ten of which will be considered, and one of which might be invested in.

Your Own Business

The next few years may be the right time to create your own business, as the UK government is hoping that entrepreneurialism will get us out of the malaise left by the financial crisis. All kinds of support are being offered to help advise and fund new businesses. So this might be the time for you to start something yourself.

We all seem to think that a new business has to be a totally new and radical concept. I hear people say, "I can't think of something new," or, "If I had a new product/idea I would start a business." Having a big idea is one way to start a business but there are plenty of successful companies that didn't develop something totally new but delivered a product or service just a little bit better, faster, or cheaper than an existing business. And some just executed their strategy better or had more effective marketing than the next guy. How did Costa dominate the UK coffee market? Do you know there were other coffee chains around before Costa and Starbucks, and that many independent coffee shops still exist? Look at all the replicas of businesses – pizza restaurants, fried chicken takeaways, frozen yogurt companies, and cupcake makers. And when you look at companies on the internet that are doing the same thing, yet all making money or at least surviving, you can see just how business ideas can be successfully replicated. If you decide to invest money in starting up your own business, carry out plenty of research, including all of the information provided by the government – grants, mentoring support, and planning documents you can take advantage of. Also visit banks that are under pressure from the government to increase their lending to small and medium-sized businesses. Lastly, look carefully at the tax situation for you, your investors and the company. And remember to file your company tax returns!

Property

When you mention investments, people frequently cite property. They sometimes lose sight of whether the place they live in is an investment or a home. It only really counts as an investment if you are willing to convert it into cash – which many people aren't willing to do with their homes. As mentioned earlier, houses aren't liquid assets, so even if you want to convert your home to cash, you may not be able to at the moment you want or need to.

However, over the past 50 years home ownership has been a good way to make money in many regions of the UK. A lot of people I know bought houses that were a mess, lived in them, did lots of work themselves to make them better and then sold them at a profit. That profit from buying and selling their home was tax-free (gains on primary residences aren't taxed) so, in some cases, they were able to make more money from doing up their homes than they did from their jobs.

The personal property market has had an upward trend for many years, but the possibility of a decrease in prices is being talked about. It is very hard to discuss this in general terms, however, as the market is very diverse. For example, house prices in London have increased hugely since 2008, while in many other parts of the UK they have not. So you need to investigate this fully and think before you buy to make sure you are making a wise financial, as well as personal, decision. By the latter I mean that you have to live somewhere so your home isn't just about how your investment performs. We will delve into property ownership and rental in Chapter 10, but I mention it here as property is a viable investment option.

There are two potential property investments to mention: Firstly, buy-to-let investments, where you purchase a property solely to rent it out. The intention is to at least break even on an ongoing-cost basis and to benefit from later capital appreciation. As you know, there are a few risks inherent in that idea. There are plenty of books covering this topic, so, if you are interested in pursuing this investment idea, get hold of one. Secondly, commercial property (offices and shops rather than living accommodation) is an area of increasing investor interest. Direct investment by individuals is difficult because of the money involved but there are other ways to invest in this market, typically through property funds (along the same lines as you can invest in equities and bonds). They are increasing in popularity at the moment due to a perception that demand for commercial space will outstrip supply, which in turn will send rental and purchase prices up. But once again, there are significant risks inherent in this business model, not least of which is the amount of capital needed to buy big buildings. Mortgages for buy-to-let or commercial properties will have higher interest rates than those for your own home because of the higher degree of risk involved.

PENSIONS

A pension is a pool of money that can be accessed at retirement age. For any individual, what retirement is and what he chooses as his retirement age can be whatever he wants. However, when you talk about retirement age in relation to a pension plan, it means the age that you, the beneficiary of the specific pension plan, have to be in order to start getting payments out of the plan fund. (The fund here is not dissimilar to the other funds I mentioned earlier – money for ultimate beneficiaries is pooled and invested under the direction of fund. The fund invests the money, balancing risk/reward across a range of equity, bond, commodity and other investment types and business sectors.)

In the 2015/16 Budget, the government took major steps to liberalise the pension regime. The most important change was the ability for anyone aged 55 and over to withdraw the money in their pension accounts rather than require them to purchase annuities which would pay them a regular income based on their life expectancy.

You can stop working well before the plan's retirement age – in fact, you can retire whenever you want, but you only get pension benefits at the age specified in the pension plan documents. The majority of people in the UK continue working past the traditional retirement age of 65 for financial and personal reasons.

There are two things that will impact the amount of money that is in the pool and therefore what you will get out when you retire. They are: how much money has been put into the plan; and how well the investments the money was put into have performed. There are three groups of pension plans that may impact you: the UK state pension that is funded by National Insurance deductions from employee and employer wage-related contributions, employer-sponsored pension plans funded jointly by employers and employees.

You may think you are too young to think about pensions because retirement is a lifetime away. But you do need to start early because the UK government has put increasing responsibility on individuals to provide their own money to live on when they are old. The government has been increasingly concerned about this and mandated that employers comply with "automatic enrolment" legislation to help more people save for later life through a pension scheme at work.

"More than 100,000 workers will retire this year with no personal pension savings. Some 15% of those expected to stop working this year will be relying solely on the state pension. Some 111,733 of those aged 65 will have to survive on the poverty line with an income below £9,500 a year." The Daily Express, May 2015.

Employer Pension Plans and Employee Contributions

When you are talking to a potential employer about a job, it is a good idea to ask about the company's pension plan and, in particular, how much the company will pay into the plan on your behalf and how much you will be required to pay. As mentioned above, the government has mandated that companies automatically enrol employees in pension plans and make contributions/deduct money from employees' gross pay. The programme has been phased in and by the end of 2018, all companies must comply. Employees joining a company who are over the age of 22 and who earn in excess of £10,000 will be automatically enrolled. This means the company will make contributions on your behalf, it will make deductions from your pay for your contribution, and the government will contribute to your pension via tax relief. If you don't meet the requirements, you can ask to join the company scheme. You can opt out of the scheme which will require you to take action. Currently, the company is required to contribute 1% of your pay, you are required to contribute 0.8% of your pay and the government, in effect, contributes 0.2% as a tax benefit (or 2% in total). In 2019, the total will increase to 5% and is expected to increase in subsequent years. For additional information please refer to www.pensionadvisoryservice.co.uk.

The automatic enrolment pension sets out the minimum level of contributions. You may find that your company will make a larger contribution to the plan and will expect you to also contribute more. These expectations will be specified in your employment contract. In every case, your contribution will be deducted from your gross pay.

The company will have retained an investment company to manage the pension monies and which will invest the money on behalf of all employees. They may provide you with choices as to what the money is invested in. When you reach the firm's retirement age you will receive payments based on what the investments are worth at that time. As the plan is based on contributions made into it, this type of plan is called a defined contribution plan. (You may be one of the very few people in the UK who is enrolled in a defined benefit plan. If you are, the benefits you will be paid at retirement age are specified and you will receive the amount regardless of how the invested funds perform. You can probably guess why there are very few defined benefit plans in existence.)

Your employer's pension plan will provide you with periodic statements explaining how much money you and your employer have contributed and what the value of the fund is (increased or decreased based on the investment portfolio's performance). You may also be provided with investment options to choose from, which typically have some sort of indication of risk level. Ask your employer to provide you with samples when you are joining the firm.

Research by Prudential has found that more than 100,000 workers will retire this year with no personal pension savings. Some 15% of those expected to stop working this year will be relying solely on the state pension. Some 111,733 of those aged 65 will have to survive on the poverty line with an income below £6,500 a year. The Daily Express, May 2015.

The prevailing view on investments choices, though you have to decide for yourself, is that riskier investments are more appropriate for younger people than they are for older people. Why? Because of the risk/return trade-off. If a high-risk investment loses money but you are young, there is time for the investment to recover its value before you need the money. Not quite the same if you are older and take a big risk!

The government is encouraging us all to sort out our own pension arrangements and rely less on what the government provides. That is a key reason behind the establishment of the auto enrolment programme which was initiated in 2012 and will be required for all firms by the end of 2018. You may need more advice than appropriate here about the balance between contributions to employer pension plans, the ISAs described above and SIPPs (self-invested pension plans, which we will turn to in a moment), but they are all tax-effective. This means they shelter some of your hard-earned money from taxes, but you do have to fulfil certain obligations to get the tax benefit.

For personal pension contributions, the tax scheme works like this: you pay income tax on your earnings before any pension contribution, but the pension provider claims tax back from the government at the basic rate of 20%. In practice, this means that for every £80 you pay in, you end up with £100 in your pension pot. If you pay tax at the higher (40%) rate, you have to claim the difference through your tax return or by telephoning or writing to HMRC. If you're an additional (45%) rate taxpayer you'll have to claim the difference through your tax return.

One in five workers are saving nothing at all for retirement, 20% are not putting enough aside, and 14% are seriously undersaving.

Since October 2012, people employed by firms that do not have a company pension scheme have been required to be automatically enrolled in one if they are over 22 years of age and earn more than £10,000. It is possible, however, to opt out. The outcome is that the majority of people are now automatically putting 8% of their salary into a pension. Even if you aren't able to participate through your employer, starting saving for retirement is a good idea, and having money deducted from your pay is the easiest way to make regular payments.

Self-Invested Personal Pensions

The final way you can establish a tax-effective pension plan is through a self-invested personal pension (SIPP). This is a personal pension plan, approved by the government, that allows you to invest your money on your own and benefit from tax relief. The government will allow you to invest in a broad, but not unlimited, variety of assets. Unlike other pension types, you are the person making the investment decisions. Like other pension types, the assets need to be segregated and in long-term investments. I won't go into details here as you will need to review the HMRC guidelines in effect at the time of making any decision about taking this approach.

In a nutshell, whilst retirement and pensions seem irrelevant at this time of your life, it is good to start thinking about them and putting money aside now. If the new rules are implemented, you will be required to make pension contributions to your company scheme as well as to the government through National Insurance contributions. If they are not implemented, you may still be able to contribute through your employment, at your employer's discretion. If you can't join a company scheme, make your own arrangements as soon as you can manage to put money aside for monthly pension contributions.

IT'S DOWN TO YOU

As you can see, once you are generating more money than you need to live on, you will have many choices about what to do with it. The most important thing is to start managing your money inflows and outflows so that you have some money left over regularly and keep yourself from spending it on things you don't really need or want. Look at the fun you can have exploring how to save and what to invest in! Even saving leftover pound coins to spend on something big after your collection efforts can be pretty gratifying. And do plan for your future and old age, despite how far away that feels right now!

Chapter Seven

Financial Basics – Pay-Related

Your Payslip

Income Taxes

Other Earnings-Related Taxes

Communications With HMRC

Expect Issues

A Few Final Words On Taxes

THE NEXT TWO chapters provide basic information about financial things you need to know about. The objective is to help you avoid the trial and error approach to learning, i.e. learning before you need to know so that you avoid making irritating mistakes. The chapters are designed for you to take a quick read-through to gain a general awareness of what to look out for. Then, when the need arises, you can dip back into the relevant pages. This chapter covers all things pay-related and the next chapter covers everything else. The tax authority rates for 2016/17 are reflected here. For subsequent years, please check hmrc.gov.uk.

By the end of this chapter you will know the answers to the following:

- How does an annual salary of £15,000 turn into take-home pay or cash to spend of £14,200?

- What is National Insurance and why do you have to pay it? Does your employer pay anything towards National Insurance?

- How do you get in touch with the taxman?

I have yet to meet a person who is not surprised when they receive their first payslip. You may have agreed an hourly pay rate, expecting to take home that rate times the number of hours worked, or you may have agreed an annual salary, expecting to take home a twelfth of that amount at the end of the month. And then, what comes into your bank account? A much smaller amount!

What you just read assumes you are employed by a company (you could be a sole trader or working for partnership) and that company is required by law to process your pay through a payroll system. Through that system your employer will be recording pay-related information, ensuring amounts required by tax and other authorities are withheld from you and paid onto the relevant parties (generally to the UK government and pension plans).

> "In this world nothing is certain but death and taxes."
> Benjamin Franklin, 1789

Your employer may not process your pay through a payroll system. You could be paid "cash-in-hand", which is your hourly rate times hours worked, with no deductions. This is most likely if you are doing short-term casual work, like painting a family friend's house or doing garden work over the summer. Or you could be paid partially through a payroll system and partially as cash in hand. This mixed arrangement is common where your pay includes a wage and tips, for example working in a pub. Be aware that under UK tax law you are responsible for taking all cash-in-hand pay into account when you figure out if you need to pay UK income tax. We will look later at how you decide if you do or don't have to file a tax return or pay tax. What you do need to do is keep track of the cash you receive throughout the tax year so you know what your situation is at the end of the year. You won't be able to recreate this information so you need to track it each time you are given cash.

This chapter is written assuming your pay goes through a payroll system, as that is how most people are paid. If that is not the case, I suggest you do a bit of research to make sure you are complying with tax requirements and, importantly, make sure that you are doing what you need to do to get working credit under the National Insurance scheme – search on "UK National Insurance".

YOUR PAYSLIP

You will probably be paid monthly, or possibly weekly if you are an hourly-rate employee. It is very useful to ask how frequently you will be paid when you are talking to a potential employer so you know when to expect to receive money. The money you earn will usually paid directly into your bank account. For all jobs you will do the work before you get paid – this is called being paid in arrears. That means that if you are on a monthly payroll cycle (usually payments are made some time after the 20th of the month) and you start work on the first of the month you will have to wait some time to get any money. The same is true if you are on a weekly payroll but the wait is obviously shorter. Whatever the pay period, when you are paid, your employer should give you, or give you access via a website to, a payslip. This includes important information, and keeping a copy in a file somewhere is important. Your payslip will look similar to the following, and an explanation of what you will see and the terminology used is detailed below.

Employee No.	Employee Name			Process Date	National Insurance Number
11	Mr. Angus Smith			24/06/2016	BA4321C

Payments	Units	Rate	Amount	Deductions	Amount
Salary	1.00	2,416.0000	2,416.00	PAYE Tax	292.60
				National Insurance	205.01
				Student Loan	83.00
				Work Pension	36.25

Mr. Angus Smith 100 High Street Glasgow G1 8HH	This Period		Year To Date	
	Total Gross Pay	2,416.00	Total Gross Pay TD	7,248.00
	Gross for Tax	2,416.00	Gross for Tax TD	7,248.00
			Tax Paid TD	877.80
			National Insurance TD	615.03
	Payment Period	Monthly	Pension TD	108.75

Tax Code: 1100L	Tax Period: 3	Dept: Marketing Payment Method: BACS	Net Pay	1,799.14

Gross Pay

This is the total amount of money you earned for the pay period and will be based on your annual salary or your hourly rate. If you are paid an hourly rate, it will be the hours worked multiplied by the rate. If your employment agreement includes extra pay for working long or unsociable hours, that should also be reflected, so check the figures carefully. If you are on an annual salary and are paid monthly, your gross pay will be 1/12th of the annual salary amount.

Income Tax Withheld Under The Pay As You Earn (PAYE) Obligations

Your employer is required to collect money on behalf of Her Majesty's Revenue and Customs (HMRC) for income taxes each time you are paid. The amount withheld from your pay cheque is mandated by HMRC, based on how much you money you are likely to earn during the current tax year. Later in this chapter we will cover how HMRC sets the withholding and how income tax is calculated, but for now, be aware that for 2016/17 the rates can vary from 0 to 45%. Be aware that the first £11,000 earned for the 2016/17 tax year (your "personal allowance") is tax-free. Therefore, there are steps you may be able to take so that your employer won't have to withhold any tax. Read more in this chapter to understand this more fully.

National Insurance (NI)

Your employer is required to deduct a percentage of your gross pay and send it to the government in the form of National Insurance (NI) contributions. These monies are used by the government to provide benefits such as retirement payments (pensions) and health services. The amount of NI withheld is reviewed annually in the Chancellor of the Exchequer's Budget. For the 2016/17 tax year, if you earn between £155 and £827 a week, you will have 12% of your gross pay withheld on any earnings between those amounts. If you earn more than £827 per week, an additional 2% will be withheld on earnings above £827. If you earn less than £155 in gross pay per week, no money will be withheld. (Your employer is also required to make NI contributions on your behalf, separate from what you pay. This has no impact on your payslip but it is nice to know.) One last thing before we leave NI – you should have received an NI number on a plastic card when you turned 16. If you didn't receive one you will need to get one in order for your employer to pay you. To ensure you get the right benefits in the long term, you need to make sure that all of your pay and NI contributions are properly recorded in the NI system. To learn more about the UK NI system, search UKNI on the internet which will take you to the right place in the hmrc.gov.uk website.

Other Deductions

There are other amounts that may be deducted from your gross pay, all of which should have been discussed with, or disclosed by, your employer before the deductions were made. If a deduction shown on your payslip comes as a surprise to you, you should talk to your manager immediately. What might these deductions be? Reimbursement for the cost of a uniform or work tool, charitable contributions you elected to make through a Give as You Earn (GAYE) scheme, private pension contributions, or insurance payments. The private pension contribution is payments to an employer-managed pension plan as described in Chapter 6. Your employer may also be providing you with other benefits which may be provided for "free" or which you choose to purchase, like insurance or use of a car. Neither of these will appear on your payslip. Later in this chapter we will cover the tax implications of these "free" benefits.

Student Loan Deductions

If you have taken out a student loan and are earning income of a certain level, as set by the government, you will have deductions made from your gross pay to repay your student loan. You agreed to these terms when you originally signed up for the loan. How this works is explained more fully later in Chapter 10.

Net Pay

This is the amount of money that you will actually get, either deposited into your bank account, or given to you in cash. This is your gross pay minus mandatory deductions (PAYE tax and NI) and optional deductions (personal pension contributions, insurance, charitable payments). Monthly payments are usually made some time after the 20th of the month, and if it is on a specific date, it will be paid the preceding Friday, or following Monday if the date falls on a weekend. If your money is tight you will want to make sure you know whether you will be paid before or after the weekend. What is really important – and everyone I know has been caught out on this, which is why I am mentioning it again – is that you get paid one month in arrears. This means that the first time you get paid will be at the end of the first month or week that you work, so you will need a money plan to get you through that first week or month.

INCOME TAXES

There are many resources you can access to explain income and other taxes (e.g. capital gains tax, value added tax) so I'm only going to cover the basics here to ensure you are aware of the impact on the income you earn from work. The hmrc.gov.uk tax website is really good at explanations and there is a helpline to call if you want to talk to someone.

Once you start earning money, you must start thinking about income taxes. Even if you are paid cash in hand you need to think about it, as being paid that way does not mean you will not have to pay tax. (If you are being paid cash, it is a good idea to put 20% of what you earn in a bank account or elsewhere where you will not be tempted to spend it until you figure out if you owe tax money at the end of the tax year.) If you earn more money than the personal allowance (£11,000 for the 2016/17 tax year) you have to make sure you have paid what is required and you may have to file a tax return and/or pay additional taxes. If you earn less than the personal allowance, or you have earned more than the allowance but the right amount of tax has been paid, you shouldn't need to file a tax return. HMRC will send you a letter instructing you to file a return if needed, but be aware that they sometimes do get it wrong. So at the end of each tax year you need to check out your earnings and tax paid to see if you need to do anything more. The tax return has to be filed with HMRC by the end of January of the year after the tax year end. (For example, for the tax year ended 5 April 2016 a tax return has to be filed by 31 January 2017.) If, however, you are filing on paper rather than online, and want HMRC to calculate your tax for you, this must be done by October of the year that the tax year ends If you don't meet that deadline you will be fined – starting at £100 plus interest on the unpaid tax amount due. If you are more than three months late the penalties will be even greater.

If you work for several employers, you need to add up what you received from all of them to come up with your total earnings when deciding whether or not you owe tax. As mentioned earlier, if you join a company it will be required by law to withhold income tax from you at the rate instructed by HMRC and that withholding will be made through the payroll system. The employer then pays the money withheld from your pay cheque to HMRC.

The amount withheld from your pay cheque is supposed to approximate what you will owe the government by the end of the tax year, but for several reasons the amount withheld may not be the amount you actually need to pay. Because it doesn't always work out quite right, you need to do a calculation at the end of the tax year to figure out if you are owed money, or you owe money to, the tax authorities. There are forms you will need to complete and submit to HMRC if you are in either situation.

You don't always have to wait until the end of a tax year to ask for money owed to you. If you worked over the summer and won't be working for the remainder of the tax year, and you have overpaid tax, you can claim it back at the end of your summer job. (How to do this will be explained later, as well as what you can do to avoid that situation.)

Important Tax Facts

The UK tax year – the tax year runs from 6 April of one year to 5 April of the subsequent year. Most countries have a 1 January to 31 December tax year. In the UK, the tax year used to end on 31 March but changed to the current date when the Gregorian calendar was adopted in 1752. What this means in practice is you need to take the pay you earned between those two dates into account when figuring out the income you earned, the tax you paid and any under or overpayment of taxes.

Personal allowance – as described above, you can earn money up to this amount in a given tax year and not have to pay any income tax on it. For the 2016/17 UK tax year the amount is £11,000. Be aware that this doesn't mean that income tax won't have been deducted under PAYE, so you need to check your payslips to make sure nothing has been withheld. If tax has been withheld, contact HMRC quickly to get it sorted.

Earned income versus taxable income – earned income is another name for your gross pay, including any cash-in-hand amounts, earned during the tax year. Taxable income is the number you get when you subtract your personal allowance from your earned income.

Income tax rates – these are the percentage rates of income tax you will be required to pay on different levels of taxable income. These rates are reviewed annually on budget day and are easy to find on the internet (hmrc.gov.uk). For the 2016/17 UK tax year, the personal allowance is £11,000, which means that until your earned income is greater than £11,000 you will have zero taxable income, and hence have no income tax obligation. In 2016/17, taxable income from £0 up to £32,000 (or £43,000 all in which is your personal allowance plus £32,000) will attract income tax at a rate of 20%, taxable income between £32,001 and £150,000 will attract income tax at a rate of 40%, and anything you earn above £150,000 will attract 45% income tax. The rates are called the "basic" rate (20%), the "higher" rate (40%) and the "additional" rate (45%).

Here are a few examples of tax you would pay based on earned and taxable income:

Taxable Income	Tax Due	Effective Tax Rate	Explanation
£ 6,000	0	0%	The money is all yours, no income tax is due, because you earned less than your personal allowance.
£ 12,000	£200	1.6%	Your taxable income is £12,000 minus £11,000 for your personal allowance, i.e. £1,000. Your tax due is £1,000 multiplied by 20%.
£ 50,000	£9,200	18.4%	Your taxable income is £50,000 minus £11,000 for your personal allowance, i.e. £39,000. Your tax due is £32,000 multiplied by 20% (£6,400) plus £7,000 (£39,000 minus £32,000) multiplied by 40% (£2,800).

Your tax code – this relatively simple concept gets incredibly complicated in practice. The purpose of the tax code is to tell employers the amount of personal allowance for each employee that should be taken into account to figure out how much tax to withhold. The tax code is used as we have done in the table above – a deduction from earned income to get to taxable income. The idea is that if the personal allowance is the right amount and all of your earnings go through a payroll system, you will not have to file a tax return at the end of the tax year.

When you start working, HMRC will get paperwork from your employer (it could be a P46 from your previous employer or if it is your first job just notification that you are starting work) and based on that will assign you a tax code. Based on that limited information, HMRC will estimate what your personal allowance should be. It will be numbers followed by one or two letters; the meaning of which is explained on the HMRC website. You should get a form in the post, at the same time that your employer is notified, of your code although every young person I have met says they never received anything. When you receive it, or when you get your first payslip, is the time to go to the website and figure out what it means and if you need to take any action.

Your tax code is HMRC's instruction to your employer of what to deduct from your earned income (or gross pay) to derive your taxable income. That taxable income is then subjected to the tax rates for each income band by your employer, who figures out how much tax to withhold from you and pay to the government. The process is messy when you first start your career for several reasons, so look at the notice HMRC sends of your tax code and check your payslip carefully for the first few months. It is also a good idea to look to see if your tax code has changed for some reason anytime your take-home pay changes. You should receive notification directly from HMRC if a tax code change is going to be made.

When you first begin your permanent working career (i.e. start work after you finish education) chances are it will take a few pay cycles to get your tax code sorted out. That is for two reasons: one is that the taxman doesn't have much information about you so can't be sure if you are entitled to a full personal allowance. The other is that you probably aren't starting work on the first day of the tax year, so the automated systems of prorating figures and treating amounts as cumulative doesn't work well.

Because of how it works you will probably find that too much tax is withheld from your first pay cheque, your second pay cheque has very little, if any, tax withheld (to compensate for withholding too much the first month), and then things normalise. What really catches people out is that first month's pay cheque. Remember that not only have you been waiting for money for a month since you started work, you may also get less cash than you expected. You need to plan for this.

There are a few things you can do to help yourself through this process:

- If you have worked before, make sure you keep your P45 (explained more fully shortly) from your previous employer and give it to your new employer as soon as possible.

- If you have not worked before or can't find your P45, your employer is likely to ask you to complete a P46 which will be submitted to HMRC.

- Look for a letter to arrive from HMRC with your tax code. Once you have it, review the information using hmrc.gov.uk to assess whether it makes sense. Note that you may repeat this process a few times until things settle down. Don't be alarmed if you are put on emergency coding, as that just means the taxman isn't sure what to do with you and is assuming for the time being that you should receive the personal allowance in full.

- If you have questions, talk to HMRC and then to your employer to make sure you understand why it is what it is and that you take whatever steps you need to in order to get it sorted.

If you feel your tax code is incorrect, it is possible to have it changed. The HRMC website (hmrc.gov.uk) provides instructions of how to do that. HMRC reviews all tax codes at the end of each tax year and after tax returns are filed, which may lead to an instruction to your employer to make an adjustment to your code.

OTHER EARNINGS-RELATED TAXES

Benefits In Kind

Your employer may offer you "free" benefits in addition to paying you a salary or hourly wage to work. These benefits could include things like medical insurance, life assurance, or a company car, all of which will have been explained to you in your employment letter. You will have been given the choice of taking up those benefits or not. At the end of the day they are not totally "free", as HMRC requires you to pay tax on their value. The estimated value will be reported by your employer to HMRC and your tax code adjusted during the year to take them into account.

Shortly after the end of the tax year, your employer will give you a P11D form which details the benefits' value. You should review the P11D as soon as you receive it, making sure it is what you expected based on your employment contract, and follow up with your employer if it isn't. If the P11D amount is the same as what was taken into account for your tax code, you don't need to do anything. However, if the amount is different from what you expected, you will either need to reflect it on your tax return, if you have to file one, or arrange for your tax code to be adjusted for the following year.

Income From Savings And Investments

This can become quite a complex area. The key concepts to know are:

- Income from savings and investments, such as dividends and interest, are taxed in the same way as earned income, which means they are subject to the same tax rates. There are some exceptions (see Chapter 6).

- Capital gains, which are gains from the purchase and subsequent sale of investment assets, are not taxed in the same way as earned income. Each individual is allowed to earn £11,100 (for 2016/17) of capital gains free of tax, and some asset sales (assets sold for less than £6,000 and your personal residence) are totally exempt from tax. The capital gains tax rate has, in recent history, been lower than income tax rates.

COMMUNICATIONS WITH HMRC

There are numerous reasons why you may need to get in contact with HMRC and vice versa. A few things to bear in mind regarding those communications and related documentation are as follows:

> ✔
> **TOP TIP!**
>
> Every time you send something to HMRC, include your name, address, NI number and phone numbers and type it and make a note in your diary to chase up in a month or so.

Your Tax Office

You will be assigned a tax office that you are supposed to communicate with if you have any tax-related issues. It is determined by the physical location of your employer. You can call the office directly (make sure you get the name of the person you talk to). I highly recommend you always follow up any conversation with something in writing to avoid any misunderstanding. And keep a copy of what you have written. If you can't figure out the tax office to contact you can look it up on the HMRC website.

PAYE P45 Form

When you stop working for a given employer, you should be given a P45 form which informs you and HMRC of the income you have earned and income tax that has been withheld by that employer during the current tax year. You will need to keep that document in a place where you can find it as you will need it to review your situation at the end of a tax year. You will also need to give one sheet of it to your next employer so that your new tax code can be sorted out.

PAYE P46 Form

When you take on your first job, you won't have a P45 to give your employer so you may be asked to complete a P46. This enables the employer and HMRC to calculate the right tax code.

PAYE P60 Form

This is the form your existing employer will give you at the end of the tax year. You will need this form to figure out if you need to file a tax return and if you need to pay or reclaim income tax. The form provides details of earned income, income tax and National Insurance withheld and student loan deductions (if relevant). Armed with your P45 forms (previous employers) and P60 form (current employer) for the year, you will have all you need to figure out what your earnings and withholdings were.

Students Working With No PAYE Deduction/Form P38(S)

If you are a student and working during the school year or during the holidays, it may not be necessary for your employer to withhold income tax from you as long as you will not be earning more that the personal allowance. To make this arrangement, you should print the P38(S) form off the HMRC website, complete it and give it to your employer. Do it as soon as you agree to do the job so your employer can deal with it before processing your first payment. Alert – I have not come across an employer who was aware of this being possible, so you will need to drive the process.

Students Working With PAYE Deduction And Later Reclaim/Form P50

If you are a student working during the holidays or during a gap year and income tax has been withheld, you can reclaim this money by filing a tax return after the end of the tax year. Or, rather than file a tax return, you can send a letter to your tax office, including your P45 and P60 forms, explaining your situation. But the quickest way to get your money back, if you are not going to work for the remainder of the tax year because you are returning to your studies, is to complete a P50 and submit that to your tax office. Again, keep a copy of your forms.

> ✔ **TOP TIP!**
>
> Set up a file where you keep your payslips and other relevant forms (e.g. P45, P46, P60, P11D) any letters or notes of discussions with HMRC and any tax returns you file.

Getting Money Back From HMRC

If you believe the taxman owes you money, you can either wait until the end of the tax year or request repayment earlier (only if you aren't going to earn anymore money during the current tax year). The easiest way to figure out if you are owed money is on hmrc.gov.uk. The site gives clear instructions that take you through the process of filing a repayment request. Make sure you print out and save a copy of whatever you provide to HMRC. In my experience, what starts out seeming straightforward takes longer than you'd expect and requires lots of letters to and from the taxman.

A clear letter to the taxman will speed the process, so make sure you explain your situation fully, including who you worked for, how much you earned, what you were paid, the fact you are not working again until whenever, and anything else that may help. Remember as you write your letter that the recipient knows nothing about you or your situation, so provide all of the information he might need. Make sure you include relevant source documents like P45s and P60s (easier said than done sometimes). And be polite and persevere, first via letters. If you have had a few goes and your money has not arrived, it is worth trying to call the person who wrote to you, as identified in the most recent letter, or call the general tax office number. As annoying as it may be to explain your story again and again, remain calm and try to ascertain what you can do to help them help you. Start by asking them what, if anything, is missing? Everyone I know has eventually received the money owed to them, though they all had moments of despair and frustration!

Filing A Tax Return

As explained at the beginning of this chapter, you will need to collect all your earnings information at the end of the tax year to determine if you need to file a tax return and/or are due to pay/receive money from HMRC. If your income has all gone through PAYE, and the withheld amounts were correct, chances are you won't have to do anything. If you get income from other sources, chances are you will need to take action. I recommend you always do an income earned and tax paid calculation and keep a record of it, whether or not you have to file a return.

To confirm whether or not you must file a return, check on the HMRC website. If you do need to file a return, you will probably be able to file it using the

HMRC online system. This is well worth doing if HMRC owes you money as it speeds up the repayment process. You may also want to file the return as soon as the tax year is over rather than wait until the filing deadline, so you get your money back sooner. If on the other hand you owe money, you may want to complete a paper return and file it on 31st January – the final return due date – so you pay the money due as late as possible. If you want HMRC to calculate how much tax you owe them, then you must file before the previous October instead.

EXPECT ISSUES

As I mentioned, when you are starting out in your career or working during summers or other holidays, you can and should expect these tax and pay issues to get a bit messy. The reason is that the taxman's systems are set up to deal with the regular wage (salary or hourly) earners. So you need to be particularly proactive.

As soon as you get a payslip you need to look at it to see if the gross pay number is right (your employer's responsibility) and if the net pay (and each deduction) is right. Check your bank account to make sure that the money has come into your bank on the day you expect it to so you don't risk going overdrawn. Companies and banks do make mistakes! And finally, don't be shy about asking your employer to cover any expenses you incur if for some reason your pay doesn't come into your bank account on the day it was supposed to. If your employer has made an error, it is totally acceptable to ask for reimbursement of lost interest and direct charges you incurred as a result, like overdraft fees.

> Assume you have a three-month summer job for which you will earn gross pay of £3,000. HMRC will provide a tax code and your employer will withhold from your gross pay the amount of tax you would have to pay if you worked and earned at the same rate all year. That means HMRC treats you as if you will earn £12,000 for the year (£3,000 times 4).
>
> If your total earnings for a given tax year were £12,000 you would have to pay tax (for the amount you earned above the personal allowance) so withholding tax from your gross pay would be correct. But, if the only money you earned during the tax year was the £3,000 you will not have to pay any tax at all on those earnings, so tax should not be withheld. See the preceding section that explains how to sort this out.

The HMRC website is very good at explaining anything to do with income taxes and the search facility makes it easy to find what you are looking for. There are three things I want to remind you to be diligent about:

- Figure out the amount of cash you will actually receive before you do your budgeting, as the impact of the above could be significant.

- Check your first few payslips carefully – gross pay, net pay and tax code – and deal with any tax code issues as soon as possible. Make sure you understand and agree with each of the employer deductions.

- Keep your payslips in a binder, drawer or box, and keep good records, so when you get to the end of the tax year it is easy for you to figure out what you earned, the cash you actually received, whether or not you need to file a tax return and whether you owe money to, or are owed money from, HMRC.

> Do your maths early to figure out just how much cash you will be getting in your pocket for your budget. When you are quoted an £18,000 annual salary, your gross pay will be £1,500 per month but the money you actually get will be less. Your 100 hours of work at £10 an hour won't mean you take home £1,000 cash.

A FEW FINAL WORDS ON TAXES

This chapter should have helped you understand what impact taxes will have on your pay. It can be quite a shock to have what seems like so much money taken out of your pay. When you read the press you will see articles about tax rates in the UK and other countries. Keep in mind that your total tax rate includes not only income tax, but value added tax (VAT) at 20% on most things you buy, other than food in shops, council tax, road tax and taxes on petrol, alcohol and cigarettes.

" I have paid all my taxes since i was 12 years old and I would certainly be happy if the rate was 60% or 0%. I wouldn't move away. I wouldn't have an offshore account. That would be totally fine, for better infrastructure and public services." Quote from Charlotte Church, singer

This seems a good place to address the frequently asked questions of: "What can I do about it?" and "How can I pay less tax?" Unfortunately the answer is "not a lot" on your earned income. Stated bluntly, if you work in the UK you have to pay UK income tax. The only real option is to move to another country. Once you leave the

UK, you will not be subject to the UK tax regime but you will be subject to the tax regime of the country you are living in. At the moment there is quite a lot of movement of people east, where income taxes are lower (17% in Hong Kong and 0% in Dubai).

The only opportunities for a typical UK employee to reduce income taxes are in the areas of savings and pensions, which the UK government is encouraging people to do and for which there are tax incentives. These opportunities were described in Chapter 6, which you may want to reread now.

"I've got enough to be comfortable – if I was reasonable for the rest of my life – but I am not reasonable." Her fortune shrunk from £25m to £11m in a year. Money week, May/June 2015. Quote from Charlotte Church, singer

During the past 20 years the primary way families increased their wealth, other than through earned income, was by investing in property. Any gain on the sale of a primary residence was, and still is, tax-free. When you could be certain that property values would increase, it was possible to turn a quick, tax-free profit from buying and then selling your home. The difference between the price you paid and the price you sold for was yours to keep. It is more difficult to achieve this now as the state of the property market is uncertain. It is hard to be confident that you will be able to sell your home for more than you paid for it, or sell it at all.

Chapter Eight

Financial Basics – Everything Else

By the end of this chapter you will know the answers to:

- When you need a loan to buy a car, is an Annual Percentage Rate (APR) of 10% better or worse for you than an APR of 5%?

- What is the difference between APR and Annual Equivalent Rate (AER)? Big APR numbers are bad and big AER numbers are good – why is that?

- Why do you get 0% interest if you leave your money in a current bank account? 1% in a savings account? Or 3% if you put it in a term deposit and commit to leaving it there for five years?

- What are the differences between a credit card, a debit card and a store card? What are the costs of each?

THE TIME VALUE OF MONEY AND THE RISK/REWARD TRADE-OFF PRINCIPLES

Fundamental economics concepts have been touched on in earlier chapters and are explained more fully in Chapter 12, but I want to remind you about two key business principles that are relevant to this chapter. These principles apply equally, but in reverse, when you have money you want to lend or are saving, versus when you want to borrow money. The impact on you depends on whether you are the borrower or the lender of money, and on the risks as perceived by the borrower and the lender.

The first principle is the time value of money, which describes the notion that money you have today is worth more to you than money you may receive sometime later. A simple way to understand this is if you have £100 and put it in your bank account on 1 January, you will earn interest on that money all year. By 31 December what you have in your bank account will be more than £100 because of the interest you earn (say £105 if the bank interest rate is 5%). However, if you received the £100 on 31 December, you'd obviously only have £100 on 31 December, not £105. Because of this time value of money, when you deposit money in the bank you expect to be paid interest on it, and when the bank lends you money it expects to be paid interest for lending it to you.

Here is another example of the same principle: if you pay an entire year's car insurance premium up front, it will cost you less than if you pay it in 12 monthly instalments during the year. Why? Because the insurance company is better off if it receives its full year's money up-front. This concept influences many aspects of finance.

The second principle is the risk/reward trade-off, which describes the notion that the higher the risk you take, the higher should be the potential reward, but also the higher the potential risk of loss. This is easy to explain using the lottery as an example. If you buy a ticket for £1, you could win millions, but the likelihood of that happening is tiny. In fact, statistically you are more likely to die of a heart attack before the prize is drawn than win the prize. Of course, by buying one ticket you haven't put much at risk. You could buy loads of tickets which would increase your chance of winning but you would have to buy an awful lot of tickets to increase your chance of winning significantly. Compare that example with a £50 ticket you can buy at an airport to win a £100,000 car. Buying one of those tickets is pretty expensive, but, as there are not too many ticket holders, you have a better chance of winning than you do if you buy one lottery ticket. A better but still not great chance. In the second case you have more money at risk, a less valuable reward, and a greater chance of winning. Sticking with the car example, if you bought all of the car tickets then you would win, but by then you probably would have paid more than the £100,000 the car would cost to buy outright. (What the raffle company is doing is betting they can get more money from tickets than the car cost them.)

The risk/reward concept applies across all aspects of life. Think about the potential financial upside and downside of someone starting their own business compared with someone working for a big company. Or how about taking a job which requires you to move to a new country – you may like it or hate it, but it may give you a career advantage. Turning back to finances, this principle explains why the amount of income you earn from lending or investing your money will depend on the level of risk you take. Similarly, the amount of money you are charged by a lender, and hence what the lender earns, will depend on the level of risk the lender thinks he is taking, i.e. how risky you appear to be.

BANKS AND INTEREST RATES

Banks are in the business of making money from money. Their motivation is to make a profit for their shareholders.

The shape and form of "retail" banking, which is the part of banking which provides services to you and me, has changed dramatically during the past 25 years. Back then there were no money machines, cheques were used extensively, credit cards were hardly used (John Lewis and Marks & Spencer would only allow you to use their store cards) and there was no internet, let alone internet banking. People actually went to their local bank and usually had a personal relationship with their local branch manager. The branch manager became a well-known person in the community, knowing everything about everyone and as a result was well-positioned to decide if someone could afford a loan. It doesn't work that way any more.

> "Fee-paying bank accounts are set to be next big scandal as complaints soar… Payouts to the people who have been missold packaged bank accounts are mounting." The Times, 3 August 2013.

Historically there were many banks to choose from, but over the past 20 years the industry has consolidated and the market is now dominated by a few players. The reason for the banking consolidation is the same as for other industries – scale is everything. Get as many customers as possible and make your processes as efficient as possible to increase your profits. Personalised service is out and centralised call centres (maybe even in India or Poland) are in, as efforts to increase profitability continues relentlessly.

The UK government is taking steps to encourage a more competitive banking landscape. The four big high street banks (Lloyds, RBS, Barclays, HSBC) service the needs of more than 70% of all consumers. The UK regulator, the Financial Conduct Authority, has "ensuring competition" as one of its statutory objectives. The regulator has also reduced the amount of capital start-up, or "challenger", which banks need to retain and is encouraging new entrants, including those using new technology through its "Innovation Hub" and "Sandbox" initiative, where firms can try out new ideas. Since 16 September 2013, banks have been required to transfer customer accounts, including all direct debits and credits, within seven days of the customer requesting it. This will be required to be even faster in the near future.

Whilst there is data to show that people are switching bank accounts, the "big four" domination will be hard to crack and, to be fair, they are working hard at meeting client needs, improving customer service and developing interesting technology.

Although this may all sound like good news for customers, as does the regulatory requirement that banks must "put their customers at the heart of every decision they make", we all need to remain vigilant. Why? Because banks are businesses and need to generate revenues and profits to remain in existence. The key is to always understand your money situation and what you need. The packaged

> "A bank is a place that will lend you money if you can prove you don't need it." Bob Hope, actor.

accounts referred to in the quote above are quite tricky – you need to look at each component part individually to be sure the offer works for you.

Banks are in the business of making money from money. Most fundamentally, they take deposits from customers and pay them x% and lend the money out to others at x% plus y%. The objective is to pay as little money as they can out to customers for their deposits (keeping competition in mind) and charge more than that to customers for the loans provided to them. And what drives the interest rate the bank gives you for your deposit and charges you for a loan? The level of risk you take by depositing money with the bank, and the risk the bank takes by lending you money. The higher the risk, the higher the rate of interest. Banks argue they are low-risk and therefore customers don't need to be paid much for the money held with them. Banks have processes for evaluating how risky you are and therefore how much they will lend you, on what terms. For these arrangements to work, banks have to have the money back from the loans they have made, to give to the customers whose money is on deposit when they want to withdraw it.

A major cause of the financial crisis was that it became too easy for people to borrow money from banks, they were lent more than they were likely to be able to repay, some of those loans were secured on properties (mortgages), and, as the property market collapsed, those properties turned out to be worth less than the mortgage amount.

> Banks will be forced to offer simple, standard and easily comparable products in a new drive to make it easier for customers to understand what they are buying. Initially the plan will cover an easy access savings account and a 30-day notice account. These products will be easily identified with a Kitemark. City AM, March 2013.

Getting customers to deposit money is a key objective of banks, as those deposits enable the rest of a bank's business. Banks work hard at attracting customers from a young age. They start with young people's accounts that are opened jointly with their parents. That works well for the banks, as the parents will probably open the account at their own bank. Banks also work hard to attract college and university-age clients, offering benefits to entice students to set up an account with them. You may be getting lots of approaches and will be hearing lots from your friends about good bank accounts. A number of incentives, such as free travel and iTunes cards, are being offered by banks. And they also offer "free" overdrafts which we will come back to later.

Statistics show that people have been very hesitant to move banks, even if they grumble about the service or interest rates, because it has been such a hassle to do so. The thought of changing direct debits/ standing orders and the penalties that could arise if payments don't arrive on time was enough to put people off. It will be interesting to see what happens now that banks are required to make it easy. We each need to keep in mind that "loyalty doesn't pay", so keep your eyes open for what works best for you.

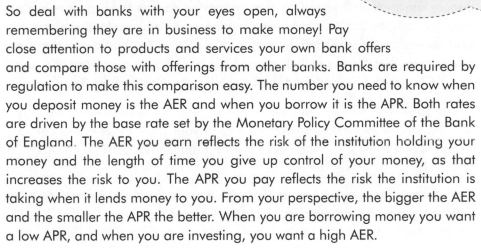

"A quarter of people under the age of 34 have never switched from their childhood bank accounts; more than half of 18 to 34 year olds have not set foot in a bank in the last three months; more than 3/4s logged into internet banking; 2/3rds have never used mortgage services; and more than 1/5th have never deposited a cheque. Study of 1,000 adults by uSwitch, July 2015

So deal with banks with your eyes open, always remembering they are in business to make money! Pay close attention to products and services your own bank offers and compare those with offerings from other banks. Banks are required by regulation to make this comparison easy. The number you need to know when you deposit money is the AER and when you borrow it is the APR. Both rates are driven by the base rate set by the Monetary Policy Committee of the Bank of England. The AER you earn reflects the risk of the institution holding your money and the length of time you give up control of your money, as that increases the risk to you. The APR you pay reflects the risk the institution is taking when it lends money to you. From your perspective, the bigger the AER and the smaller the APR the better. When you are borrowing money you want a low APR, and when you are investing, you want a high AER.

> Both AER and APR are expressed as percentages to make it easy to compare products. AER is the amount of interest income you earn on your deposit/investment for a year, divided by the amount of money you have deposited/invested. APR is the amount of interest you pay to borrow money for a year, divided by the amount of money borrowed.

A few people explained to me that they saw no benefit in saving money at the moment, as the AER on any savings is so low. Fair enough, but, if interest rates on deposits increase, so too will interest rates on loans. Those two interest rate numbers are always correlated. Whatever the raw numbers, the banks will always charge customers more for their loans than they will pay customers for the money they have on deposit with the bank. That is the only way they can stay in business. It is the same when you change money into a different currency for holiday. The exchange rate board will show two prices – whether you are buying foreign currency or changing it back, you always get the worst price.

Let's look at more things bank-related:

Current Accounts

You have probably had a current account for some time, as the only other option is to have a mattress account, which is where you keep your money under your mattress (not usually a good idea). You may laugh, but, whilst this is a rare occurrence in the UK, it is not unusual in some lesser developed countries or those with mega-high inflation. When inflation is really high, people are better off spending their money as fast as they can rather than saving it, so they don't bother taking the money to a bank. Mattress accounts also spring up when people lose all confidence in the banking system and are worried that if they put their money in a bank they may never see it again (think Cyprus and Ireland, and the UK during the Northern Rock collapse).

> Transactions that decrease the balance in your bank account are called debits and transactions that increase the balance are called credits.

Your parents may have taken you to open your first account and chances are you are still with that same bank today. Or you may have switched banks or may hold accounts at various banks. As an aside, make sure you keep track of what accounts you have. If you have lots of cash, you will want to split it across banks to make sure all of your money is protected under the government guarantee (£75,000 per account per bank).

> Depositing money into a bank account: if you want to deposit cash into your account, you will probably have to go into a bank, prepare a deposit slip and hand it to a cashier. The deposit slip just needs a date, the amount and a signature. The cashier will count your cash and stamp the slip, which you should keep for your records. If you want to deposit cheques, you can do the same as with cash or you can post them to your bank. Use a deposit slip as described above. If you do this by post, check your account balance after a few days to make sure the cheques have been processed. If they don't turn up at the bank you will have to notify whoever issued the cheque to cancel it and send a new one.

Most of your money transactions will flow through your current account. Money goes in, or is credited to your account when you deposit cash or cheques, your parents put your allowance in, or your employer transfers in your monthly/weekly take home pay. Money goes out, or is debited from your account, when you withdraw money from a cash machine, use your debit card to pay for something, or when money is withdrawn under a direct debit or standing order made by a vendor under your instructions. Both direct debits and standing orders are automatic payments (usually monthly) taken out of your account. These are set up so you don't have to remember to send a cheque or instruct a payment every time a payment is due. You will know that you have done this because you will have signed a contract authorising the payment. Examples of these could be your mobile phone bill, housing rental charges, university fees, council tax and utilities. The difference between these two is that under a standing order the same amount goes out every time (think rent) and under a direct debit the amount will change based upon your usage (think phone contract). These debited amounts will appear on your bank statement.

Whenever you use your contactless debit card to make a payment, it will be going through this account. If you use a contactless credit card, the amount charged will be listed on your credit card statement (currently a £30 per transaction limit). Do be careful that only one contactless card gets near the payment reader and that you check your bank and credit card statements to make sure you haven't had a card clash (where a contactless payment card is in the same wallet or purse as another and the reader detects more than one card to take payment from).

If you write a cheque, it will be drawn on your current account. To fill one in: date goes in the upper right; payee is the name of who you want to pay the money to (this needs to be the legal name of the payee or the bank will reject it, e.g. my bank account is in my maiden name); amount to pay is included in figures on the right and must include two decimal points; amount to pay is written in words under the payee line. Make sure the numeric and word amounts are the same. Then sign it. All this may sound straightforward but I have sent unsigned cheques, I have had cheques rejected due to writing the wrong name, and I have had cheques rejected for illegible or inconsistent amounts. Remember to write all of the relevant information on the slip in your cheque book.

As you can see, this bank account is an important one, as most of your financial transactions will go through it. It holds a lot of information about what is going on with your cash, so you want to keep a close eye on it. It is a good idea to check your account balance every time you go to a cash machine and review monthly every transaction that has gone through the account. (See Chapter 4 on Budgeting.)

As you review your transactions each month, make sure you agree with every item that is listed as touching your account. Any direct debits, standing orders and direct credits will have identifiers that tell you who originated the entry, which you should recognise. Cheques you have written will appear individually; if you deposit one cheque, the individual amount will be shown, but if you put a few cheques in as one deposit, only the total amount of the deposit will appear. If there is anything you don't recognise, get in touch with your bank immediately. Also consider if there is anything missing. In accordance with regulations, your bank has to reverse charges you think are incorrect, subject to investigation. This is described in the terms and conditions that you will have been given when you set up your account and are also available online.

One last thing to mention here is about the timing of money movements in and out of your account. This can be quite annoying. A quick step back for a moment: payments in and out of your bank account, except for cheques, are automatically processed via technology. This includes instructions given by phone, via internet banking and through direct debits/direct credits/standing orders. Under the UK Faster Payments Service initiative, the amounts processed that way will be debited/credited to your account pretty much immediately. This is not the case for cheques.

If you do go overdrawn, review what happened carefully. Until fairly recently, if you had money coming in and going out of your account, the bank could process the outgoings before the incomings for the same day. As a result, people were going overdrawn simply due to that sequence. I am sure you will agree that seems unfair. So, good news, under recent regulations: before charging for overdrafts, banks are required to take the full day's incoming transactions into account, even if it means running their internal processes twice.

The process is different when you deposit a cheque at a bank: the money will not count as yours for several days as the funds need to be cleared by the bank. "Clearing" is the bank's processes that make sure a cheque is legitimate and the cheque writer has the funds available in his account to pay over. It is during this process that a bank may find that the friend who gave you that cheque had no money in his account, so the cheque will be bounced! (More about "overdrafts" and being "overdrawn" soon.) This clearing process takes a few days, so you can't use that money until the process is complete. The same process happens on the flip side when you send a friend a cheque for something.

Packaged Accounts

There are an increasing number of bank accounts and credit cards that offer the consumer a combined package of services. One that has been particularly popular is the Santander 123 account which offers cashback and savings. It is critical that you review the details of the offering very carefully and evaluate whether the deal is a good one for you.

Debit Cards

You probably have a debit card issued by your bank and connected to your current account. It is called a debit card because each time you use it the money is debited (i.e. removed) from your account, reducing the amount in the account. This is the card you use to get money out of cash machines and to pay for things in shops, restaurants, and everywhere else. Any payments made with the card go out of your current bank account immediately and appear on your bank statement as of the date of the transaction. There is no charge for using the card. You need to keep close tabs on the current account the debit card is attached to, avoiding the possibility that you will spend more than the amount of money you have available in your account.

> Using a bank debit card will take money out of your bank account immediately.

Free Overdrafts, Authorised Overdrafts, Unauthorised Overdrafts And Being Overdrawn

You need to make sure that you are carefully monitoring the amount of money that is in your current account. If the balance goes below zero, you are overdrawn, the implications of which I will explain in a moment. Banks offer overdrafts to some customers which are like a safety net on your current account. Overdrafts allow you automatically to borrow up to a certain amount when there's no money in your account and can be useful to cover short-term cash flow problems. You don't have to use it, but it is there if you need it.

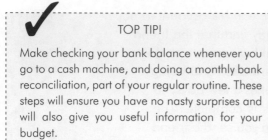

You may have a free overdraft, which means the bank will not charge you for borrowing that money. You do have to pay the money back. If you don't have a free overdraft you can ask your bank for an authorised overdraft. They will decide whether or not to give you one based on your bank record and you may have to pay a fee to set it up. You don't have to use this overdraft either. You will have to pay the overdraft back, plus interest plus a usage fee (typically £5). Read the overdraft terms and conditions carefully.

If you go overdrawn without your bank's authorisation (this means below zero in your account, including money from an approved overdraft, free or paid for by you), which the bank calls an unplanned/unauthorised overdraft, the charges will be higher. It is common practice to charge a fee of £10 for each day that you are overdrawn, capped at around eight days. You will also be charged interest on the amount you have borrowed. Your bank may also bounce (refuse to pay) cheques you write or refuse to pay direct debits. You will be charged fees of around £10 for each refused transaction. This seems to catch a lot of people by surprise! The reason for this is that the bank on the other side of your transaction, which is trying to collect on the cheque or direct debit, is likely to keep asking for the amount due to be paid and, each time it fails to get paid, your bank will charge you the fee.

If you are a student you will probably have been offered a free overdraft from your bank or other banks (to attract you as a new customer). Is it really free? Be very careful, as this is basically a loan that won't cost you interest now but may in the future. Many students told me about being offered several free overdrafts which they took "because they were offered". Once they graduated, they started to get charged interest on them. No one remembered getting warned in advance of the change, but it may be that they just didn't notice (see next paragraph). The interest rates were high and they had to work hard to pay the balances and interest they had accumulated. They were all pretty cross about their naivety and wondered how could they not have realised they would not be free forever. Every one of them said they wouldn't have spent the money they did if they had understood how it worked.

As your student days draw to a close, the bank(s) that has been providing you with an overdraft will probably change the terms of your overdraft agreement.

Banks handle this transition differently, but in all cases they aim to eliminate the interest free nature of the overdraft. (That is because now that they have you as a client and you can, in theory at least, afford to pay interest they want to make money from you.) Whatever the change, they are required to notify you in writing well in advance of it. (I have seen these letters arrive at my own home so I think they do get sent.) Your bank or other banks may offer you a "graduate loan", which allows you to bring any and all overdrafts you have outstanding into one. I have no personal experience with these, but have been told by numerous people that it is not a good idea. This is because whilst it is great to have all the overdrafts in one place, making it is easier to keep track of what is going on, the interest rates charged are higher than what they were before. The best thing for you to do is to get your overdrafts paid off before the new, tougher terms kick in. If you can't pay them all off at once, pay the ones with the highest charges first.

About 40% of people I talked to had bank overdraft arrangements in place as an emergency backup that they only used to cover them for short-term money shortfalls. They drew some money on them but made paying them back a high priority, cutting spending in the near-term to address the shortfall. This is a prudent way to use the overdraft to get you through the financially challenging student and early post-student years.

Account Controls: Reconciliations And Errors

Problems with your bank account? – Did you or the bank make a mistake?

The content of this section relates to savings accounts as well as current accounts, but I have included it here because it is more time critical in relation to your current account than to your savings account. There are two things that can go wrong with your account which you need to be on top of.

The first one is that you can make a mistake. The worst result of a mistake is that you go overdrawn. So another plea to keep close tabs on what is going on within your bank accounts. Look particularly carefully at cheques you send to your bank for deposit, as they take a few days to get credited to your account. The second is that the bank can make a mistake. Money you are sure had gone in doesn't get credited to your account or payments are taken out of your account that you haven't authorised. Or maybe some money has appeared in your account that you don't recognise – don't spend it if it's not yours. Any of these could be a genuine mistake made by the bank. The key is to find them as soon as possible and take action.

TOP TIP!

If you find yourself with a growing balance in your deposit account, you will want to explore ways to earn more income from your money. Take a look at Chapter 6 to get some ideas.

Let's say a direct debit has been made to your account for things you don't remember authorising, or standing orders that you thought you cancelled still show up as coming out of your account. If you catch these early, you will have only one month's charges to untangle, which is much easier than backing out of several months of payments. As soon as you spot a problem call the bank; typically it will be a call centre. Keep in mind that the call centre person spends his entire day dealing with problems so try to make it easy for him. Explain your situation fully. Be as precise as possible on dates and amounts, aiming for both of you to have a full understanding of the bank's and your side of the story. Hopefully the issue will be resolved to your satisfaction. Do not hesitate to ask for compensation if you have incurred a financial loss, and don't be surprised if the bank takes back any financial gain.

If you do not feel the situation has been satisfactorily resolved, you should make it clear to the person that you want to "file a complaint". By using that specific word, you will be letting the bank know that it is a serious problem and chances are the person on the phone will escalate it to his manager. There has been a huge amount of focus on the way banks handle complaints (or don't!) and several have incurred regulatory fines. Banks are required by the regulators to address any issue you raise with them within 80 days. That doesn't necessarily mean giving you exactly what you want; it means treating you fairly. If you are not satisfied with how you are treated you are free to file a further complaint with the Financial Ombudsman Service (FOS). Plenty of people do, so don't be shy about it. The FOS publishes a list of number of complaints by bank twice a year and the numbers are high. The big three UK-headquartered banks (Royal Bank of Scotland, Lloyds Banking Group, Barclays) tend to head the list every time, but to be fair they do have an awful lot of accounts, so the numbers are bound to be big.

Savings And Deposit Accounts

Your bank has probably offered you a "deposit" account. It may be convenient to have a deposit account at the same bank as your current account but, with the UK Faster Payments initiative, the importance of this has diminished. (It used to be that same day money movements between bank accounts only happened if the accounts were with the same bank.) Make sure you are being given immediate credit for money transfers between all of your accounts.

Banks will give you interest on your deposit account money. The AER you will earn and the timing of interest payments will be documented in writing, as required under banking regulation.

TOP TIP!

If a financial offering sounds too good to be true, it probably is.

Generally interest earned will be calculated and paid monthly, based on the average balance in your account (though some banks use the lowest balance in your account during the month) multiplied by the rate of interest, divided by twelve. Right now the interest rate is low for a few reasons. These are: the Bank of England base rate (on which all other interest rates are based) is low; you are taking no risk by leaving the money with the bank; and you can access your money whenever you want.

In short, it is convenient and safe to keep any savings you have in a deposit account with your bank, but the interest you earn on those savings will be the low because of it.

It is easy it is to get caught up in trying to find the best deal on a deposit account and lose sight of the actual difference it would make in terms of interest you will earn. Let's say you have £1,000 on deposit. If you have that money in a bank for a full year at 2% or 4% interest, you will earn £20 or £40, respectively. That income may be subject to tax, so the difference to you may be even less. If you have £10,000 on deposit for a year, you will earn £200 and £400, respectively. That is worth thinking about. But why would a bank offer a rate of interest double that of other banks? Suspicious? The answer is likely to be that that is the only way they can attract money in. And that should raise alarm bells with you as it must mean the bank is higher-risk than others. The old risk/reward trade-off again!

Security And Technology

Information on a related topic, Take Steps to Avoid Identity Theft and Other Crimes, is included in Chapter 11.

You will probably do most of your banking, other than getting cash, via the internet. That will include giving payment instructions, checking your balance and reviewing transactions. There are masses of criminals perpetually trying to access bank account information. Losses and fraud are becoming commonplace and it is in your interest to be vigilant. You'd be surprised to learn (as I was when I heard recently) that most hackers get into accounts by guessing people's security codes, and they do that quite easily. Apparently people are not too clever in picking these codes. You know why? Because it is a pain to remember complicated codes, especially if you have lots of them. Record your codes somewhere, ensuring they are not easily accessible, and are nowhere near other bank information.

Protect yourself from becoming a victim of a hacker by:

- Making sure your password has a combination of upper case letters, lower case letters, numbers and symbols.

- Never giving information out about yourself or your bank account details to anyone, even if the request is via an email or phone call that is supposedly from your bank.

- Calling or emailing your bank independently. If you are contacted by your bank, don't respond to that call or email. Hang up the phone or ignore the email and call/email the bank yourself (don't press the dial back button). When you originate contact, you are in control of who you are talking to, but if you are responding to a call or email you can't be sure.

- Accessing your bank's website directly, not through links in emails they appear to have sent you.

Whilst we are talking security, let's turn our attention to cash machines.

- Have a good PIN number that no one can guess, e.g. not your birthday.
- Don't give your PIN to anyone, ever.
- Change your PIN if, for any reason, you think someone may have it or has figured out what it might be. This is easily done via the internet and at some cash machines.
- Be careful when you are getting money out. If anyone is around you, don't feel awkward about covering your hand as you put your number in. You may feel like a weirdo but so be it. The same goes for using a PIN with your credit or debit card.

CREDIT CARDS

A credit card is issued by a bank or other financial institution (e.g. VISA, MasterCard, American Express). Unlike a debit card, when you use this card money is not automatically taken out of your account. Instead, every time you use it, the money gets added to a running tally. On a monthly basis the credit card company will send you a list of transactions and will require you to make a minimum payment – currently around 2.0% of the outstanding balance or £5, whichever amount is greater. You are always allowed to pay more than that minimum amount.

The financial institution is issuing you with a card because they are willing to lend you money and they hope to make money from you by charging you interest on the balance outstanding at the end of each month. However, the majority of money earned by the companies is through charging vendors that accept your card a percentage of whatever you spend with them.

> A recent survey showed that roughly 66% of 18–25-year olds pay off their credit card bills monthly. Center for the Study of Financial Innovation, July 2012

If you pay the full balance owed every month, you will not incur any interest costs and the bank will make no money from you, only from the seller you purchased from. But if you don't pay the card balance off, you will be charged interest on the balance. The rate of interest charged is currently around 14% per annum for purchases; the issuer is required to contact you if the interest rate changes. You can also find the rate on your monthly statement and on the issuer's website. If you withdraw cash, however, the rate is likely to be around 27% per annum. Importantly, you will be charged that higher rate on the full balance of the card even if you pay the card balance off fully when the account falls due. Read the card's terms and conditions carefully on this – I know many people who learned this the hard way.

Prior to issuing a card, the issuer will carry out a credit check on you. The terms of the card will include a credit limit which is the amount you are allowed to have outstanding on it at any time – in effect, the size of the loan the issuer is willing to give you.

As this can be an expensive way of borrowing money, you want to avoid spending so much on the card that you can't pay it off at the end of the month (at least most of the time). The interest is calculated and added to your balance on which the next month's interest is calculated, so you end up paying interest on interest.

If you have a £1,000 credit card balance and make the minimum payment required every month, it will take 14 years and 11 months to pay it off. You will have paid £882 in interest.

Each month you will get a statement from the credit card company. It contains key information and will look something like this:

Credit Card Statement

Account Number	Name	Statement Date	Payment Due Date
4321-123-456	John Jones	01/08/2016	25/08/2016

Credit Line	Credit Available	New Balance	Minimum Payment Due
£1200.00	£1074.76	£125.24	£20.00

Reference	Sold	Posted	Activity Since Last Statement	Amount
875FRT657		25/10	Payment – Thank You	−168.80
862GYI191	12/10	15/10	Music Mania	14.83
764HUH182	13/10	15/10	Big Eat Central	30.55
098RTE854	18/10	18/10	TK Travel	27.50
009EWM522	20/10	21/10	Superstore UK	12.26
416POF121	09/10	09/10	Surf and Shop	40.10

Previous Balance (+)	£168.80		Current Amount Due	£125.24
Purchases (+)	£125.24		Amount Past Due	
Cash Advances (+)			Amount Over Credit Line	
Payments (−)	£168.80		Minimum Payment Due	£20.00
Credits (−)				
Finance Charges (+)				
Late Charges (+)				
New Balance (=)	£125.24			

Finance Charge Summary	Purchases	Advances	Send Payment To:
Periodic Rate	1.65%	0.054%	PO Box 6543, London, UK
Annual Percentage Rate	19.80%	19.80%	For Customer Service Call:
			0800-456-9876
			For Lost or Stolen Cards Call:
			0800-456-6789

The statement will give you a date by which you have to make a payment on the account. As mentioned earlier, you must pay the minimum amount indicated on the statement but you are allowed to pay as much as you like above that. You can make your payment by sending a cheque, in plenty of time for the company to receive and process it before the payment due date, sending a payment instruction via the internet, having a standing order in place for a monthly fixed payment, or having a direct debit in place to pay the full balance monthly. Don't miss the payment date as these companies are ruthless about charging you. If you decide to set up a direct debit or standing order, make sure you have enough money in your account to cover the amount as of the payment day (shown on the card statement).

You will receive the credit card statement in advance of the payment due date which gives you a chance to review the statement in detail, ensuring any incorrect charges are fixed before the payment goes out of your bank account. So make a point of reviewing the credit card statement in detail as soon as you receive it to confirm that the balance it shows you as owing is correct. Take a look at the total and see if it makes sense. If it looks too big, the first thing to check is that your previous month's payment was processed in time. (I once forgot to sign the cheque I sent to my credit card company, which I only discovered because the payment wasn't credited on my statement. I noticed there was a problem and sorted it out in time to avoid any interest charge.)

> Be aware that some companies you buy goods or services from will charge you a fee for paying with a credit card, with the rate sometimes varying by credit card provider. This practice started with discount airlines but is spreading. What is annoying is that you usually don't see this until you are nearly at the end of the buying process. Assuming you want to proceed with the purchase, take a moment to think about the incremental cost before deciding which card to use – a debit or a credit card. And note that some credit cards are most costly than others.

Using a credit card can be a useful money management tool if you pay the balance off before you incur any interest charges. The first reason is due to the time value of money. You get to use the card to buy things all month and only have to pay for those things at the end of the month. Unlike when you use your debit card, you have the use of your money all month rather than paying out cash as you go along. If the money you use to pay the card company is in a savings account you may even be earning interest on it. The second reason is that your monthly statement gives you an excellent record of the money you spent, when you spent it and what you spent it on. Once you have confirmed that the total looks reasonable, get out your pile of credit card slips and follow the processes detailed in Chapter 4 on budgeting.

If there is anything on the statement that you don't recall spending, you should get in touch with the credit card company immediately. Credit card fraud is a big problem and you want to protect yourself from it. Even very small amounts should be investigated. As with the debit card, you need to do this on a timely basis so you don't have to try reversing out months of charges.

Three more things to mention whilst we are on credit cards:

- **Lost or stolen cards** – as soon as you notice your card(s) are missing or stolen, you should contact the card provider. Once you do so, the provider will put a stop on your card, which means it cannot be used. If it has been used by whoever took it, the card company will reverse those charges as they are fraudulent and the provider is required to bear those costs. The sooner you report the missing card the better – it reduces the cost to the provider and the hassle to you of arranging the reversal of charges. Contacting the provider can be, at least momentarily, challenging, because without the card you won't have the phone number to call readily available (it's on the back of the card) and you probably don't know the card number (I've been caught out on that a few time). If this happens, you can find the helpline number on the provider's website and usually on your statement. It is a good idea to have a list of card helplines somewhere easy to find. But perhaps the best thing is to limit the cards you have, so you will notice if one goes missing. Losing cards is a pain, especially if you lose the one you use most often (that is always the one you lose!) as it can take a week or more to receive a replacement.

- **Card protection services** – you can buy a service where you give a company details of your cards and if your wallet gets stolen they handle the cancellation and reissuance of everything. I know people who have this but to me it seems like an unnecessary expense. If you have a well maintained list of all your cards, their numbers, and contact information you can easily do this yourself. The most well-known provider of this service, Sentinel, provides add-on services, including replacement of missing handbags and briefcases, providing emergency cash advances, and protecting your personal identity documents. Before you take this out, review your home insurance and travel insurance policies, as you may find some or all of these add-ons are provided under insurance policies you already have.

- **Payment protection insurance** – this is insurance that card and loan providers offer you so that if, due to ill health, loss of job or some other catastrophic event you cannot make payments on a credit card, the insurance company will pay on your behalf. This sounds like a good idea, but the execution was fraught with problems, the main one being that people who thought they were covered found the insurance companies would not pay out when they thought they would. The companies (banks that offered the credit cards and insurance) all had to make good on these misleading and inappropriate sales, which cost them billions of pounds as you may have seen in the press. As a result, it is unlikely you will be offered this and, if you are, read the documentation very carefully.

As mentioned earlier, whilst the credit card company is making money from you if you don't pay your credit card balance on time, they make most of their money from the companies that accept their cards. Every time you use a credit card the provider takes a fee from the company you bought your goods or services from. Why do sellers agree to this? Because it makes it easier for people to buy from them if they can use a credit card rather than pay cash. In addition, not handling cash reduces the seller's risks as cash can be stolen, sales people can make mistakes when they give change back to a cash buyer, and someone has to reconcile what is in the till at the end of the day.

STORE CARDS

It is hard to imagine, but in the 1980s the only retail chains in the UK that had store cards were M&S and John Lewis, and in those two stores the only cards you could use were their own. How often, when you go into a high street shop, do they try to get you to register for one of their cards? Usually they will offer you 20% or more off today's purchases. I find that discount makes it really hard to say "no". If you say "yes", though, you will need to go through their credit check process which may result in your being turned down. (Read more about credit ratings in Chapter 9.)

Why do shops offer these cards? No surprise – it is another way for them to make money – in a kind of bankish way. Usually there is a finance company behind the company you are dealing with. They are hoping that you will use the store card to make purchases and then be unable to pay off the monthly bill so that they can earn money, in the form of interest, just like any other credit card.

Why would you not want to take up the store card offer? The answer is simple – because of the rate of interest you will be charged. The APR for these cards is currently around 30%, so significantly higher than your credit card. Pretty outrageous really. So why do people do it? They simply can't bear to miss out on the upfront purchase discount or they can't borrow the money they need to buy whatever it is they feel they need from anywhere else. The first reason is easy to tackle – do it, pay the bill as soon as it arrives and then put the card somewhere you won't use it ever again. The second reason is not a good one – adding to an existing financial problem. The store may well save you from yourself on this one. If they check your credit and see that you are high-risk with significant debts already outstanding, they may well turn you down.

> 40% of store card users do not know the interest they are being charged (thisismoney.co.uk)

One more reason to avoid these cards – the more cards you have, the harder it is to keep track of where you are financially.

BUYING ON CREDIT

It wouldn't surprise me if you haven't come across this yet, but you will probably start to notice it now, particularly in advertisements. It is not unusual to see stores offering deals like interest-free credit, pay nothing until two years from now and similar promises in relation to big purchases like furniture and electronics. You should approach these offers with a lot of caution.

CREDIT?

PAY LATER ○

PAY NOW ○

Why would companies offer such a deal? Well, firstly they are keen to sell whatever it is they are selling, so they are trying to entice you to buy it by making it easy for you to do so. For example, they could have too much stock and they want to get rid of it, even if they lose money on it. Or they could be about to get next year's models so they want to shift the old stuff. At the same time the seller, or the financing company behind the seller, are hoping to earn interest from you. So look very carefully at the APR and payment terms. Are you able to pay when you want to, or do they fix you onto a schedule that means you will be forced to pay a high interest rate? You won't want to incur that cost if, during the ensuing two years, or whatever the time frame, you have the cash to pay the whole amount off.

BUYING "FREE" STUFF ON THE INTERNET

Have you ever been tempted by those adverts for free trials that you can cancel whenever you want?

It sounds so easy, but somehow it can turn complicated. I have heard plenty of horror stories from people who were enticed into buying something by an advert of this type. You will be asked to provide your credit card details when you sign up for the "free trial". The vendor will then send you whatever it is you wanted and you have to remember to cancel your order. And that cancellation has to be in good time. And it has to be in writing. And it is really hard to find out where to send it. And there is no number to call, or, if there is, it is a number that cost lots per minute and you wait ages to be put through to a human being and then you finally give up. And...and...and it seems to end in tears all too often.

Based on the stories I have heard, it seems to me that, even when you think you've followed the right process with these offers, a charge you didn't expect may appear on your credit card statement and you have to work to get it reversed out. That takes time and effort. This is a good example of why it is important to review your credit card statement, as well as your bank account, very carefully every month.

BORROWING FROM A BANK – LOANS

The subject of bank loans appears in several places in this book because banks are where most of us turn when we need to borrow money. When I say "bank" I also mean other lenders of money that you will find if you do an internet search on "bank loan", "car loan" or "personal loan". In this chapter we will focus on what I call planned loans; by that I am excluding the short-term financial crunch need to borrow money described in Chapter 5, Handling A Money Shortfall. The fundamentals of how banks decide whether they will lend you money, how much they will lend you and the terminology used are consistent, regardless of what you want to borrow the money for. The principles underlying loans are the fundamental principles of the time value of money and the risk/reward trade-off.

Let's start with a quick recap: banks use the money on deposit that people have placed with them and lend the money on to other people. The strategy employed by banks to make money from this process is straightforward – pay the depositor a lower rate of interest than you charge the borrower. The actual rate of interest provided to you for the deposits you leave with a bank will be impacted by the Bank of England base rate and by the amount of time you commit to leaving the money with the bank. The longer the committed time, the higher the rate you can expect to earn. The third determinant of the rate you are paid is the risk to you of leaving your money with the specific bank – the higher the risk to you that something will happen to your money before you get it back, the more interest you will expect to be paid. The interest rate a bank will charge to lend you money will reflect the base rate as a starting point, increased to reflect the bank's perception of how risky you are.

A bank will decide whether or not to lend you money based upon how likely they think you are to pay the interest you owe during the term of the loan and to pay them the full amount of the loan back ("principal") at the end of the term of the loan. The lender's starting point in thinking about lending to you will be to assess your credit worthiness, asking you to provide information and/or using a credit rating agency (refer to Chapter 9 to read about credit ratings in greater detail). The bank will base this evaluation on personal information about you, your housing arrangements, employment history and credit history. Loan providers are required by the UK regulator to ascertain that you can afford the loan, meaning you will be able to pay the interest and principal when they come due. One other factor that features when a financial institution is deciding whether to provide a loan is whether the loan is "secured" or not, meaning whether the loan backed is by something tangible the institution can get its hands on if you don't pay when you are supposed to.

Let's take a mortgage. A mortgage is "secured" against a property. Therefore, if you fail to meet your interest payments, the bank can force you to sell the property and the proceeds of that sale can be used to pay off the mortgage. There are lots of people grumbling about the 25% deposits that are currently being required, particularly for first-time buyers. The reason banks require this is for their protection. If the bank provides a mortgage and the borrower puts down a 25% deposit, the property would have to decrease in value by more than 25% before a forced sale of the property would fail to pay off the loan. You can see why the 100% mortgages that used to exist provided lenders with very little security, and negative security if house prices are falling. The lender will expect you to protect its interest in the property by having homeowner's insurance on the property. (See the Insurance section later in this chapter.) Personal loans differ from mortgages and other secured loans because in many cases the assets the loan is associated with are not containable, i.e. you could not sell it on its own (think kitchen upgrade) or the bank chooses not to make the loan specifically secured. The best example of this is a car loan where the bank will require you to take out insurance and, if the car is ruined, the insurance proceeds will be used to pay off the loan, but the bank will not put the effort into securing the loan, as the amount involved is likely to be small. Because of the lack of security, personal loans attract higher interest rates than secured loans. Personal loan providers, their rates and conditions for lending are very easy to find on the internet.

> A banker's draft is a cheque where the funds are drawn directly on a financial institution rather than on your personal bank account. When you give someone a banker's draft in payment for something, they treat it as if it were cash; i.e. they will not wait for the cheque to clear as they would with a personal cheque. A bank will charge you around £15 for this service.

Each type of loan is explored further below:

Personal loans – these loans can be used for a wide range of purposes and you have to explain the purpose in detail to the lender. They are typically for a specific, containable need. A few examples of purposes of these loans include buying furniture, paying for a wedding, or building a garage. A personal loan would not be provided to cover general living expenses.

Car/vehicle loans – lending institutions will treat these as personal loans, but, as this is the most likely loan you will take out in the near term, I wanted to include additional information about the processes involved. Once you have made a decision to buy a car or another vehicle (read Chapter 10 when you are working through your decision), there are a few ways a bank may get involved or you may bypass banks altogether.

If you buy the vehicle directly from another person:

- The seller will want cash from you which means, unless it is really inexpensive, you will provide the seller with a personal cheque, provide a banker's draft or instruct your bank to make a payment via online banking or in person at your bank.

- In order to do that, you will need to have the money in your account already, or you need to get it there. Getting it there may mean borrowing it from your bank or other lender. The process for obtaining a car/vehicle loan is much the same as for any other loan. The bank will ask you questions and gather information from other sources to assess your credit worthiness, i.e. how certain are they that you will make your payments as they fall due?

- The bank will also ask questions about the vehicle because, whilst the loan won't be secured against the vehicle, the lender will want to get some comfort that, if you don't pay back what you owe, it can force you to sell it to get back the money it lent you. Therefore the bank will be interested in what you have agreed to pay for the vehicle and, depending on the amount of money involved, it may takes steps to gain comfort that the purchase price is reasonable. The bank will also want to see the vehicle's registration papers to confirm that you will have good title to it. Good title means that the person you are buying it from has the right to sell it to you because they legally own it. You will also have to show an MOT (Ministry of Transport) certificate if the car is more than three years old, to demonstrate the car is roadworthy. And you will have to show that you have made arrangements to insure the vehicle. (Insurance is described more fully later.) Having insurance is important to the bank because it is loaning you money on an asset and if something happens to the asset (an accident) the bank wants to make sure it will still get its principal back. If, for example, the car is written off as a result of an accident, the insurance money will go to the bank to pay off the loan.

- Regardless of where you are getting the money from, the seller will not let you have the vehicle until the money is confirmed as being in his account. So if you do a wire transfer, or provide a cheque, he won't let you have the vehicle until the money is cleared by his bank. You will remember that the way banks work it will take a few days between putting a cheque in the bank and getting credit for it, whilst a wire transfer will be effective nearly immediately. If you provide a banker's draft you should be able to take the vehicle with you when you present the draft.

- Note that first-time buyers are more likely to buy from individuals rather than dealerships. Sometimes that works out well, though I have heard of people buying cars that they thought were a good deal but then they had to spend a lot of money on repairs. Therefore I encourage you to get any car you are thinking of buying checked out by a garage you trust.

If you buy the vehicle from a dealer:

- A dealer will typically help you navigate the purchase process as he is likely to be keen to get the deal completed. Whilst the dealer may offer you funding, the actual provider will be a financial services institution.

- You may be offered money for the purchase through two different types of arrangements. These are either a loan, just like one provided by a bank, or a leasing arrangement. The latter is more common for new rather than used vehicles. Dealerships offer financing arrangements because it makes it easier for people to buy their vehicles. They in turn will have an arrangement with a bank to handle the financing arrangements. It could be the same bank that you use, but the deal could be better than if you walked into your local branch to arrange the financing yourself. There are business reasons for this, but for now just make sure you ask both the dealer and your bank about the cost of a loan so you have a complete picture of your options before making a decision.

- Buying from a dealership makes finalising the transaction easier when compared with buying from a private individual for three reasons: the dealer will have the car's registration documentation ready. The dealer will be able to arrange insurance quickly for you, although this insurance is typically more expensive than if you arranged it yourself. And, perhaps most importantly, the dealer may offer you a guarantee on the vehicle you purchase. That guarantee may provide for engine and other repairs, at no cost to you, during a specified period of time, which helps you with your financial planning.

I remember vividly the interest rate on a mortgage I had, a 95% mortgage, and the interest rate changed from 8% to 13% in less than a year. Absolutely horrible and it forced us to sell the house. In order to do that, we had to promise to protect the buyer against further interest rate increases for a year, i.e. we promised to pay him cash if the rates went up.

Housing Loans – Mortgages

This is a huge topic and is covered in detail in Chapter 10. The same concepts apply here as to the other loans we have covered. You are buying something valuable and the bank will be interested in: what you will be paying for the property; what the bank's surveyor assesses the property to be worth; and how much money you want to borrow. Once again, the bank will want to evaluate your creditworthiness and that will include assessing your ability to "afford" the loan – paying the loan and the monthly interest back. Regulations since 2014 have required lenders to collect a lot of personal information about your money, so be prepared! A mortgage has two distinct payments to think about – monthly interest payments and repayment of the loan itself (the principal), a portion of which may also need to be paid monthly. Because a mortgage is a long-term proposition (the most common term is 25 years) and lots of things can change over that time period, it is a risky decision for both parties. Therefore, both you and the bank will invest a great deal of time to finalise a deal.

Until recently, banks capped the mortgage loan offered at 75% of the property purchase price or a 25% deposit – the same thing. Now, banks have relaxed their requirements and are more willing to lend with only a 10% deposit. Some banks are now offering 100% mortgages if you have a parent who is willing to guarantee the mortgage will be paid. Before signing up for a mortgage you need to think about your long-term risks. Most importantly, think about how large a loan you could afford to pay interest on if interest rates increased dramatically. It may be hard for you to imagine, but I can tell you they can change quickly. In the late 1990s, our interest rate went from 8% to 13% in less than a year – nightmare!

INSURANCE – BUYING PROTECTION

This is an important feature in managing your money effectively though you may not have thought of it that way. In fact you may not have thought about insurance much at all. The first time you may have become aware of insurance may have been in relation to getting your driving licence and wanting to drive a car. Maybe your parents paid the cost of insuring a car for you to drive or maybe you had to pay for it yourself. If you don't know what that insurance cost was, go online and see what it might have been. I suspect you will find the numbers shockingly high. And how was that rate set anyway? How come the annual payment to the insurance company was more than the car was worth? Or near to it anyway, especially if you factor in several years of insurance?

> Insurance provides financial protection against a potential future loss.

Insurance Fundamentals

Insurance has a terminology all of its own, so let's work through it.

Insurance is a policy you buy on something that is of value to you. You use it to make sure you don't lose out if that something is lost, stolen or damaged. The amount of insurance you take out on the thing of value depends on what the thing is worth; what it would cost to replace. You can insure just about anything. Musicians insure their hands, dancers their legs, horse owners their horses. If you have pets you may have pet insurance, so that if your pet gets ill the insurance company will pay the vet bills.

Life assurance has many of the characteristics of insurance with the exception that you are not buying protection against a possible future event (death is still inevitable) but merely the timing of it. To keep things simple I will explain life assurance as if it were insurance. On a related note, Accidental Death Insurance provides money if death results from an accident – it is insurance, as it's only a possible event.

Policy periods and renewal refer to the period the insurance coverage will be in place and therefore how long you will pay the premiums. Most policies cover one year and then you are given the option to renew the policy. One thing to look out for is the timing of the renewal.

One thing I find annoying is the fact that insurance companies almost assume you will renew with them. So they send you a renewal proposal a few days before the policy runs out, giving you very little time to research other options. Every time I get a renewal the price goes up, but if I look around I can usually get my current insurer to reduce the price or find something less expensive with a different provider. I finally figured out that I needed to get control of this, so now

I once asked my daughter to research my car insurance renewal and offered her 10% of whatever she saved me. The only savings she gained was from turning a series of monthly payments into one annual payment. I did honour my commitment, taking the opportunity to explain the time value of money. I pointed out that when she starts paying her own premiums she may not have the option of doing an annual payment as she may not have the cash available.

I have a diary note to myself to remind me a month before the renewal is due. The UK regulator is now focusing its attention on this renewal process, and is cracking down on firms to give customers more notice – more good news for consumers!

Premium refers to the payments you make to the insurance company for providing you with the insurance policy. Usually it will be a monthly payment made by cheque or via a direct debit to your bank account. However, you can also make an up-front annual premium payment. That amount will be less than twelve times the monthly payment amount you are quoted because you are paying the full amount up-front. (This goes back to the time value of money principle.)

Factors that impact the premium amount: the premium amount is determined based on: the value of what you are insuring; how good/comprehensive your insurance is going to be; the excess level; and what limits there are on what the insurance company will pay out to you. The insurance provider will also take into account your personal track record of claiming money on the insurance policy. Let's consider these concepts in turn using car insurance as an example (with one small deviation at the end to clarify one concept):

- **The value of what you are insuring**. This is pretty self-evident. Ignoring everything else for a moment, it is going to cost you more to insure a brand new Maserati than a 10-year-old Ford Fiesta, or even a new Ford Fiesta. The cost of the car is taken into account as is the cost of repairing the car.

- **How good/all-inclusive the insurance policy is**. There are two types of car insurance policies – fully comprehensive and third-party. UK law only requires you to have third-party insurance. Fully comprehensive means that the insurance company will cover your costs, as well as the costs of whoever you crash into, if the accident is your fault. Under third-party insurance, the company will only cover the cost of damages to the car/person you crash into. In actual fact, and disappointingly, the cost difference between the two types is negligible these days, because, as I was told by my insurance company, "We can't estimate the value of what you will crash into."

- The **excess level** is the amount you will spend on repairs before the insurance company starts to pay up. If you offer to pay the first £200 of expenses to repair your car, your premium will be less than if you have no excess which means the insurance company pays for everything. If you offer to pay the first £500 of expenses, the premium will be lower still. Many insurance companies are now requiring all young drivers to have a mandatory excess of £300. If you have an accident that costs £199 or £499 to fix, under the two scenarios here, or something just a bit higher than the excess, it may be financially advantageous to pay the repair costs yourself. This is because, when your policy comes up for renewal after an accident, the insurance company is likely to increase your premium because of the costs they had to pay out for you. You are required to notify the insurance company of any accident, whether you claim costs back or not, so they may increase your premium regardless.

- **Limitations on what is covered** under the policy will reduce your premium. This is along the lines of third party/comprehensive for cars but has much more applicability in, say, medical insurance. You can get lower premiums if certain medical problems are excluded – because the insurance company is limiting the likelihood that you will make a claim. Insurance companies exclude pre-existing conditions which are medical conditions that are known and likely to continue to be conditions and the insurance company won't insure them.

Insurance Providers And Their Business

Where do you go to get insurance? Some of the main brands you will come across are Aviva, Direct Line, Admiral, Churchill, AXA/PPP, and BUPA. Some of these are owned by insurance companies and some are owned by banks. Supermarkets are increasingly offering these products through arrangements with insurance companies, so next time you go into Tesco or Sainsbury's take a look at the booklets at the tills. Lastly you can go to an insurance broker, which is sort of like a travel agent for the insurance industry.

Insurance providers are in the business of making money. They set premium rates with the expectation that they will receive more money from premiums than they will have to pay out to people claiming on the policies. To increase their probability of getting that right, they assess the likelihood of a bad event happening and factor it into their pricing. They do that based on masses of data. For cars they have found that younger drivers have more accidents than older drivers. Young men also used to have higher premiums than young women, but the EU courts recently decided that setting premiums taking that

> **TOP TIP!**
>
> If you have been covered under your parent's or family insurance plan you will need to look to see when that cover will stop. Some policies will state an age limit, some cease coverage when formal education ends, and others use different criteria.

into account was discriminatory (despite the facts) so gender can't be figured into premiums – bad news for girls and good news for boys. Powerful cars with big engines tend to have more costly accidents than 1.2 litre engine cars that go slower. Cars kept on the street are more likely to get stolen than those parked in garages.

Insurance companies will take this generic information into account, as well as your specific information, when they provide you with an insurance pricing proposal. If you have had any accidents, it is going to cost you more to insure a car than if you have had none. Same goes for speeding tickets. Getting through the first three years of driving without a traffic violation or accident is a good goal for lots of reasons, including money.

You may think, "Maybe I'll go without car insurance." But you can't, as it is against the law for the owner of a car not to insure it. The police use automatic number plate recognition equipment to find uninsured cars as they move around or are parked. When you go to buy a car you will have to show you have insurance before you take the car away, and when you pay your annual road tax you will also have to provide proof of insurance. It is the government's way of making sure that people on the roads can pay if they crash into other people – to repair their cars and pay medical bills if someone has been hurt. The same applies if you rent a car – you will need insurance, which will be provided by the car rental company at a cost to you. That is usually an incremental cost to the cost per day you were quoted for the rental, so watch out! If you plan to drive a friend's car or let your friend drive your car, talk to the relevant insurance company in advance to make sure the car will be insured – don't just assume it is. A recent change in the law makes this harder to achieve than it has been in the past.

The pricing principles explained above apply to all types of insurance. The insurance market is highly competitive and can be a bit confusing when you try to compare what different companies are offering. There are some great websites to help you get the best deals. The most advertised at the moment are gocompare.com and confused.com (be mindful, as Admiral Insurance owns this site) and similar services are emerging all the time. I have found that these websites compare key, but not all, information, so read any policy you are considering very carefully, and perhaps go back and consider some of the policies you rejected. It definitely pays to shop around every time you renew insurance. Remember to put a note in your diary a month or two before the renewal is due so you have time to do your research.

Types Of Insurance

- **Life** – you may not have given much thought to this yet but you will once other people start to depend on you. Your employer may provide life assurance for you (which will have tax consequences as noted in Chapter 7). The deal with life assurance is that, if you die, the insurance company will pay a lump sum to whoever you have designated to receive it. The sum paid is either described as an amount, or if the assurance is being provided by your employer it is likely to be stated as a multiple of your base salary. It is very important that the assurance company or your employer has something in writing that states who should get the money if something happens to you.

- **Accidental death** – this is a lump sum payment made to whoever you designate if your death is due to an accident rather than natural causes or illness.

- **Medical** – as you know, the NHS provides medical services to all of us free of charge, although not totally free as we pay National Insurance and other taxes to fund the NHS. When you travel within the EU, you will be provided with medical care but you may need to have your EU medical card (EHIC) with you. If you get ill or injured when you are on holiday, that will be covered under your travel insurance (see below). But what about when you are here in the UK? What if you don't want to wait for the NHS all the time? What do those doctors do when they are doing private work with private patients?

  Private health insurance, or medical insurance, is becoming more common in the UK, as the NHS faces increasing challenges with balancing its costs and the services it provides. An increasing number of private companies are providing it to their employees (with P11D tax implications) and an increasing number of people are buying it privately for themselves. If you have private medical insurance you will still need to see a GP in the first instance – either your NHS one or a private one (at your expense) – who will then refer you to a specialist. You can find private doctors via internet search engines. It is seeing the specialist and having additional tests and other procedures performed under his direction that this insurance covers.

Do make sure you get any treatment pre-approved by the insurance company, which should only take a phone call to arrange. This insurance also covers surgery in private hospitals and will usually result in your being treated more quickly than under the NHS, particularly for those medical treatments that are not "life critical".

- **Dental** – this type of insurance was nearly non-existent in the UK twenty years ago. As it gets increasingly difficult to get NHS dental care, people are turning to private dentists and looking to insure themselves against those potential costs. A common provider is Denplan, though a selection can be found using insurance websites like moneysupermarket.com. In order to encourage their clients to maintain good dental health, the insurance premium may include reimbursement of twice a year dental check-ups. This insurance may be provided by an employer or purchased directly by you.

- **Travel** – if you have done much travelling on your own you are probably aware of this insurance. It provides protection if your trip is cancelled, if you cannot go through with your plans for medical reasons, if you lose something while travelling, or if you get ill whilst in a foreign country. (It's best to always charge a trip or flight to a credit card, if possible, as you then have additional protection, e.g. if the travel firm goes bankrupt you are more likely to get your money back than if you paid cash.) You need to read the small print very carefully to make sure you understand what is and what is not covered. High-risk sports like hang-gliding are frequently excluded; skiing and scuba-diving frequently require additional premium payments. Many people were reading their policy small print to figure out what was and wasn't covered when volcanic ash made flying across Europe impossible in late 2010. And again when tons of snow fell right before the 2011 December holidays, leaving many travellers stranded.

  Travel insurance can be purchased for one trip only, for multiple trips or for a period, typically a year. Most travel insurance policies won't cover you if you are going to be travelling for more than 90 consecutive days. Watch out for that, and always read the small print.

- **Home and contents** – whilst living with your parents you didn't have to think about these types of insurance, as your parents will have dealt with them. What would it cost to rebuild your home? Replace everything in it? Home insurance is designed to protect you if your home is damaged or destroyed, and contents insurance covers you for damage, destruction or theft of everything that is inside the home.

If your parents own their home, as opposed to renting it, they will have insurance. If your home has a mortgage on it, the lender will require you to have home insurance. Why? Because the lender has secured the loan against that property and therefore will want to make sure that its value is maintained. The lender always wants to make sure the property is in a state where, in a push, it could be sold to pay off the mortgage. So, if your home was totally destroyed, the insurance company would pay you the money it promised and that money would be used to rebuild the home or pay off the mortgage.

Whether your family owns or rents its home, you will have contents insurance. Contents insurance protects you from losses incurred from your possessions being damaged, destroyed or stolen. Take a moment to think of all the stuff you have in your home and how much it would cost to replace it. Under this type of insurance policy, you insure for an overall amount and can also insure specific items. An expensive computer, a family heirloom, an expensive piece of jewellery, artwork and other valuable items can be specifically priced into the contract with the insurance company. Look carefully at the terms to see if items are covered even when they are outside your home. You want that computer or jewellery insured wherever you take them.

It is highly likely that your family's contents insurance will cover your possessions when you are away at college or university. However, you need to check it out. It is also likely that the contents insurance requires you to lock your room, flat or house, or bike or car to protect them from thieves. If you don't do that, the insurance firm is unlikely to cover the cost of any stolen items. If something is stolen you should report it to the police as soon as possible. You should inform the insurance company quickly if your possessions are stolen or damaged and you plan to file a claim. As an aside, if you are burgled and it looks like the burglar is still on the premises, do not enter the premises for safety reasons.

- **Professional indemnity** – if you are a budding entrepreneur running your own business, you will be providing services and/or products to clients. That means you will need insurance to protect you against any claims those clients make against you. They typically include negligence, non-delivery on commitments, and mistakes. I wanted to make you aware of this, hence the mention, but that is all I will say about it.

There you are. The financial fundamentals you need to know. There are others of course throughout this book, so keep reading!

Chapter Nine

Your
Credit
Score

A CREDIT SCORE (the term "credit rating" is also used and means the same thing) is a numerical assessment of a person's creditworthiness. Or, put another way, it is the quantification of risk assessment – what is the risk that someone will not pay what he committed to? You will have made your own risk assessments of this type, without even thinking you are doing it. Think about what you do when a friend asks to borrow some money, just for a grocery run or trip to the pub, nothing big. You will probably think about whether or not that friend is likely to pay you back. If you have lent your friend money a few times and struggled to get it repaid, you probably won't be too keen to lend him the money. On the other hand, if he borrowed money before and repaid it, you are quite likely to lend it.

> A credit score is an assessment of your creditworthiness; an evaluation of how likely you are to meet your financial obligations of interest payments and principal repayments.

You are in essence credit-scoring your friend. That is the same thing a bank or other lender does when you ask to borrow money. Those institutions will evaluate you and decide how likely you are to pay or not pay back what you borrow. Unlike the situation with your friend, they don't know you, so they will collect data from you and other sources in order to do their evaluation.

INTERESTED PARTIES

Every time you do something financial you are adding to a picture of your creditworthiness in the outside world. It is very easy for people to see your credit score and history online using services like experian.co.uk, creditexpert. co.uk, noddle.co.uk and others, which you can find if you search on credit score. Whilst your credit score is important for lenders, be aware that other interested parties will also use the information available from credit agencies. Most employers will do so before you join them as it is an important reference for them, just like a reference from a previous employer. If you are going to work in a regulated or security-related industry they will definitely check. There are two reasons why these credit checks are done: first, it is easy to do; and second, it tells you something about the person if he can't manage his own financial situation well.

So there are a few reasons why, besides being able to borrow money when you want to, you really should keep a clean credit record.

And last but not least, you are an interested party. You might want to check yourself out on those websites and, if you are turned down for credit and you are surprised, ask for an explanation. To keep an eye on your credit score without any cost, check out noddle.co.uk, an independent service recently launched by Call Credit.

HOW A FINANCIAL PICTURE OF YOU IS DEVELOPED

As you move up the financial ladder you create a credit picture for others to see. Let's see how that happens:

Bank Current Account

You created the first personal financial record on you when you opened your first bank account. You create a new record each time you open a new account. For regulatory purposes, whenever you open an account you have to prove that you are who you say you are. The bank will ask you to provide a passport or driver's licence and produce a bill or two that shows your current address to meet this requirement. Each time you go to a new bank you will have to repeat this process. In addition to regulatory checks, the bank will check to see if you are on the electoral register and also look to see if there is any bad money information about you.

When a bank provides you with a debit card, it will only perform limited credit checking because its exposure to you is limited by the amount of cash in your account plus an overdraft if you have one.

Bank Overdrafts

When a bank offers you an overdraft they are in effect agreeing to lending you money. An overdraft is like a safety net attached to your bank account. If your bank account balance goes below zero, cash will be provided from the overdraft facility. As mentioned in Chapter 8, some banks use this as a way to encourage new customers, particularly students who are offered free overdrafts.

Managing any overdraft you take on is important to your credit score. A potential lender will ask you what overdrafts you have outstanding and will ask about your track record of managing those previous overdrafts. It is very helpful if you have a financially responsible story to tell.

Once your student days are completely over, banks will do more creditworthiness checking before they offer you a loan of any sort, including overdrafts. This general borrowing, not for a specific purpose and not secured on any assets, is higher-risk than secured or specified borrowing so you may find the interest rate you are offered is quite high. You may be better off waiting to get a loan once you are borrowing with a need in mind.

Credit Cards

When your existing bank offers you a credit card, the process is likely to be fairly straightforward as they know quite a bit about you already. They have held your money on deposit, can see transactions in and out of your current and savings accounts, and can see what your overdraft(s) look like and if you have gone overdrawn (unauthorised overdraft). If your bank offers you a credit card, you will need to complete an application and the bank will want to know if you have overdrafts, loans or other credit arrangements with other banks.

Assuming your bank offers you a credit card, it will set a limit on the amount you can have outstanding on the card at any time. If, at a later date you want to have that limit increased, the bank will review your financial records again to assess whether they think you can manage a bigger limit. I cannot emphasise enough how critical it is that you always pay at least the minimum monthly amount due on your credit card by the specified due date.

Other Extensions Of Credit

When you apply for other credit cards or store cards, or buy goods on credit, or take out smallish bank loans, the potential lenders will always follow the same basic process. You will be asked to complete a questionnaire, the lender will take steps to validate the information you provided, and the lender will check if you are on the electoral register. The lender will also check the credit score you have at one or a few of the credit agencies.

Home Loan/Mortgage

When you apply for a mortgage the lender is going to do a great deal of work before lending you money. (See Chapter 8 for more information.) At this stage just understand that lenders

> **TOP TIP!** ✔
>
> Getting a credit card from your bank, using it for purchases and paying it off regularly is a good way to build a credit history and rating. Without a borrowing and paying record, it is very difficult to get any other credit. Someone I knew had £2,000 invested in an ISA and had paid his mobile phone bills himself for years, but was rejected for credit when he tried to switch the mobile phone account to his name from his mother's.

will have specific criteria for you to meet in order to approve a mortgage. This is where a good credit record is really important. Their starting point for the amount of mortgage they offer will be a multiple of your base salary. Banks are very forthcoming about the multiple so that no one's time is wasted.

Once you figure out the bank you want to use, you will have to go through a detailed application process, beginning with a questionnaire. They will confirm your salary with your company. Expect to be challenged hard by the bank to verify your earnings if you are self-employed. The point system banks use awards additional points for stability, including being with an employer for several years. They will want to know all about your financial history, current position and future potential. All of this is aimed at assessing whether they feel comfortable that you will be able to make interest payments as they come due as well as pay back the principal. The UK regulator is putting additional pressure on banks to make sure they do enough work to satisfy themselves that the mortgage provided is affordable by the client so expect even more questions and paperwork demands.

> You can pay a monthly fee (roughly £15) to check your credit score regularly on Equifax, Experian or Call Credit. Noddle.co.uk will provide you with the same information free.

HOW CREDIT SCORES ARE CALCULATED

Credit scores are calculated based on answers to a pre-specified set of questions, including the following:

- Name – always use your legal name and include prior names if any have changed.

- Current address and how long you have lived there. If you have lived there less than three years, provide your previous address.

- Owner or renter at your current address?

- Are you on the electoral register? (You need to be.)

- Are you an employee or self-employed?

- What company do you work for? How long have you been working there? How long were you at your last employer?

- Provide a list of credit cards, the average balance, average monthly payments and credit limits.

- Provide debit card details.
- Provide details of any other indebtedness including totals, monthly payments, and interest.
- Declare any county court judgments against you.

As you can see this is pretty basic information. But it can go wrong for you if you haven't been at your address or in a job for a reasonable period of time. The lender's point system will allocate points for each answer and the points will be added up to create a total score. This score will be turned into a yes or no for credit approval. If you have been working for the same company and living in the same house for 10 years, you are more likely to be given credit than if you just moved to your house (and you move annually) and you haven't had a job for the past 10 years. They will also consider how much credit/debt you have outstanding or could have outstanding. How many credit cards and loans do you have? How many store cards do you have? And what is your track record of paying back what you borrow?

This score is based on factual information provided by you in the first instance and then, depending on the amount of money involved, validated and/or supplemented by external information sources. For example, if you are buying furniture on credit, the company may well contact your bank to confirm information about your relationship with them. They may want to confirm your employment information. Or they may want to confirm the amount of rent you pay.

CREDIT SCORING AGENCIES

Historically many credit providers (e.g. banks, building societies, credit card and store card providers) did their own scoring. With the development and expansion of credit rating agencies, lenders of all types are increasingly relying on information provided by those agencies to make their credit decisions. The credit scoring agencies collect information about you from many sources. With that information (they also have access to data about credit cards, lines of credit, court orders for non-payment and bankruptcies) they derive a number that is classified as good, mediocre or bad. A potential lender simply obtains your rating from an online system and, based on that, decides whether or not to lend you money. And that is why you want only good data about you available in the market.

KEEP IT CLEAN

When you think about it, it's obvious that you want a good credit score. That can be quite difficult to get when you are coming out of education and starting your career. Firstly it is hard because you tend to move quite a bit – keeping up to date with registration at doctor's surgeries is hard enough, let alone electoral registers! But the electoral register is vital, so you need to keep that information up to date. That is quite easy to do; you just need to remember to do it every time you change your address. What is harder is accepting that, if you don't have a job or haven't been in the same one for some time, you are not going to get much credit. A good credit rating is not a reason to stay in a job, but you can impact the timing of a move, so try to avoid changing jobs when you are in the middle of trying to get a loan.

What is helpful is to stay out of anything that would make you look high risk to a lender. Keep out of trouble by making payments on time, don't go overdrawn (i.e. have any unauthorised overdrafts), don't try to get a bunch of store cards and max out on them; and don't leave unpaid debts with utilities companies or rental agents. Yes, those latter two can muck up your credit rating even if you are in the right in a dispute.

YOUR PERSONAL INFORMATION

It may seem somewhat scary that people are collecting information about you and you don't know about it. Sometimes the age of technology doesn't feel very comfortable. You can see your credit records using one of the services listed earlier. If your credit application is turned down, you have a right to ask the potential provider for an explanation of why you were rejected. It is possible that your application was turned down inappropriately; the lender may have received incorrect information.

You will also want to check out some of your underlying data occasionally. I was shocked when my credit card application was rejected. When I investigated, I found that my home address was incorrect on Experian's records so I didn't appear to be listed on the electoral register, the first test the lender applies. Easy enough to fix and I have done it, but what a lot of trouble due to the transposition of two words.

YOUR CREDIT SCORE – KEY POINTS

So, in a nutshell what you need to know:

- Anyone thinking about lending you money will do checks on you to evaluate how likely you are to meet your payment commitments.

- They will do the work themselves or get data about you from other sources like credit scoring agencies.

- Keeping a good credit record is critical. It will give you financial options because people will be willing to lend you money. To keep your record clean, pay your bills on time and don't borrow more than you can afford.

- On the flip side, getting a bad credit record reduces your financial options. You may find yourself unable to borrow money, be offered borrowings, but at very high interest rates to reflect perceived high risk, or only be able to borrow money from alternative sources, such as pawnbrokers and unauthorised money lenders. Getting a bad rating is easy – just don't pay your bills on time.

- Turning a bad credit score into a good one is hard work.

- Remember that other people can see your credit score. Remember that prospective employers have an established practice of performing credit checks.

- You can check out your credit score and underlying information for free on some webpages, so remember to do it from time to time.

Chapter Ten

Making Big Financial Decisions

T IS LIKELY that most of your money decisions so far in life have been fairly straightforward and short-term. Most of the effort you spend on managing your money may be aimed at working out how to get from month to month, keeping your inflows and outflows of cash in synch during the month, and perhaps trying to figure out how to earn more money without sacrificing other parts of your life.

Perhaps you have had experience already – and if you haven't you will soon – with making some bigger and/or longer-term decisions. Bigger means making a decision that may involve saving money, borrowing money or spending a substantial amount of money you have been saving. Longer means making a decision that commits you to making ongoing payments or having money tied up for a lengthy period. Some of these decisions will feel complicated, especially as there is lots of new terminology that people will use. Don't let that get to you or let yourself feel pushed into a decision before you are ready. Ask questions, take your decision step by step and you will figure it out.

In this chapter we will take a look at where you can go to get help in making big financial decisions and explain what you may want to consider as you make some of these decisions. Because you will probably spend a large proportion of your earnings on housing costs, part of this chapter covers the issues of renting, buying and comparing finances across the two. I got a lot of advice from people about renting properties, so there is quite a bit about that. And having heard a great deal as well about buying versus renting property (including grumbles about the amount of deposit required), I have included information about that too.

WHERE TO GO FOR GUIDANCE

Think back to when you last tackled a complex issue. Maybe you had a moment or two of thinking "I can't figure this out" and somehow in the end you did figure out what to do. How did you figure it out? Where did you turn for help? The good news for financial stuff is that most people will be facing, or have faced, the same types of issues as you. So there are plenty of places to go for help including:

- **Family** – this includes aunts, uncles, brothers, sisters, cousins, and even parents. Parents, speaking as one, always like to be asked for advice and generally do recognise that things have changed since they were your age. They also have experience of money which is valuable to you. Family friends are also a good avenue to explore – they are interested in your wellbeing but may be more objective than your own parents.

Going back to values from earlier, it is really useful to get the views of people who you know view money issues differently from you. Make sure you get the input of both a cautious spender and an extravagant spender.

- **Friends** – this is a great place to start, especially if you have friends who have gone through a similar situation and are kind of in the same place financially. Any friends you have who are just a bit older, who have been through the same thing a year or two before you, will have good insights as their learnings are fresh in their minds. (I once gutted and fixed up a house right after a friend did hers. I just replicated everything, from the choice of builder to the door handles – made it easy!)

- **The internet** – it is so hard to imagine what we did without the internet. There is tons of information to support big financial decision-making – almost too much. Start with general searches. Throughout this book there are references to existing websites that you will find useful. They keep changing all the time – in a good way. My advice is to just jump in and start looking. Use searches like "How do I buy a scooter?" "What are the steps in the flat rental process?" "What do I need to know when I look for car insurance?" You get the idea. And keep notes of what you learn and from what sites so you can refer back to what you found.

- **Visit providers** of whatever it is you are thinking about spending money on. You want to buy a car? Go to car showrooms and find someone who is willing to take the time to explain everything you need to know about cars and financing options. You want to buy a flat? Do the same at estate agents, lawyers and surveyors. Need to borrow money? Go to your bank and other banks to ask about financing terms. And in any of these places, if the people you talk to say things or use words you don't understand, get them to stop and explain.

You may hesitate to ask questions, thinking "I should know" or "they're busy", but let me share a secret with you. People love to talk about what they do. And that is what you are asking them; it gives them a chance to share what they know! Do a bit of research before you start your visits so you look serious about whatever it is. Doing some planning around what you want to ask. Writing a list of what you need to learn will make your discussions more productive.

Of course, at the end of the day, the responsibility for the decision and outcome is yours. You want to do enough thinking, calculating and gathering of information to help protect yourself from any future regrets. No regrets doesn't mean you won't make any decisions that you wish you hadn't. What it means is that, whatever the outcome, you know with hindsight that you made the best decision at the time, based on the best information you could gather.

Let's now take a look at some of these big and/or long-term decisions, going from smaller to larger money amounts.

INADVERTENT COMMITMENTS

Sometimes you can find yourself committing to something that is long-term without thinking about it in that way. Or you may decide to buy something big, as in costing a lot of money, on the spur of the moment just because you could. Maybe you are just cash rich and you felt like it. Think clothes, shoes, electronic equipment. Try using those escape routes we covered earlier – or at least counting to ten before you hand over your money!

There are several ways you can end up committing to something that, whilst not a lot of money in the big scheme of things, may be long-term and therefore lock you into a spend. Think free offers, magazine subscriptions, gym membership, or buying one of those restaurant and club cards that gives you discounts. What experiences do you have of committing to something that was a bit longer-term than you realised? Any trouble ending the contracts, or is it just me? Most of these commitments run for about a year, but frequently the onus is on you to cancel the contract when the year is up. Make a note in your diary a month before the year runs out, to make sure you complete the paperwork to make the agreement end, if you want it to, otherwise the deal may inadvertently roll over for another year!

TRANSPORT – BIKES

Bikes are increasingly used as a means of transport, including in big cities. The price range is huge, so deciding on how much to spend and what you need in a bike can be complicated. Deciding how tempting your bike will be to thieves and how to protect it against theft is sadly an important factor to take into account. Most bike purchases will be made with savings or credit cards, and perhaps a personal loan. You will need good insurance in the event the bike is stolen (every city cyclist I know has had at least one stolen). Your bike may be covered under your home insurance, but you may have to increase the coverage for it. It is worth calling the insurer in advance to learn what the incremental cost will be. You will need a really good lock and must use it all the time. Insurance companies are unlikely to reimburse you for a stolen bike if it wasn't locked.

If you live in London, and perhaps in other UK cities now, consider whether you need your own bike or if a rented bike (Santander bikes in London) will do. You can use them for free as often as you like if you keep the usage to half-hour stints. Please wear a helmet and reflective gear all the time!

TRANSPORT – SCOOTERS, MOTORCYCLES AND CARS

What do you need to think about when you are buying a scooter, motorcycle or car? The first thing of course is how much you can spend on buying it – the purchase price. How much money do you have? Do you need a loan? Who should the loan come from?

There are quite a few other costs that you need to take into account, in addition to the purchase price. These will vary for the three types of vehicles but in principle they are similar.

These include:

- **Petrol** – a fuel-efficient car will save you money. Consider a diesel engine as they get better mileage per gallon than petrol engines. Take the cost of diesel and petrol into account when estimating your running costs. You can also consider cars that run on gas and electricity, though these are less common at the moment, so there are other implications like vehicle purchase price and availability of energy source to think about.
- **Repairs** – engine repairs, replacement tyres, oil changes and other servicing work, to keep it working well, will all have to come out of your cash flow so need thinking about. Bear in mind that, in general, diesel engines last longer than petrol engines.
- **Insurance** – this was covered in detail in Chapter 8. Remember that you will want to have some money in reserve to cover the excess or repair costs you want to pay for yourself in the event of an accident.

- **Road tax** – when you buy a car, you will need to pay tax on it. The amount of tax varies based on the size of the engine and the environmental impact of the car. You can tax it online at www.vehicletax.service.co.uk, at the post office or over the phone, and the DVLA will also verify that the car is insured. You need to pay the tax before you drive the car and don't drive without it as the government can confirm if you have paid this by running a check on the vehicle's registration number.

- **MOT** – if your car is more than three years old you will need to have an MOT (see direct.gov.uk for a full explanation) which is a test conducted by a garage to certify that your car is roadworthy. That test has to be conducted annually, at your expense, although some garages will give you a discounted rate for doing the tests if you bought the car from them. It is worth negotiating to get free MOTs if you are buying the vehicle from a garage, as every little bit helps. You need to factor in the cost of the test and any repairs needed to make the vehicle roadworthy. There always seems to be something that needs doing! Don't even think of driving without a valid MOT. As with road tax, having a valid MOT is a legal requirement – the fine for not having one is £1,000.

- **Parking** – consider where you will keep the vehicle. Can you park it for free or will you need to rent a parking space?

Do your sums objectively – there is quite a bit of emotion around buying a car!

If you decide that owning a car is too expensive, particularly for the amount you will use it, there are a variety of rental alternatives. There are the classic daily car rental companies – e.g. Hertz, Avis, Enterprise. There are also firms that provide rentals on an hourly basis, so you pay only for the time you actually use the car (e.g. easyCar, Zipcar) and also peer-to-peer rentals such as WhipCar. These firms are only in major cities so far, with cars parked in designated spaces around the city. If you have an occasion that requires a really fancy car (think Maserati, Porsche) there are rental agencies that provide these as well. With all car rental companies, ask early on about minimum age or driving experience requirements. Similarly, ask about additional charges they will put on if you are a young driver. And look out for insurance costs!

If you decide to buy a car and find you don't use it as much as you planned, you can rent it out to others for hours or days. This would make you a provider in the peer-to-peer market which is mentioned above.

Buy New Or Used?

An important consideration when buying a vehicle is the purchase price and evaluating whether it makes more financial sense to buy brand new or used. You will hear people say that, from a pure financial perspective, it rarely makes sense to buy a brand new car as cars drop in value (estimated at as high as 30%) as soon as they are taken off the forecourt. This is because, from the dealer's perspective, a new car becomes a used car as soon as it rolls out on the road. Bear in mind however that financing a new car through a leasing agreement with the dealer can bring sizeable financial benefits, especially near the end of a model year. You may also get peace of mind from having a warranty that covers repairs for the first few years and being the only owner, so you control how well the car is maintained. Do make sure you keep the service records up to date.

It can be worth buying new if it enables you to take advantage of a good financing deal, typically a leasing arrangement (covered in Chapter 8). A dealer may also offer you free insurance, though, as mentioned before, the dealer's insurance price is usually higher than if you arranged it independently. The important thing is to shop around a lot, see what offers the car dealers can give you, and look at the current price of similar cars that are on the used car market. Don't forget to consider going to a car auction, though do take a mechanic with you to check the car out before you buy.

Financing Options

There are several ways to finance a car purchase which are explained in Chapter 8. In a nutshell, you can pay cash, get a loan, or take a lease from the dealer. There are quite a few options so work through them, figure out which is best for you, and ask lots of questions.

GAP YEARS – SOONER OR LATER?

Several young adults I talked with described their gap year planning (pre- or post-university) as a big learning experience, including financial learning. If you decide to do a gap year trip, you will need to figure out how much money you will need, which is complicated by the choice of places to go, how you plan to get there, who you travel with, and what you want to do during your travels. Then, armed with your "money needed" figure, you will have to figure out how to earn it and how you are going to save it. It can be a great test of your willingness to save for a longer term goal and forgo short-term pleasures.

Remember that the taxman may be withholding money from your pay cheque, so factor that into your earnings calculation. A few people told me that they purposely earned the cash they needed and let the employer collect the tax monies, even though they knew they would get the money back later. Then as they left for their travels they filed their tax reclaim and were happy to have money in their bank when they returned from their trip. If you don't want income tax withheld as you earn, read about how to arrange that in Chapter 7.

Whilst gap years have typically been taken around university time, it can be done whenever you want. In fact, a big trend is for the over-50s to take gap years. Sometimes people take time away between jobs as that can be a natural break point. Once you get into the work/career thing it can be more complicated to plan. If you take a gap year once you start your job/career, there are a few additional questions to consider: is this the right time to do this? What am I planning to get out of the travel? What will happen to the job I am postponing or stepping away from? What impact will this have on my career? Can I take my full personal leave time for the year all at once and supplement it with some unpaid leave? If you are going to do this and hope to remain with the same employer upon your return, talk to them as early in your thinking as possible. There are some careers that offer paid or unpaid sabbaticals as a matter of course, ranging from several months to a year.

Two important things to mention: when buying airline tickets for a long multi-step trip, it is usually less expensive to buy a round-the-world ticket (currently around £1,300) than individual tickets. Check out your travel insurance, as many do not cover you if you are travelling for more than 90 days in one go, so you may need an additional policy.

UNIVERSITY – GO, NO GO, ALTERNATIVES?

Across the UK, the cost of university differs. Scottish students do not incur tuition fees if they attend a Scottish university as the government funds them, although they do incur living costs. English and Welsh students have to pay to go to Scottish universities as if they were going to an English or Welsh university. The fee information below reflects the English structure. Remember that even if you don't have to pay fees, you do have living expenses!

In a recent survey of young adults, findings showed that many did not understand how student loans worked and were surprised by the interest they were charged. Centre for the Study of Financial Innovation, July 2012.

As mentioned in Chapter 2, the cost of going to university in England and Wales has tripled in the last few years and the impact of a university degree on current and long-term earnings is not clear. It was not long ago that the government's aim was to have 50% of all sixth form students go to university and the tuition cost was zero or a relatively small amount. There was also general acceptance that university graduates would quickly out-earn those who did not go to university. The targets and earnings projections no longer hold true. Unemployment and underemployment amongst young adults is at a very high level, with both university graduates and non-graduates being impacted.

Let's concentrate on the money issues here. In Britain and Wales, the first time university students were required to pay for their tuition was in September 1998 and the maximum they could be charged was £1,000 per year. In 2004 that amount was increased to £3,000 and in 2008 it went to £3,290. From September 2012, universities were permitted to charge up to £9,000 a year for tuition. In addition, students need to cover living expenses which, depending on where in the UK you are living, typically run between £150 and £250 a week.

The government has established loan programmes to support these students. The details are clearly explained at direct.gov.uk. The key points to be aware of are:

- Full-time students may take out government loans for the full amount of tuition fees, up to a maximum of £9,000 per year; part-time students may be eligible to borrow up to £6,750 per year. The tuition fee loan is paid from the government directly to the university and you will be required to pay the loan back.

- Students may be eligible to receive maintenance loans to help them with living costs. These amounts vary depending on whether you live at home and where your university is located. The maximum amount is £10,702 if you attend university in London and live away from home, and up to £6,904 if you live at home. Maintenance loans are subject to means testing, i.e. based upon your family income, and these details are available on the website. The maintenance loan money is paid directly to your bank account at the beginning of the academic year – so you need to manage that money carefully to last you all year. You will be required to pay the loan back.

- It is also possible to obtain additional government funds for tuition and maintenance expenses if your family income is low or for other reasons detailed on the government's student finance website. There is also the possibility that your university might offer you a bursary, so, if finances are an issue, do explore that avenue as well.

As explained above, these loans will have to be paid back. The government is becoming more assertive in seeking payments including those payments from graduates who have gone overseas following graduation. At the bottom of the direct.gov.uk student loan page is a section titled More Useful Links, and the second item you will see and should click on is "Paying back your student loan". This will take you to a page that explains the repayment process.

Once you finish university, you will be liable for the total amount you borrow under these loan arrangements. The arrangements differ depending on whether your course began before or after 1 September 2012, so make sure you look at the right webpage.

Key points:

- Interest is added to the initial loan amount from when you get the money. The rate of interest varies depending on when you started your course and is quoted relative to the Retail Prices Index (RPI). The Student Loan website sets out the interest rates and provides information on how repayments are calculated.

- The government will collect the money from you via payroll deductions (explained in Chapter 7) once you are earning more than £15,795 a year, if you started your course before 1 September 2012, and £21,000 if you started after 1 September 2012. The repayments will be deducted from your gross pay (see Chapter 7) from the April after you leave university. The payments will be 9% of any income over £21,000 and the website can be used to figure out what your monthly loan repayments will be. You can make additional payments if you wish to repay your loan earlier.

- You should receive an annual statement of your loan situation from the Student Loans Company, but you can check your balance online at any time, as explained on the website.

And remember, you can do paid work whilst attending university. Several students I have met said it was definitely doable, though it does require a bit of self-discipline. They also mentioned that by working part-time they avoided spending money going out as much – a double benefit!

> The City & Guilds vocational rich list shows the UK's vocational (non-university) elite are worth about £17.6 billion...and include Jamie Oliver, John Frieda, Rick Stein, and James Dyson.

The sharp increase in university costs has made people think a bit harder and longer about attending university for two reasons: the high cost of attending and the likelihood of landing a graduate-level job after graduation. An increasing number of students are considering vocational learning offered at colleges, which includes a wide range of courses, involving practical experience organised by the college. In some cases, such as accountancy, they are an alternate route to the top accounting firms. These colleges are preparing themselves for increasing application rates, so if you are interested plan well in advance, as popular courses fill up early. Similarly, businesses are offering more apprenticeships than before, which are another good route to a career. When thinking about the finances of university, both in earnings and expenditures, use the web to your advantage and fully research your options.

If, when you finish university, you are in the fortunate position of having cash to pay off your student loan, think carefully. Whilst you may be keen to get rid of the debt, it may not make sense financially. For example, if the rate of interest the loan attracts is less than the interest rate you can get on savings, you will be making money by letting the loan continue. And you may want to keep the cash lump sum ready for another use – say making a deposit on a property – so if you use it to pay off your loan it won't be there when you want it.

According to a survey 2/5ths of those aged 14 to 25 were unable to tell the difference between being in credit and overdrawn on a bank statement; one in eight did not know what an overdraft was; and 28% did not know that a lower APR rate was better than a higher one. The Times, June 2013.

UNIVERSITY LATER OR RETURN FOR AN ADVANCED DEGREE

Nearly everyone I talked with about university felt that the university decision was a one-off, something decided immediately after completing college/sixth form, when in fact it is an option available to you forever. I just read about someone earning their first degree at the age of 94! There are groups anticipating that the average age of university entry will increase, as potential students decide to pay for their studies with money they have saved up rather than complete university burdened with large debts. (It may help many of them enter with a clearer idea of what they want to study and how that study will transfer to their life's work.)

If you do begin working and head to university later, there will be other financial issues to consider, many of which are similar to the gap year questions included in that section of this chapter. A few are: when is the right time to give up paid employment for a period? Will you be able to return to your existing employer if you want to? Will the university course enhance your current career or lead you to another? What are the financial implications of a complete career change? Is your employer willing to cover the costs of university?

These questions, as well as others, will also be relevant if you decide to return to university to pursue an advanced degree. You will be forgoing earnings for a period, which requires thought. As an advanced degree student, you are likely to have opportunities to work at your university within your field of study whilst a student. (I taught accounting to cover my Master's degree costs.)

HOUSING ISSUES

Chances are your first big financial decision has been, or will be, about where to live once you have moved away from home. If you go to/are at university chances are you will have to figure out your own accommodation at some point. And at some point you may look to buy a property. Either way you will need to think about who you share living space with so we will start there.

Deciding Who To Share With
The first and most important thing to think about for many reasons is who you want to share with and how many of you will be in one property. In some ways, sharing with more rather than fewer people is good, because you can share costs. On the other hand, sharing with a big group can make basic household arrangements like paying shared bills, cleaning the place, and keeping the kitchen in order a nightmare.

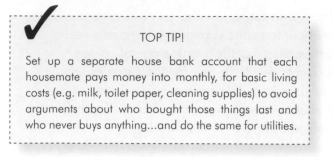

TOP TIP!

Set up a separate house bank account that each housemate pays money into monthly, for basic living costs (e.g. milk, toilet paper, cleaning supplies) to avoid arguments about who bought those things last and who never buys anything...and do the same for utilities.

When you pick your housemates it is worth thinking about their money values. A few thoughts come to mind on this: how do their money values match yours? Are they big spenders compared with you? Are you on a tight financial package compared to them? Or perhaps it is the other way around as you are flush and they aren't? What will you do if they have to move out? Are they likely to honour their rental commitments for the full period of the lease? It is amazing how good intentions and general agreements disappear in the heat of the moment. What have I seen? A friend who let the others down on a one-year lease by not turning up for university – and left her friends to cover her costs. Disagreements over noise levels, who can bring guests over when, and, mostly, why didn't people tidy up after themselves? Also, people not paying their share of bills in time so others had to cover or the whole house would face the implications of things like losing their electricity.

An important discussion to have is whether everyone will pay the same rental amount, assuming all bedrooms and bathrooms are not equal. Or will you decide on different room rates? And how will you then decide who gets which room? Think in the first year about what will happen with the room allocations if you stay in the property more than one year? Will you switch rooms? Change the rental amounts?

You can't really ask the person you are hoping to share a place with what he will be like to live with but you can reduce the risk of a clash. Do talk about lifestyles – e.g. big partyers or not, hard workers or not, tidy or untidy. Think about what environment you want to live in. This may mean you can't live with some of your friends, but at least they will stay friends if you figure that out before moving in together. Several people I spoke with said they thought it was easier to live with people who weren't really close friends. They felt that negotiations over money and other things were easier to do with acquaintances.

TOP TIP!

Organise a cleaning rota and agree what "clean" means.

Organise a watertight lease for all the sharers to sign and have their parents sign, though don't assume that means people will deliver on commitments.

Lastly, you may have a friend who offers you the chance to rent a room in their family property. There are plenty of good reasons to do so, but approach the lease and arrangements with the same rigour as if it were a deal with someone unknown to you. That way you are more likely to make sure everyone feels they were treated fairly. That includes doing a full inventory on the way in and on the way out of the rental, which can feel a bit odd.

Renting Property
The All-In Cost

Once you have figured out who you want to live with and how much you want to spend, you have what you need to know to start looking for a property. You will find there is plenty of help at hand. Use the internet, look in papers, look in estate agents windows and register with them as well. If you don't have people you want to share with, you can easily identify places to share using websites like flatshare.com, roommates.com, sofasurfer.com, gumtree.com and plenty of others. Be careful, though – do not pay any money over, until you see the property you are planning to rent, even if the person says there is "lots of interest and you may not get it if you don't pay now!"

When you start looking for a rental property, it may seem straightforward to compare places and their prices, which will be quoted as a weekly or monthly amount. However you do need to take the full costs into account which may mean asking a few questions of the agent and/or existing tenants. Key questions to consider:

- **How long is the lease?** If you are only going to need the property for eight months while you are at university, do you have to take a 12-month lease? Can you sublet some rooms to other people for the last four months?

- **How much money do you have to pay to get the property?** In general the landlord will require you to pay two months' rent upfront, when you sign the lease. One month is for the landlord to keep as a deposit to use if he needs to fix things when you move out (see below) and the other is the first month's rent. You always have to pay rent in advance of the month you are using the rental property.

• **Is it furnished or unfurnished?** Renting unfurnished is straightforward – there will be nothing there when you move in though white goods (fridge, cooker, oven and maybe a washing machine or dishwasher) will be included. A furnished place is less straightforward. If you are considering furnished accommodation, make sure you are absolutely certain before you sign the lease as to what furniture comes with the property. This is particularly important if there is a tenant already living in the place. When you look around, think about any additional furniture or equipment you may need. Typical additional needs include: more kitchen chairs, a table, a desk, bookshelves, an ironing board, a hoover (that works) and a reasonably sized kitchen bin. Check out the kitchen equipment, e.g. plates, cutlery, pans, to make sure there is enough for the number of you living in the place. Check out the curtains or other window coverings. Confirm whether bed and bath linen is included.

• **What is the cost of utilities and are they included in the rental price?** Usually the tenant is responsible for the cost of electricity, gas, water, and heating of whatever type. Ask what you can expect the monthly bills to be. Ask about the winter and summer costs, as you may be surprised by how different those two numbers can be. These estimated costs will be impacted by the living habits of you and your housemates. For example, leaving lights on all over the place is not a good idea but you can negotiate that amongst yourselves later – that usually happens after the first bill arrives! Also clarify whether or not you have to pay a deposit up front. And remember to think about internet connection, TV and a phone landline.

• **What about the council tax/rates?** The estate agent should be able to provide this information and in some places it can be surprisingly high, e.g. Scotland. The tax is what you have to pay for local services, such as rubbish collection. Whilst you are a student you are likely to be exempt, but to get the exemption you will need to complete paperwork to notify the council of your student status. If you have students and non-students in your place the council will give you a reduced rate, but you have to notify the council to get the reduction. If you have a student and non-student mixed household, you will need to agree up front who will be paying the tax.

- **Do you need insurance?** Think about what if something happens to the property and the stuff in it? Responsibility for insuring your stuff is your responsibility. Do you have insurance, perhaps through your parents, which will cover the cost of replacing whatever was destroyed or stolen? The landlord is responsible for insuring the building, the fabric of the building – though dilapidations are your responsibility (more on that later).

- **What else might cost you money that you need to ask about?** A lovely garden that you need to contribute running costs to? Someone to clean the entrance? Any sort of maintenance? When you are renting, those costs should be covered by the landlord, but it is best to be certain.

Signing A Lease

Like all things, this can be more complicated than it seems. That is because it is new to you and you don't know what to look for. It is worth asking one of your friends who has done it before, or your parents or someone else you trust to review the document. The legality of the document can be a bit off-putting. In a nutshell, the lease commits you to do certain things – e.g. pay rent, maintain the property in good condition, not put holes in wall to hang pictures, not sublet the property. In return the landlord lets you live there. It seems a bit one-sided and that is how it will read – lots of obligations on your part and few on the landlord's part. But he is responsible for ensuring the house is safe to live in and to repair things that break. Before you sign the lease, make sure the property has what you need in it as you will be signing to take the property on as it is unless specified. There is no point asking for things like smoke alarms to be put in, repairs to be done, additional furniture or a dishwasher after the fact. Once the lease is signed, there is rarely any appetite on the part of the landlord for negotiation. If you are in Scotland, make sure that any property is HMO (Houses in Multiple Occupation) licensed; and similarly in England, if five or more people are going to live together.

You need to look carefully at the lease period. For university student rentals it can be common for landlords to offer nine- or twelve-month leases. To be honest, if they offer a nine-month lease, it is usually the same total cost as for a full year just divided by fewer months. For other rentals, it is common practice to have a one-year lease with a six-month break clause, which enables either the landlord or the tenant to end the agreement any time after six months. The person ending the arrangement typically has to give two months' notice in writing. That means that a six-month lease becomes an eight-month commitment. Read this part of the lease very carefully. I heard a story about someone who took a lease that did not have a break clause, so when he took a lower-paid job and could not afford the rent, he could not get out of the agreement. It is not unusual in your first few years out of education to move jobs or locations, so you should try to keep things flexible.

If you are renting with others, you will have to decide collectively how you are going to be held together legally to meet the lease commitments. The landlord may have a requirement about this. Let me explain what I mean in terms of your renting group. You can have one person sign the lease, which means that person is liable for the property and lease. Then everyone else is obligated to him to abide by the terms of the lease. If you do it this way, you should put something in writing for each person to sign to demonstrate their commitment to do what is expected. The alternative is that each person signs his own lease with the landlord.

Sadly, despite everyone's good intentions, these arrangements can go wrong. I heard a story about a group of seven students, each of whom signed a lease and so did their parents. The contract was written with joint and several responsibility, clearly setting out that each person would pay their part and make good if the others did not. And would you believe it, one of the sharers decided not to come to university and left everyone else high and dry! They went on to find someone else, but it was so late that the remaining sharers had to absorb part of the monthly rental for the year. Another story – one student rented a place in her name for a year and didn't ask her friends to sign anything. Eight months later she gave everyone two weeks' notice that she was off. Depending on your values you may find these stories a bit disheartening or you may think "well, whatever". So talk it through with your planned sharers, including exploring various difficult "what if" situations.

One more thing to consider in the lease is what the lease renewal clause says. What you are looking for in the lease, whether or not you plan to stay for longer than the proposed lease term, is an option to renew the lease. And you want the clause to state that the rental increase for the new lease will be limited – typically to the increase in inflation or the Retail Price Index, both of which you can find on the internet. Without this clause, the landlord will legally be able to set the new rental rate at whatever he wants.

Moving In

Right, you have rented your perfect place or the best you can afford and it is moving-in day. You will have organised the electricity, water, and anything else to be changed to your/someone's name. The landlord/agent should have helped with that, as the previous tenant will have removed his name from the bills. Don't get too upset if when you walk in the place doesn't look the same as it did before. Empty places nearly always look worse than occupied ones.

What is incredibly important is that you do a detailed moving-in inventory. At the risk of being unfair, I have found university town estate agents to be rubbish at this when you move in, but really good at finding everything they think is wrong when you move out – and charging you for it. So, before you move all your stuff in, walk around the place looking at everything carefully. The agent is required to give you an up-to-date list of the condition of the property and the contents. As you walk around, make sure that list includes a hole in the wall where a picture was, a broken shelf, a door that doesn't close quite right. Remember to check under and behind furniture. If the place is furnished, the list should include everything in there, down to the last spoon and plate, so check those details carefully as well. Check the loos are flushing, the kitchen equipment works, and electric plugs work – check everything! And document what you find. That includes taking photos so there is no question about the condition of the place when you took possession.

A repeat warning here: make a note of any holes or other marks on the walls from pictures and posters. If the lease says you cannot make holes in the walls and if you do you have to return the property to its original condition, don't put anything on the walls without the landlord's permission.

Moving Out

Whilst it would be unfair for me to say that every young person renting a place gets ripped off when they move out, based on the stories I hear, it happens an awful lot. If the property is not in the same condition as it was when you took over the lease, less reasonable wear and tear, the landlord is entitled to withhold money from the deposit you paid at the beginning of the lease. He is then supposed to use the money that he withholds to return the property to the state it was in when you moved in.

You can take steps to ensure that your exit from a property is free of financial penalties by taking a few precautions. The biggest issue that arises is a disagreement about the condition of the property when the lease started. This is really easy to avoid if you document everything when you move in, along the lines explained earlier. The other cause is that people don't plan their move out in advance so it is a mad rush, with no time to clean the place, repair any damages, or do other things to avoid penalties. So the first point is think ahead. The fundamental principle is that you have to leave the place in the exact same condition that it was in when you moved in, less wear and tear. (Do be aware that I have yet to see a landlord who views wear and tear in the same way as the tenant, so just aim for leaving it in great shape – what you would want if you were moving in.) You and your friends have to plan backwards from when you have to be out of the property and allow plenty of time to get it into a landlord-ready state. Start with the end-of-lease date and plan a good chunk of time for cleaning.

Since it is easier to clean if the place is empty, figure out how/if you can get your stuff out. If you can't get the stuff out, at least move it so you can clean around it. And you really have to clean everything – crumbs out of drawers, skirting boards, windows, curtains. It takes a huge amount of time to do this well. You may find that the lease requires a cleaning by professionals for that reason and you have to bear the cost. You can reduce this cost by doing the best job you are capable of before the professionals turn up; and try to arrange it so that they charge you by the hour rather than a fixed rate. If the landlord doesn't require a professional clean, he will check it out after you do your clean and charge you for any additional cleaning that needs to be done. You absolutely want to have someone from your group there for the check-out which is when the landlord or his checker will identify what they think counts as dilapidations or things that need further cleaning. If you are not there to discuss or document differences of opinion, you won't be in a good position to challenge the decisions later.

The biggest issue is with putting stuff on the walls. Chances are your lease says you can't put any holes in the wall or stick anything using Blu-Tack. And chances are you have done that. I have just found the answer to this – 3M produces picture hanging strips called "Command Strips". If you don't make it look good, the landlord will do it and charge you for it. The landlord may decide that it doesn't turn out well enough if just the hole is filled and paint dabbed over the area. This happened to a friend of mine where, due to one or two holes, the landlord repainted the whole flat and then charged her for it!!

You also need to plan in advance to have your water and electricity meters read and the utilities bills changed to the new tenant's name. You don't have to worry about the new people, but you do have to worry about getting final bills and ensuring you don't keep getting bills after you move out. It is worth having one person from your group take responsibility for this. It is best if the person responsible is the same one that set it all up originally as there will be user names, PINs and passwords to use – hopefully written down somewhere? The bills you received from the utilities companies whilst you rented will have the number to call to make these arrangements on them. They will also have an account number and an account holder's name. That "account holder" will be whoever set the accounts up in the first place and will have to be the one doing the calling. All due to the Data Protection Act – don't ask!

Buying A Property

Once you have been renting awhile and are earning a regular income, you may start thinking about buying a property. The timing of your thoughts will depend a bit on what you were used to growing up, so whether your family home was rented or owned, and also by your values and aspirations. The UK has one of the highest home ownership rates of any country – something to do with our national psyche. When you think about the financial crisis, though, you can see that a root cause was too many people owning homes they couldn't really afford, as mortgages for unrealistic multiples of salaries and 100% mortgages on properties were available. As a result of the crisis, banks have clamped down on mortgage lending and particularly first-time buyer mortgages so, even though interest rates are really low, it is hard to get a foot on the property ladder. Banks and homeowners have also realised that house prices can go down as well as up, which many people had never seen, and didn't believe could happen.

> **TOP TIP!** ✔
>
> Do not take out a 12-month internet contract if you are only going to live in the place for eight months. Service providers are willing to give contracts for the length of time you need. You can get internet-only contracts, where no television or landline phone is supplied.

You may feel pressured to buy, hearing people say things like "Renting is throwing money away," and "The cost of renting is the same as owning/paying a mortgage." That first statement is merely a value judgement. There are many reasons to rent rather than buy, money being just one of them. The second statement may or may not be factual, although I often hear it said. In this section of the chapter we will review all of the expenses involved in buying a property, as we did for renting in the previous section.

When you are making a "rent versus buy" decision, you have to consider some things that are totally known and some that are not, for which you will have to form a view about the future. The two things you will have to take a longer-term view on are: what do you think will happen to interest rates, and what do you think will happen to property prices? The first will directly impact the cost of owning as you will have to service your mortgage. The second will directly impact the potential capital appreciation of your property, i.e. the price when you eventually sell it compared with the price you paid to buy it. If the ongoing costs of renting and buying are exactly the same but you think that the price of property is going to increase, you would lean towards buying a property as you could make money when you sell it. Alternatively, if the ongoing costs are the same and you think property prices are going to go down, you would lean towards continuing to rent rather than buy.

In addition to financial thoughts, there are other life events that you may want to factor into a potential property purchase decision, which include:

- What would happen if, after a certain amount of years of moving in, you lost your job?
- What would you do if you were offered a job overseas, or in another city?
- What would happen if you got into a relationship where you wanted to live with your partner? And what if that partner owned a property too, or lived in another city?
- What if your employer moved to another part of town or to another town?

Those questions remind me of a fundamental property truth: it is not a liquid asset. That means that you may not be able to sell your property when you want to; or there may not be someone wanting to pay the price you want to sell it for. I hope your experience is different from mine, but every time I have wanted to sell a property the market was not good, my house was in the wrong place, I couldn't get the price I wanted, or, even when it all seemed right, I couldn't get the process done fast enough! The crux of the matter is you can't assume you can get out of an owned property as quickly as you will want to and you can't assume the maths will work out the way you planned. If lots of people want to sell their properties at the same time, due perhaps to economic events (like the break-up of the euro if you have a place in Greece) the price will fall and there may be no buyers! Read about supply and demand in Chapter 12.

Despite a UK cultural bias towards owning, renting is a good option in many respects. The two best aspects are: you can be confident of what your monthly costs will be; and if something breaks the landlord has to fix it. Renting also gives you a great deal of flexibility. With six- or twelve-month leases being the norm, you won't be tied into the arrangement for too long. In your early years of post-college/university work, renting is particularly attractive from a budgeting and cash flow perspective.

Compare Ongoing Owning Versus Renting Costs

In the renting section you learned about the all-in costs of renting a place – e.g. rent, utilities, council tax. If you are starting to weigh up the rent/buy decision, it is worth jotting down all your numbers and think back on anything that came up during your rental that surprised you.

In order to do a full comparison, you have to list, item by item, of what costs there are under both options; and it is easiest to do this if you start by looking at ongoing running costs – though the upfront costs of owning are significant, so we will come back to those in a bit.

> When people say that the cost of owning is the same as renting, they are usually just comparing a rough estimate of monthly mortgage payments, none of the other costs. And, whilst this is likely to be the biggest cost, the other things do add up.

The primary ongoing costs once you own a property include:

Mortgage Payments

This is the amount you pay the bank (monthly) for the loan they have given you to buy the property. The amount paid is determined based on the amount of money you borrow (the principal), the type of mortgage and the interest rate on the loan. A bank is required by regulation to ascertain that you will be able to meet your mortgage payments as they fall due. That means your monthly payments and, if you have an interest-only mortgage, the principal at the end of the mortgage term.

Key mortgage terms to understand include:

- **Salary multiple** – the starting point for banks when they are deciding how much money they will lend you is your base salary. The maximum amount they will lend you is typically expressed as a multiple of your salary. Pre-financial crisis, the multiple figure had reached the level of eight times salary, and dropped to around four times salary or three times joint-salary. However, the emphasis now, following regulatory changes in 2014, is on affordability, with lenders looking closely at your budget, including details of your income and what you spend money on.

    Lenders prefer lending to borrowers who can demonstrate they have been working for a while (say a year) and who are employed by a company rather than self-employed. This is because it is easier for them to confirm what you say you are paid and having regular salary payments makes them more confident that you will be able to pay them what you commit to.

- **Deposit** – the bank will also require you to provide a lump-sum of cash towards a home purchase. For new buyers, it is currently around 10–15% of the purchase price, although this will vary by lender, with some accepting just a 5% deposit. In March 2016, a bank advertised an offer of mortgages of 100% of the property price as long as the buyer's parents signed a guarantee. Getting that money together may take quite a bit of saving on your part. As described in Chapter 8, this deposit represents protection for the bank. The bank wants to make sure that if you can't meet your payments and they take your home back, they can sell it and get all of their money back. If you have paid a 15% deposit they only have to sell it for 85% of the original price to recover all their money.

    The government is trying to help first-time homebuyers and has set up a few programmes under help to buy schemes. These include several arrangements, including shared ownership and shared deposits. If you are considering buying a home and it is your first or you earn a low income, you should check out the government programmes on their website: gov. uk/affordable-home-ownership-schemes. Some banks have created new mortgage-related products already, e.g. ones where a family member can offer his property for security on a young person's mortgage, and more are sure to emerge, so keep an eye on this.

> "Use the 'Ultimate Mortgage Calculator' on the moneysavingexpert.com website to compare the cost of mortgages, including fees."
> MoneyWeek, June 2013.

- **Fixed rate interest versus variable rate interest** – there are many different types of mortgage products, and particularly mortgage rate options on the market, but at the end of the day they come down to types of interest rates – fixed or variable. With a fixed rate mortgage you agree at the beginning of the loan what the interest rate will be for a set period of time. This means you will know exactly what your monthly payments will be. You have to pay for that certainty, so the interest on these will be higher than a variable rate mortgage. The set period of time is rarely more than three years and more typically two years. Look carefully at what happens at the end of the fixed term.

With a variable rate mortgage you agree to having the rate of interest you pay change over the term of the mortgage in relation to a specified benchmark. The benchmark is typically the Bank of England lending rate, or it may be a "tracker" that aligns with movements in the stock market. Obviously this means that you can't predict exactly what your mortgage payments will be, so it can cause you some cash management angst. Banks are required to communicate rate changes either in a letter to you or publication in a major newspaper as detailed in the terms and conditions of the loan – the change won't happen overnight.

As mentioned before, when you decide to buy a place, you will need to take a view on what interest rates will do. If you choose a variable rate mortgage you have a risk that the rate will go up, but you could benefit from the rate going down, as many homeowners did when interest rates plummeted during the financial crisis. Interest rates can change dramatically – in the late 1980s mortgage rates were 15%!

- **Principal (or capital) repayment mortgage versus interest only** – it is highly likely that you will only be offered a capital repayment mortgage, which means that each monthly payment you make will be comprised of two components – interest on the loan and a repayment of the underlying loan. If you keep the mortgage until the end of its term (usually around 25 years) you will have repaid the full loan amount through these payments. With an interest-only loan, your monthly payments are comprised only of the interest, none of the principal. These are rarely offered these days.

• **Offset mortgage** – if you keep your savings and hold a mortgage with the same bank, you may be offered this type of mortgage. In this instance the bank calculates interest daily, and when the calculation is done the bank takes into account the balance in your savings account, offsetting that balance against your outstanding mortgage principal amount. As a result your interest costs will be lower. Do read the fine print on any arrangement of this type so you are clear about what cash balances will be taken into account and if there are any constraints on how long the cash is in the bank.

• **Mortgage arrangement fee** – this is really important to consider when you think about your actual borrowing costs. It is the cost the mortgage provider charges you for setting up the mortgage. It is typically a fixed amount and can be a pretty big number. You need to add this to your interest payments to figure out what the real cost of your borrowing will be; and you may be surprised at what a difference it makes to your APR. If you see a mortgage deal with a surprisingly low interest late, look at the arrangement fee. It is likely to be unusually high, and vice versa.

• **Early repayment/termination** – this is important to consider, not because you are thinking that you will be able to repay your mortgage off soon, but because you may want to change your mortgage deal as interest rates change. Many mortgage arrangements will have a relatively big lump-sum fee you will have to pay to break the deal, so read this section of the mortgage agreement carefully before you sign. As an example, if you are on a fixed rate mortgage and rates fall significantly you may want to change deals, but the cost of termination may make that prohibitive. And the cost of termination plus arrangement fee for a new mortgage may make it doubly so.

Utilities

Whether you rent or own a specific property, the utility costs will be the same. But utility costs can differ significantly by type of house. Charismatic old

properties are frequently draughty and expensive to keep warm. New properties are usually more environmentally friendly, which also means wallet-friendly too. Whether a place has electric, oil or gas heating and the type of cooker and other white goods will also impact utilities costs. A good starting point is to ask the estate agent about the prior owner's bills. You can also check out the environmental rating of a property online.

Council Tax

This too is the same whether you own or rent the same property, but the amount will differ based on where you live. This is because the tax is the cost the local council is charging you for services it provides to you. Better services are more expensive. The annual tax should be disclosed on the estate agent's property particulars. Bear in mind that this figure can change year by year and the amount of change differs by council. So do your research on what is happening in the area you are looking to buy in. Keep in mind that you can pay the council tax in ten monthly instalments rather than as a lump sum. And keep in mind that students do not have to pay council tax, but you need to alert the local council to the fact you are students. If your household has students and non-students you will be charged council tax at a reduced rate and will need to figure out which housemates bear that cost.

Ground Rent/Service Charges

You will see the word "leasehold" or "freehold" when you look at estate agent's property particulars. Put simply, if you buy a freehold property you own the land and if it is a flat, you own part of the communal areas (e.g. hallway). If you buy a leasehold property, someone else owns the land, and the communal areas. Either way, if you are buying a flat you will need to figure in costs for your contribution to running the communal areas. In some cases everyone in the building will pay a monthly or quarterly amount to build a fund ready for use when the roof needs redoing or the lobby needs repainting. In other cases you will be told to contribute as and when something needs doing. You need to ask about this so you are clear about what the financial demands on you may be. My sister's flat had a lift replaced at a cost of hundreds of thousands of pounds and it was not a big building! She was on the fourth floor, so it was important for her, but I wonder what the people on the ground floor felt about having to contribute. If the property is in a building of flats, the cost of insuring the whole building is likely to be included here.

Building Insurance

When you rent a place, the building itself will be insured by the property owner and the cost will be factored into your rental payments. When you own your own home you will have to arrange your own building insurance and it can be surprisingly expensive. If you buy a leasehold property it is possible that the cost will be included in the ground rent. But it is more common practice that the overall building is covered that way and you will need to arrange insurance for your own part of the property (i.e. your flat). This insurance covers things like fixing the place if you have a fire, smoke, or water damage and fixing the flat below you if you have a leak that messes up their place.

Contents Insurance

You will have insured yourself for loss (including theft) or damage to your stuff when you rented which may have been for a substantial amount of stuff if your rental was unfurnished. Once you own a property you will probably have more stuff to insure. You will need to estimate the total value of everything you own in order to get insurance quotes (remember curtains, clothes, equipment). It is a good idea to keep a folder of invoices (in a waterproof and fireproof cabinet) for any high-value things you buy, as it will make life easier if you ever have to file an insurance claim. It is also useful to review that file when your contents insurance comes up for renewal. And if you buy valuable things in between insurance renewal periods let the insurer know immediately by phone, followed up by an email or letter.

Armed with the information described above, you will have what you need to do an easy analysis to help you make an overall buy-versus-rent decision. This will give you a general feel, but if you decide to buy you will want to do a detailed, property-specific analysis as you narrow down the properties you want to consider. It is definitely worth taking your time on the maths. And importantly, play around with the mortgage figure as that is the one that can change dramatically due to factors outside your control – changing interest rates.

One final thought: in doing your analysis you may figure out that you want to buy a property with a spare room to rent out to someone. To incorporate that into your figures, calculate your total running costs and then include an offset amount for the rental you will charge. Investigate the tax benefits of renting out a room on the HMRC website and also check your insurance policy and council tax requirements for potential money implications. Remember that the rental rate you charge a tenant will be driven by market rental rates, not your costs, so do your rental research. Consider also which expenses in your analysis will be shared (so tenant pays in addition to rent), in keeping with standard rental property practices and set up offsets for those items in your analysis as well. Also remember that the rent you charge will only change when the lease is renewed, not when your owning costs change.

If you decide to rent a room to a friend, it is good to do that as if it were a stranger when you make your arrangements such as organising the lease, talking about wear and tear costs, moving-in and moving-out logistics. Take a look at the ARLA (Association of Residential Letting Agents) website for standard lease agreements.

Buying Costs

There are three key financial things to consider when you are buying a property:

- **Property purchase price** – the biggest decision is how much money you want to spend, probably impacted by how much you can borrow. As explained in the mortgage section above, banks will limit how much you can borrow, and how much you can borrow will impact how much you can spend. The other constraint will be how large a deposit the lender requires. You may be able to pay that in cash from your savings or you may borrow that money from other sources – but not from another bank because your main bank won't allow that. The amount you spend will also be impacted by the anticipated running costs – the bigger the place, the higher the costs to run and furnish! And you will also want to consider the cost of any repairs or planned refurbishments or decorating.

There are lots of ways to find properties, with estate agents nearly always involved in some way. Always remember that estate agents are working on behalf of the person selling the property and it is in their client's and their interests to get the highest price possible, whilst also getting a deal done. When you are the buyer, they are not really concerned about you, though if they are really good they may make you feel as if they are. Agents are paid a fee by the seller – usually two to three per cent of the final price. All of this applies whether you visit an estate agent's office or find a property online.

When you start looking at properties you will get a good feel for pricing as the market is very transparent. The area you look in will influence the price of a property. In London, Chelsea is more expensive than Elephant and Castle. In Manchester, Deansgate is more expensive than Fallowfield. And in Bristol, Clifton is more expensive than Hotwells. There are plenty of market forces at work and, with experience, you will get pretty good at figuring out what a reasonable price for a property is. When picking where to live, you will want to consider what it will be like to sell the property when you want to move.

In general, properties in more desirable areas are easier to sell and hold their value better than those in less desirable areas. But they are usually more expensive to start out with as well. Some say it is all swings and roundabouts. What else to think about – how close is public transport, are there restaurants and shops nearby, and are there good schools in the area? In London, for example, property prices near Barclays bike stations and areas near the new overground stations increased recently. Frequently, there are articles in newspapers, particularly the Sunday ones, about up-and-coming areas that can offer good value in terms of cost of purchase and a potential value appreciation.

- **Legal fees** – finding a good lawyer who will help guide you through the purchase process is really important. Ask others you know and trust and who have been through the process themselves for recommendations. The role your lawyer fulfils is critical, making sure you have good title to the property, checking to see if there is anything planned in the area that could impact the property price and quality of life there, e.g. a motorway being built on your doorstep. Lawyers will also handle the movement of monies and the necessary negotiations with the seller's lawyers. It is a good idea to ask the one you select what the likely cost of services will be, but in reality there are many factors that will have an impact on the cost. You don't want to worry about making social chit-chat with your lawyer, as he charges you by the minute. You do want to plan your meetings with him in advance. You can ask for periodic, e.g. monthly or weekly, spending updates and bills, so you always know how much money you have spent.

- **Property surveyor fees** – you will also need to find a property surveyor whose job it is to visit the property you want to buy and inspect it closely. He is looking to see if there are any major repairs needed and give an estimate of what he thinks the property is worth. You want him to find everything that is wrong and the seller wants him to find nothing wrong! Once he has done his assessment, he will provide a written report that lists what he has found and his view of the property's price.

Armed with the report, you will need to decide if you want to proceed with the purchase and, if so, whether or not you are still happy with the price you originally agreed. If major work needs doing, you may want to negotiate the price down. Typical examples that are big spends for which negotiation is likely include roof replacements, damp-related repairs and woodworm repairs. The most frequent finding is that a property has subsidence, which means that the house is moving as the foundations are probably not deep enough. You want to know that for sure, as the seller can claim the cost of repair on his insurance. You may feel differently about asking for a price reduction if you were getting a bargain in the first place versus if you felt you were paying top of the market. If other people want the place at the full price, you may not have much room to negotiate. The important thing is to be fully informed before you finalise the deal by signing the papers.

The surveyor will send his report to your lawyer and mortgage provider. There will be a problem if the surveyor's estimated value of the property is below the price you have agreed with the seller because the lender may no longer be happy about lending you the full amount you wanted to borrow. (I say this assuming that the mortgage amount relative to the value of the property is a large percentage.) The reason is that the lender wants to be absolutely sure that if you can't make your mortgage payments and they force you to sell the house, they will get the full amount of their loan back.

- **Stamp Duty** – this is a tax imposed by the UK government on property purchases and is paid by the property buyer. The tax charged is zero for a property valued up to £125,000; 2% on the value between £125,001 and £250,000; 5% on the value between £250,001 and £925,000; 10% on the value between £925,001 and £1.5 million; and 12% on the value in excess of £1.5 million. Check the HMRC website for the current taxes early in your decision-making process to confirm these rates as they can change. Beginning in April 2015, the Scottish government introduced a Land and Buildings Transactions Tax and the details are available at www.revenue.scot/land-buildings-transaction-tax.

If you sell a property, you will bear the additional cost of estate agent fees.

Costs Once You Own A Property
The costs don't stop coming in once you own the property. There are potentially purchases you will want to make in three main categories:

- **Furniture** – first things first, you need to get some furniture. You don't have to fully furnish your home immediately – it is well worth pacing yourself. New ways to shop economically keep emerging, but for starters, use eBay and IKEA and think about secondhand purchases through websites like furnitureswapshop.co.uk, loot.com, preloved.co.uk and netcycler.

co.uk. And look at freecycle.org for all sorts of free used things ranging from washing machines, to shelving, to furniture. Once again, do some research, make a budget, seek advice from others. You may be offered free credit if you buy at certain shops, which could be a good way to finance what you are buying, but read the financing terms thoroughly. If you work at it you shouldn't have to pay full price for anything big. Wait for the mid-year sales for sofas, chairs, tables and negotiate at every shop, including the big retail chains. Look out for floor sample sales where you can really bargain on pricing as the shop is trying to clear out what they have in stock to make room for new goods.

- **Appliances** – these can be quite costly. Hopefully the place you buy will come with what is essential. But essential is a funny term. For example, a washing machine and tumble dryer is something you may expect but it won't necessarily be included. You then have two choices: buy one, or do your laundry at a launderette. Nothing wrong with spending a few hours there – I suspect your parents did at one time or another. Quite a few boy-meets-girl films take place in them. Is a dishwasher a must? A fridge is a must, though it doesn't have to be huge one.

These are pretty big investments and if you buy them you want to check out the warranty period they come with. It is financially helpful to be able to fix something that breaks at no cost to you, which is what a warranty provides. The retailer will probably offer you an extended warranty at the time of the sale, which requires you to pay an additional fixed amount up front to cover repair costs after the original warranty expires. In order to decide whether or not you take this, you have to do some maths. You need to consider the warranty cost versus the value of what you are buying. You could end up paying for the machine several times over in warranty costs. I have to confess, I am not a big fan of extended warranties. I have read that retailers make more money from selling them than they make from the original sale of appliances. I find that, if I start with a good-quality piece of equipment and I take care of it, it tends to last well.

Let's turn back to budgeting and saving...at some point you will have to think about saving money in case a machine breaks down and needs repair or replacement. Most repairmen will take credit cards, but that will cost you interest if you can't pay the credit card off at the end of the month.

- **Garden Equipment** – how about the garden you so wanted? That can require quite a bit of money. Suddenly you have to buy a lawnmower, and a rake, and lots of other tools. And you want nice plants and flowerbeds. If you aren't a lover of doing your own garden, think about getting a property that gives you access to a communal garden that someone else takes care of.

There you have it – the big money decisions you are likely to face and things to think about to help you make the most informed decisions and therefore the best decisions for you.

Chapter Eleven

Avoiding
Money Pitfalls

Don't Be Rushed Into Making A Decision

Be Wary Of The Upward Financial Spiral

Never Mix Short- And Long-Term Debt

Pay Attention To Details

Remain In Control

Manage Any Rental Property Carefully

Choose Who You Live With Carefully

Buy Stuff On The Internet With Care

Evaluate The Cost Of Borrowing From
"Payday" Money Providers Versus Banks

Think Before Lending To, And Borrowing Money From, Friends

Take Steps To Avoid Identity Theft And Other Crimes

And Some Good News

THIS SOUNDS LIKE a nasty chapter, doesn't it? In this chapter we are going to revisit some of the financial pitfalls covered throughout the book. As you will see, some of them are personal, or value-based pitfalls, and some are purely financial. Remember that the goal of this book is to help you be in control of your money destiny and that means you need to make financially and emotionally informed decisions. The best advice I can give you is to pause, think and investigate before you make any major financial decision.

So keep this list in mind as a sort of alarm bell inventory and pay a little closer attention to what you are deciding when you come across them.

DON'T BE RUSHED INTO MAKING A DECISION

Take your time making any decision that involves big money; the bigger the amount involved, the more time you want to take to think the decision through. If someone is rushing you into something, saying "you'll miss this chance if you delay", it's highly likely you should give it a miss. This is not to say you can't make the occasional little punt – say, bet on a Grand National horse, or play the lottery – but invest time in making your decision if the money and time commitment is significant.

BE WARY OF THE UPWARD FINANCIAL SPIRAL

It is all too easy to get caught up in a cycle of taking on more debt. This is because banks, credit card companies and other lenders seem to offer money all the time. It also happens because, once we each start earning money, we think we will earn more money. So we buy bigger houses needing bigger mortgages, buy bigger cars, and generally acquire more stuff. The root cause of the 2008 financial crisis was decades of easy borrowing around the world, resulting in millions of people living in houses they couldn't afford, driving cars they couldn't afford, taking holidays they couldn't afford and on it went. People were living beyond their means and the lenders were earning money so they were happy too. And then it all crashed.

When people or families find themselves in difficult, overextended financial situations, life can get pretty uncomfortable. It's like you missing out on the budget targets we talked about in Chapter 4, but the numbers involved getting bigger quickly. Imagine if you were in that situation and had family members depending on you. A pretty crummy situation to be in, made worse by the fact that you did it to yourself. The stress can be horrible (and I have seen it a few times). Having debt collectors calling you, sending you those red notices (had one for your electricity yet?) and badgering you is all unpleasant stuff.

Sooner than you think, you will be making decisions about how much money you allow yourself to borrow. How much money do you want to commit to renting a property? How big a mortgage will you be willing to take on to buy a home? How should you finance buying a new sofa? There will be lots of big decisions. What you decide for those and other situations will have been shaped by the money habits and values that you develop now and in the next few years.

Of course, always spending too much can become an accepted part of your life. One guy who worked for me was very dissatisfied with his year-end bonus. He explained, "It takes a lot of money to dress like this," as a justification of why he deserved more money. Think carefully about the lifestyle you want and what it will cost to maintain. And make sure you have money in reserve in case things change suddenly. If things start to go wrong take action fast!

NEVER MIX SHORT- AND LONG-TERM DEBT

A big mistake that people make, and you should avoid, is ever paying off a long-term loan with a credit card. That will accelerate the deterioration of your financial situation because a long-term debt (e.g. mortgage) will have a long-term borrowing rate which will always be much lower than the short-term credit card interest rate. Put simply, if your mortgage interest rate is 5% and your credit card interest rate is 16%, it doesn't make sense to shift the debt to the higher-cost lender.

PAY ATTENTION TO DETAILS

Read the small print on anything you are thinking about committing to. That includes things like mobile phone contracts, property leases, and ordering stuff on the internet. And work through detailed thinking around worst-case scenarios that could happen relative to your decisions. Things like: what if the value of the home you buy decreases by 50%, what if you wreck the car, what if you lose your job, what if interest rates go up, what if interest rates go down?

REMAIN IN CONTROL

Always remember that there are several groups who are always keen to get their hands on your money, so make it your job to remain in control when you deal with them. Let's take a quick run-through what we have learned about who wants your money and what to look out for:

The Tax Authorities (HMRC)

The tax system is set up to assume that you work all year, so it is likely that when you work during summer and other breaks, and when you start your first permanent job, you will, at least initially, have more tax withheld than you will owe. Pay close attention to your payslip each time you are paid. You are allowed to earn up to your personal allowance (see Chapter 7) before you have to pay any tax. If you think the tax code and hence amount of tax withheld from your pay is incorrect get in touch with your employer's tax office as soon as you notice it. You will need to have your National Insurance number handy. Make sure you make a note of who you have spoken with and follow up with a letter or email to document the conversation.

The Banks

- Once you have a current account with a bank, you need to be careful to avoid going overdrawn. I have heard of too many nightmares of young people trying to get costs reclaimed from banks due to their going overdrawn. If you don't have enough cash in your account and someone you have written a cheque to tries to cash it, you could get charged multiple fines, from each time the other bank tries to get the money from your bank. A friend of our daughter wrote us a cheque and our bank kept presenting it, resulting in £50 of fees to her.

- Think twice about getting an overdraft. If you are offered a free one and therefore feel you must accept it, make sure you can pay it off before it turns into a graduate overdraft, when you finish your education. The bank is required to notify you in writing when the overdraft terms change, including interest rate changes.

- Reconcile your bank account regularly and check the balance every time you get money out of a cash machine.

- Manage the use of your debit card (like cash) and credit card closely.

- Shop around if you are looking for a loan for personal use, buying a car, or buying a property. Your current bank is not necessarily going to give you the best deal – remember that loyalty doesn't pay. It is now very easy to change your bank, as banks are now required to make a transfer of all of your information within seven days of your request.

Anyone You Sign A Contract With

Take the time to read the contract carefully and always ask any questions you can think of. Pay particular attention to the term of the contract – how long is it, are you able to cancel it part-way through the contract term, what is the cost of early cancellation? A few specific examples:

- **Mobile phones** – figure out what you really need (that is different from want!) in terms of call minutes, texts and data usage. Review your last six months' of itemised bills so that you negotiate based on call minutes and texts actually used, rather than what you think you have used. Be careful about making and receiving calls and text messages when you go outside the UK. You may incur very large additional costs (currently under review by the UK government), so stick to WiFi to reduce costs and remember to turn off data roaming. Remember that pay as you go can be the most appropriate option for you and avoid being tempted by the coolest phone!

- **Internet access** – this can involve big numbers, so make sure you fully understand the deal. A good friend of mine (who has earned lots of money in his career) was ranting about being ripped off for years by his internet deal at home. He was paying for something he didn't even need. He obviously had too much money so he wasn't paying attention. We get caught out when our daughter and son come home and our allocated download amount gets exceeded due to film downloads, with huge bills as a result. It's hard to keep up with all the technology options and interconnected technology deals. I don't have an answer as to how to manage this, other than to suggest that, each time one technology-related contract is up for renewal, you should think about all of your technology contracts collectively.

- **Gyms** – gyms sign up more new members in January than in any other month. If you sign up, make sure you will use it. Add up the all-in cost and estimate how much you will use it, taking holidays into account. What is the likely cost per visit? Is it worth it to you? One way to look at it – if you had to pay the per-visit cost at the door as you entered, would you still do it? Consider other options: government-supported gyms, exercising outdoors or having a few pieces of equipment at home (easy to buy at deep discounts on the internet).

MANAGE ANY RENTAL PROPERTY CAREFULLY

As you read in Chapter 10, there are plenty of potential pitfalls when you rent a property. Starting with the rental agent, get totally clear about what is and is not included in the rent and do your full sums before committing to the lease. Think about how, amongst the group sharing, you will handle the financial arrangements. Consider a house account that everyone pays into in advance of bills coming in and regular account top-ups by all flatmates. Moving in at the beginning of the lease and moving out are high money-risk moments. When you move in, do a full inventory – write lists of what is there, what marks are on the walls and take pictures so no one can later question the state of the place when you moved in. And when you move out, do the same. Restore everything to the condition it was in when you arrived and make sure it is mega-clean.

CHOOSE WHO YOU LIVE WITH CAREFULLY

As we covered in the "renting property" section of Chapter 10, think carefully about who you share with. Remember that it can be easier to live with people who aren't your best friends than those who are. This is even more important if you decide to buy a property jointly with someone else. I have heard quite a few stories about partners buying property together, followed by a break-up of the relationship and a nightmare process of unwinding the property deal. The same can be true of renting property.

BUY STUFF ON THE INTERNET WITH CARE

You can be enticed into buying many things – diet pills, magazines, music downloads, food – with the banner free trial that says "You can cancel at any time." If only it were so easy. Untangling yourself from one of these can take a great deal of time and effort and those arrangements may leave you open to fraudsters. It's as if your payment information gets passed on somehow. We once experienced a problem with a firm that took out only a few pounds every month so we didn't bother chasing it, but when it was month after month, we realised it was a scam. When we called the credit card company (who are required by law to sort it out and get it off your card immediately) they were well aware of the scamming company.

IF YOU NEED TO BORROW MONEY FOR A
SHORT TIME, CHECK YOUR OPTIONS CAREFULLY
AND MAKE SURE YOU WILL BE ABLE TO PAY IT BACK

Chances are at some point you will have a short term money need – if you do, think carefully about the options for borrowing. Payday lenders (search under that on the web) are now fewer in number than previously due to stricter regulation. They are likely to be your quickest route to cash. If you don't pay the money you borrow back on time, the penalties will be limited to 100% of the amount you borrowed but your credit rating will suffer.

If you do find yourself needing short-term funds review all of the options available (see Chapter 5) before you commit.

THINK BEFORE LENDING TO, AND
BORROWING MONEY FROM, FRIENDS

In general, mixing friends and money is not a good idea. Even seemingly little amounts can go unpaid and strain a relationship because the lender isn't quite sure how to ask for the money back. The only suggestion I can make is to write money borrowed or lent down as soon as the money changes hands. This even goes for the casual tenner when you are out and about. (It may be tough to write it down then and there, but make a point of the fact you are lending it and mention it the next day.) Someone said to me, "If you can't afford for your friend not to pay back the money, don't lend it in the first place." And if someone lets you down with repayments, don't keep lending to him. If you do borrow or lend a significant sum from or to a friend, do it on a commercial basis. That means giving/getting more interest than a bank would charge so everyone wins.

TAKE STEPS TO AVOID IDENTIFY THEFT AND OTHER CRIMES

The price of using technology in relation to money is that we are open to the risk of other people accessing our money through that technology. Criminals are always inventing new ways to get money through illegal means. Therefore you need to be vigilant. I am increasingly hearing unpleasant stories from friends, and particularly young friends, of someone accessing their bank account, using their credit card details or otherwise getting access to money when they shouldn't. You need to be careful, sometimes verging on neurotic, to protect yourself.

Here are some pointers:

PIN codes – never tell anyone else what your number is, and make sure no one sees the numbers you punch into any machine.

Credit cards – in the UK we use chip and PIN and the same warnings as above apply. But in other countries, where you may have to sign a credit card receipt, you will want to keep a copy of the receipt you sign. In lesser developed countries your card may be run through a funny machine that has carbon paper in it. If so, you want your receipt copy and the carbon paper.

Credit card slips – you will be holding onto these so that you can tick each one off against your credit card statement for budget purposes, as explained in Chapter 4. Rather than carry the slips around with you, stick them in a box, envelope or something at home until the statement arrives. Once you have done your reconciliation you should destroy those slips – run them through a shredder, tear them up into small pieces or burn them.

Cashless payments – payments can now be made in lots of different ways: tapping a debit card (up to a limited amount), tapping a credit card, tapping your travel card, tapping your phone and who knows what next? Two important risks are emerging with these. First is "card clash", where two of your cards get charged for the same thing. Think Oyster and debit card as you go through the tube barrier or get on a bus. Keep your cards separate and only put one next to the reader. Second is when a thief passes his card reader by your card and "collects" money from you. I have heard of this happening at crowded tube stations where the thief quickly collects thousands of pounds. This makes it increasingly important that you check your bank account frequently and make sure you investigate any irregularities as soon as you see them!

Cash machines – it is hard to imagine life without these, and sometimes we can forget that they pose risks. It is best to use machines that are located in or outside a bank branch. If you notice anything at all unusual about the machine as you are using it, immediately cancel the transaction and get your card back. If the machine swallows your card for no apparent reason, report it immediately. Don't let anyone look over your shoulder as you are using the machine, even if they are trying to be helpful in some way.

Avoid wallet/handbag theft – this of course isn't totally under your control but you (don't think this is just women) can take a few precautions. Make sure your handbag can be closed properly and make sure your wallet is at the bottom of

the bag. When you are in crowds, including tubes and buses, keep your handbag closed (my wallet was stolen from my unzipped handbag on a crowded tube); for guys, keep your wallet in your front jacket or trouser pocket. Backpacks are great but it is easy for someone to slit the bottom and take what they want, so keep it in front of you when you are in a crowd. It is a big mistake to leave a handbag, backpack, laptop or anything else on the back of a chair, on the floor, on the table in a restaurant or any other public place, as it very easy for someone to steal it. (I know more than a handful of friends this has happened to.) If it does happen, call your credit card companies immediately. They will ask you what the numbers of your cards are – how are you supposed to know that if the card has been stolen (I always think) – so keep a list of the cards you have, the card numbers and contact information stored somewhere in case you need it. Somewhere separate from your handbag and wallet of course. The information is also on the credit card statements – another good reason to keep them around.

Avoid getting mugged – this clearly has implications beyond money and technology but this seemed like the best place to include it. Keep these in mind:

- Trust your instincts. If you are uncomfortable about someone sitting next to you, walking near you or something else, do something about it. Don't worry about causing offence or being embarrassed which are the reasons I hear for not taking action.

- Stay away from deserted areas, and, on the flip side, be extra vigilant in large crowds.

- Be aware at all times. This means not walking down the street with your iPod on, talking on your mobile phone or texting/emailing. Step out of the stream of people traffic and stop walking to do anything on your phone. You will see people doing these things all the time and totally oblivious to their surroundings, which puts them at risk – I have seen some potentially fatal near-misses with cars and buses and people). Avoid this risk to yourself.

- If you are mugged, give the person what they want. You can even throw your bag, wallet, phone, computer or whatever it is the mugger wants aside so the mugger goes after that and not you. This is not the time to think about anything other than your personal safety.

Get to know your credit card helplines – the more your credit card company knows about you, the more it can do to protect you. Ring to tell the company if you are travelling to ensure you won't get stuck being unable to use your card in some distant place as they think your card has been stolen. (Note that the ability of firms to track and use this information is a fairly new development.) Respond quickly to calls from your credit card company's fraud department. These calls are initiated because, for some reason, their data-mining work has indicated that someone may be using your card fraudulently. You will need to respond to a series of questions about recent purchases. To make it easy for the company to find you, make sure your contact details held by them are kept up to date. Don't be alarmed if a vendor gets an instruction to ring the card company when you go to use a card, as the company may be just checking for fraud reasons.

Protect your information – whenever possible, put security codes on your laptop, tablet, mobile phone and any other equipment. By doing so, if you do lose it, at least the information won't be available to whoever has it to cause damage by incurring costs.

AND SOME GOOD NEWS

There is plenty of support to help you make informed money decisions all the time. Resources include:

- The internet is a great source of information on all things money-related. Relevant websites were mentioned throughout the book and new ones will continue to emerge. Do make sure you are aware as to whether a given site is independent or not.

- Newspapers also are good sources of information on money issues. The money sections of the Sunday papers are useful as they include topical pieces. Newspapers also provide information about the political, social and financial environment, all of which will impact you and your money.

- Travel plans are best made early using comparison websites such as expedia.co.uk and kayak.co.uk. And the very confusing train travel pricing is best conquered via the internet, as no one could possibly be on top of an explanation of all the available options. One of the easiest ways to stretch your cash is to plan ahead. Of course, that is easier said than done!

- Fashion can be a cheap product now, with shops like Primark, and lots of discount shopping available on the internet. But if you want to buy quality pieces at a discount, wait for the major summer sales at the main shops or specialist high-quality internet sites like net-a-porter.com. There are new ones springing up all the time.

- Using coupons is a great way to save money – vouchercloud, Groupon and myvouchercode are all accessible via smartphones or the internet. You can also take advantage of paper-based offers, and make sure you use loyalty points awarded in stores, on airlines, and all sorts of other places. Sometimes I feel like a real dope when I pay full price for something!

This covers key pitfalls in quite a summarised way, so take a look at the relevant chapters if you want to remind yourself of details.

Chapter Twelve

Some Things Are Outside Your Control

The Impact Of UK Politics On You
The Three Most Pervasive Economic Principles

B Y NOW YOU should have a good understanding about how you make earning, spending and savings decisions and about how the world of money works. You are hopefully also feeling well-positioned to control all money aspects of your life. So, before we part company, let's talk about the things you can't control that will impact your money situation – a quick dip into economics and politics.

As you know, the economic and political climate directly influences your life and financial situation. That became really clear to everybody during the global financial crisis that began in 2008, continues to impact us today, and will impact us for many years to come. Sometimes it can feel that in the UK we are in the middle of things and sometimes on the periphery – sitting outside the euro currency and possibly about to leave the European Union, but a member of the G7, a seat on the UN and an active participant in global events. Talk about people having problems balancing budgets! Greece for one certainly had more money going out of its government than it had coming in for generations and are still verging on bankruptcy and elimination from the euro despite a bailout in mid-2015. Ditto for Cyprus, Portugal and Spain. After the UK vote in June 2016 to leave the EU, the future of the EU and the euro remain a question for perhaps many other countries.

Closer to home, what the UK government is trying to do is the same as you, just on a bigger scale. The "money coming in" bit is hard to influence, although they are attempting to in altering taxes. The "money going out" bit appeared easier to influence, although as spending cuts are proposed, the government is getting a lot of resistance and so change is slow. Unlike us, the government has to steer many factions into one direction (e.g. politicians, unions, citizens). There is keen interest in the economy and banking from all quarters. While there is mostly bad news about banks – PPI and interest rate swaps misselling, regulatory penalties, and leadership changes – there is also some good news for consumers. The banking financial results are improving and there are expectations that one of the bailed-out UK banks will return to private ownership in the near future. There is also evidence of additional banks coming on the scene, and the government is incentivising new entrants. The economy seems to be recovering – which will affect you and your money situation.

THE IMPACT OF UK POLITICS ON YOU

The UK political and economic situation directly impacts your money situation in a few tangible ways that I want to highlight.

UK Budget Day

Having grown up in the US where changes to spending and taxes take months of debate, my first UK Budget Day was a shock. On a specified Wednesday in March, the government in power sets out plans for the country's fiscal policy and an annual budget for the country. What is communicated that day impacts all of us, and it does so immediately. The Chancellor of the Exchequer declares what components of government income will go up and down and what government spending will go up and down. There will be quite a bit of speculation in the press in the run up to Budget Day so the declarations are usually not a total surprise. Key areas that will impact you that are frequently adjusted include: personal allowance level (remember this is how much money you can earn before having to pay income tax); the amount of tax on wine, beer, cider and spirits; the tax on cigarettes; income tax rates; the tax on petrol (as an aside do you realise that petrol is a commodity and the only thing that makes it more or less expensive in countries is the tax imposed by that country!); and lots of other things. Make it a point to read the papers after the next Budget Day to see a full list and the economic debate that follows.

Which Party Is In Charge Of Running The UK?

Each political party (Conservative, Labour, Scottish National Party (SNP), Liberal Democrat and UK Independence Party (UKIP)) have very different views about how to manage the country's economy. Therefore you will be directly affected by who is in power. The tools they have at their disposal to manage the country's finances include tax rates, interest rates and inflation rates (though they say the Bank of England controls these last two) on the income side. They have differing approaches to managing the spending side as well, which are managed via government budgets by department. From where I sit, irrespective of political party, politicians have overspent in the US, the UK, across the EU and elsewhere. And now each of the political parties is trying to convince citizens that they have the answers to get us all out of the financial mess.

There are political party biases which I will depict here a bit in the extreme. The Labour party is on the socialist end of the scale – big spend, big government and greater benefits to the less well off in society. Conservatives – less government, less taxes, fewer benefits to the less well off. The Liberal Democrats set out fiscal policies which were more closely aligned with Labour than with the Conservatives, in many respects, but they ended up running a coalition government with the Conservatives from May 2010 until May 2015. The SNP is concerned with independence, although there are questions as to whether full fiscal independence would be viable. You can see the fundamental differences in approach really hit hard when they get into debates on education (like university fees) and the health service. Keep your eye on politics!

The Press
It is worth reading a range of newspapers and magazines and listening to news and other broadcasts to help you get a broad and balanced view on financial matters. Turbulent political times frequently go hand-in-hand with opportunities to stir things up about the government's money management capabilities. The press is good at highlighting financial changes that may or may not materialise around interest rates and inflation and, as they report these things, you can learn more about them. Most papers have pretty good money sections on weekends that give investment ideas, mortgage rates and other money and economy-related stories.

Taxes
The rates for income tax, capital gains tax, value added tax, petrol tax and other taxes are all set by the government and they all impact you!

Interest Rates
The Head of the Bank of England heads the Monetary Policy Committee (MPC) which sets the base rate of interest in the UK. The Governor of the Bank of England, Mark Carney, has indicated that interest rates will remain low for some time to come. How long that is remains unclear. That rate is important to you as any lending of money is done at a rate pegged to the base rate. The Bank of England also tries to manage the rate of inflation.

The Rate of Inflation
This is the rate at which the overall cost of living, meaning the cost of buying the same things now as you did before, is increasing. You will often see inflation rate referred to in the press.

Interesting Percentage Dynamics

- If the rate of interest you are earning on your money on deposit in a bank is less than the rate of inflation, you are losing purchasing power by keeping money in the bank rather than spending it, or investing it somewhere else where you earn a higher return.

- If earning a higher interest rate isn't possible, consider ways to increase the underlying capital to generate higher overall returns (e.g. through shares or property as described in earlier chapters).

- If your earnings (i.e. salary) are not increasing at least as fast as the rate of inflation, you are losing purchasing power.

We are living in weird economic times but there have been lots of "weird economic times" in the past. In the past 25 years I have seen the following:

- One British pound worth one US dollar; one British pound worth two US dollars.

- Mortgage interest rates at 15%; mortgage interest rates at 3%; and mortgage interest rates at 0% for some borrowers.

- Money on deposit in a simple bank savings account earning 6% interest; money on deposit earning no interest.

- The top rate of income tax on earned income at 60% and 98% on unearned income (interest and dividends); a top rate of tax on earned income at 40%.

- The rate of inflation at 6% a year in the UK and more than 100% a week in South Africa.

- Lots of planning needed to get money out of a bank – no money machines, no chip and PIN on credit cards (that came in around 2007), banks were open 9am to 5pm, credit cards were hardly used, and cheques were written for just about everything. And now, cash machines are available everywhere as well as contactless cards where you don't need a pin or anything to pay for items up to a limited amount (up to £30 for the time being).

THE THREE MOST PERVASIVE ECONOMIC PRINCIPLES

These three principles came up throughout the book, which is indicative of the ongoing impact they have on each of us and our financial situation. There are lots of books you can read, or if you studied economics you will have read, that explain these in detail. In summary:

The Risk/Reward Trade-Off

The fundamental concept is that the more risk you take, the more you should expect to be rewarded for it. And by the same token, the less risk you take, the less you should expect to be rewarded for it. So if a lender is considering giving you a loan and you look like a high risk, the lender will expect to be paid more for taking the risk is rated a low risk. All the work a bank does before it gives you a credit card or loan is aimed at figuring out just how risky you are; i.e. do they think you will pay them the money you are lent plus interest? The bank can reduce its risk in various ways, for example by reducing the amount of mortgage it gives you relative to the value of the property you are buying. Take a minute to think about everything we have gone through so far and just how much has to do with this concept. It is a notion you can use in all aspects of life and it is a principle that helps make sense of many things in life.

Here are a few examples:

- **Careers** – if you take a safe, reliable, easy job, you may earn a steady salary but you are unlikely to make a huge amount of money. If you try to set up your own business, the risk to you is much higher. You may fail or you may get it right and make millions. There has been plenty written about Richard Branson – it is no surprise that one of his teachers told him he would either end up in jail or very wealthy.

- **Earning interest** – I have an example of this for you. In the run-up to the financial crisis, interest rates in the UK were falling and people with cash were frustrated because they could not earn much of a return on the money they held on deposit at their banks. Along came Icesave, from Iceland, offering interest at way above the market – well 3.5%, which seemed like a lot at the time. So individuals, businesses, local authorities and charities I know invested their money there. People didn't give much thought to why the interest rate was higher, or what would happen if Icesave had problems (remember the UK government provides guarantees on the first £75,000 you hold at a bank. When it did go bankrupt, people lost all their money. They took all that risk to benefit from a 3.5% interest rate rather than 1.5% and the risk became a reality. Happily for the investors, the UK government bailed them out in the end.

- **Current interest rates** – why do banks currently give you so little interest if you have funds on deposit with them? Quite simply, the Bank of England base rate is low and the banks don't need to reward you for the risk of leaving deposits with them as they are unlikely to fail. As we covered in the investment section, whilst the bank doesn't have to pay if you keep money in a current account, and only pays a bit if you hold money in a savings account that you can access at any time, they do have to pay you extra if you commit to letting the bank have your money for a longer, fixed period of time. The longer the period of time, the greater the relative amount they need to pay you, because the risk of needing it and not being able to get to it is a risk that you are bearing.

- Asking people out – the trade-off works here too. Every time you ask someone out, you are taking the risk that you may be rejected. But if you don't ask, there is zero chance of going out at all.

Supply And Demand

This concept is fundamental to setting the price of goods and services. It is a really simple concept that looks at the relationship between people wanting to buy something (demand) and people providing what it is those other people want to buy (supply). In practical terms, and relative to the price of something today:

- if there is a large supply of something and little demand, the price of that something will go down

- if there is a limited supply of something and lots of demand, the price of that something will go up and

- if the supply and demand for something are pretty much in balance, that something will remain at the price it is.

Manufacturers of products can control the pricing of their something by controlling the supply. They can influence demand to an extent by having a great product everyone likes, but then copycats appear, which rebalances supply and demand. Think about petrol and the changing prices you see advertised on station forecourts. They go up each time we think the Middle

East may reduce oil production. Think also about the price of tickets to football matches that are influenced by how well the team is performing during the season. Or the price of clothing depending on what shop or designer is in fashion.

On the flip side, think of areas where you have seen prices decrease. The first one that comes to mind for me is technology – mobile phones, laptops, and tablets. Each new model starts expensive and then decreases – sometimes quickly.

This concept will impact your spending but also your earnings. If you follow a job or career path which anyone can do and lots of people do it, you are unlikely to get paid a high rate. If, on the other hand, you end up in a job that few people are in but for which huge demand develops, your pay is likely to increase. Of course it is hard to predict what jobs/careers will be in demand, so that is not a good basis on which to make a job/career decision, but it is useful to understand that this principle is at work. The concept also applies to you personally and your reputation at work. If people know you for being great at what you do, employers will want you to work for them and will be willing to pay you extra to get you working for them.

The Time Value Of Money
This concept works equally but opposite on earning and spending money:

*   Getting money now is better than getting money later. Why? Because you can earn interest on that money. And if someone pays you money later you expect to get paid for waiting for your money, in the form of interest.
*   Paying money later is better than paying money now. Why? Because you can earn interest on that money until you have to pay it.

Keep a close eye on the economic and political scene in the UK, Europe and beyond, as it will impact your financial situation in the short and long term. If you understand that and keep the three economic principles in mind as you work to make sense of the world of money, you will be well-positioned to make good decisions!

Chapter Thirteen

Relevant Readings

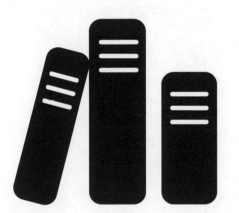

WHILST RESEARCHING this book I came across a great deal of useful information that I wanted to share but I couldn't find the right place to fit it within the main chapters of the book. I have collected it here, as article excerpts clustered by topic, for you to enjoy. The highlights are mine to help you pick out the topics you are interested in.

***

"**Wealthy people are more likely to have misgivings over their lack of financial self-discipline despite having more spare cash,** a survey from Barclays Wealth reveals. One-third of wealthy individuals wish they had more self-control over their financial behaviour. **Almost half (45%) of people worth over £10 million expressed a desire for greater self-discipline**…Younger people are far more likely to be discontent with their financial self-control, the report also found." *City AM.*

***

"**Student debt takes 11 years to pay off** – Crippling student debt will take 11 years on average to clear says uSwitch research. Almost four in ten graduates (38%) are putting big life decisions such as getting married or starting a family on hold because of student debt…and, as fees go up, students run the risk of even bigger debts. But without a degree, getting a job in today's stagnant market may be even harder. **Two-thirds of these graduates said they underestimated how much debt they would incur.**" *City AM.*

***

"Vocational training – **for years we have been sold a complete load of rubbish, told that if you want to get on in life you have to go to university.** Where did that get us? Thousands of useless courses and hundreds of students with huge debts and no jobs, that's where. Jobs like plumbing, carpentry, electrics – you know, the useful ones – have been downgraded in society. One step forward might be to stop using terms like 'vocational' – a word that plumbers like me never use. **We should be talking about 'getting a trade', something that parents used to aspire to for their kids as recently as the 1970s.**" Charlie Mullins, MD of Pimlico Plumbers, quoted in the *Guardian* in *The Week.*

***

"Who needs a degree: not these self-made tycoons – **A-level students worked about running up big debts to secure a degree should take note – many of Britain's richest tycoons never went to university**...Dragons' Den panellist Deborah Meaden, TV chef Jamie Oliver or JCB industrialist Sir Anthony Bamford. The trio have made their millions and climbed to the top of their chosen professions with just an apprenticeship under their belts. With fees of up to £27,000 for a three-year degree, there is an alternative to the world of academia said the body for City and Guilds qualifications. An astonishing **94 of the richest 100 Britons have made it on their own merit** according to the *Sunday Times* Rich List...Sir James Dyson, John Frieda, Sir Jackie Stewart. Celebrity chefs who started their careers having completed a vocational catering qualification include Jamie Oliver, Rick Stein and Gary Rhodes. **The City & Guilds Vocational Rich List 'proves you don't need a degree to succeed'.**" *Evening Standard*.

***

"...**would you pick a well-paid job with a less happy lifestyle or a less well-paid job with an easier lifestyle?** The answer we're expected to give, by happiness gurus, is that we'd forfeit the stress, dosh and status to be more content. Some of us have always doubted this. We are the ones working in August, the types who balance our work laptops on our knees while watching *The Killing*, so we miss the vital clues while we're sending a late email. But we're not just made workaholics according to some of the latest research. Recommending that people pursue happiness rather than economic wealth doesn't necessarily go with the grain of human nature. *Researchers asked thousands of students and graduates at Cornell University to choose between a job that paid comfortably and let them get a full night's sleep and one that paid more but left them less free time. Most of the sample agreed that the first option would make them happier – but promptly chose the second... Deep down, a lot of us work harder than we strictly need to because for all the tensions it is satisfying and makes us money. A sense of purpose, higher professional standing and sense of control motivate us as much as a pursuit of ease or balance does: and that's all right. A lot of today's graduates in the midst of an uncertain recovery will have to take jobs they don't want, for wages they think are too low and with shaky futures. I don't envy them that climate but they will learn the lesson that the wellbeing gurus forget. We graft for all sorts of reasons and don't always expect it to make us happy. That's why they call it work.*" *Evening Standard*.

***

"The true path to happiness runs through the office – *Rush: Why you Need and Love the Rat Race*, written by Todd Buchholz, is different from the other happiness books. **It is a relief to find that the true path to happiness involves doing what most of us do all the time, whether we like it or not – work. Stress he says, makes us happy.** Competition is good; without it we would be more than just unhappy, we would have died out long ago. It doesn't make us selfish it makes us co-operate. Retirement is bad as it makes you stupid. Working weekends is fine as it shows that you are needed – which is all most of us want. And earning lots of money is also all right because it a sure sign someone appreciates you...It is easier to see the joy of competition if you are the one getting the prizes...He deploys anthropology, economics and neuroscience in support of his thesis. We get a surge of dopamine and serotonin when we take on a new task; we are bathed in warmer oxytocin as we chat to colleagues; when we succeed, we get a shot of beta-endorphins, which are as good as cocaine...**I know I am at my happiest when I'm working hard and well.**" *Financial Times*.

***

"**When Katy Young decided to save for a deposit,** she knew she had to take drastic action. The 28-year-old made a resolution to **go a whole year without buying clothes.** Ms. Young has gone to seven weddings this year – wearing a different outfit to each – without spending a penny. And she is putting away at least £150 a month. She has started attending guilt-free clothes swapping events and is even sewing to recycle old clothes. 'I don't get the same buzz as **I've realised how wasteful it is.'**" *Metro*.

***

"I leave feeling several stone lighter than I did before. **How do I make sure I never end up in a mess again?...do everything in cash.** Take out a set amount of money each day then leave your card at home. Your spending will plummet. I think people **register physical money** in a way that they don't when they buy everything on their card." *City AM*.

***

"...riffles though statements to put together a realistic budget...**discomfort looking at statements is a bad sign.** 'You've got a problem as soon as you stop opening your statements. You need to know precisely what you spend on everything to get things under control.' MoneyNet's Andrew Haggar. 'You need to do this regularly. Making a note of everything you spend throughout the year.'" *City AM.*

***

"Citizens Advice Bureau inundated by debt-laden young professionals – The centre in Islington [London] has been inundated with **requests for help from first time homeowners unable to pay off large mortgages and women 'maxing out' on storecards** from firms such as Waitrose and M&S. The centre is the first to open in London in about 20 years and sees up to 70 clients a day…for years it was mainly the poorest residents who sought debt help. Jeanette Daly Mathias, manager, said that people are **making poor choices of credit** and suffering with loans secured against their homes. In one case a **woman found she owed £80,000 over 20 credit cards**. CAB workers advise people to pay off emergency debts first and then try to negotiate around other financial commitments." *City AM.*

***

"**Only facing up to your debt problems will stop the stress: tens of thousands of people spend more than they earn every month and are struggling to make their credit card payments.** Stephanie Broll explains how she stopped being one of them…the average household debt in the UK excluding mortgages is £8,055…**I was a student and every time I skirted close to my credit limit, it would be increased automatically. This is dangerous when you're a fresher and your loan is paid in lump sums every quarter. Somehow money just doesn't seem real.** I now have more debts than I can cope with and end up skint every month 15 days before payday. A good APR is out of the question if you've missed payments in the past…even missed phone bills will count against your credit rating nowadays." *City AM.*

***

"**Putting small amounts of money into an emergency ISA fund every month is a good idea.**" *City AM.*

***

"Tips of the week – **how to save money at university**:

- If you have done holiday work, remember to claim back overpaid taxes. Most students pay an emergency tax rate of 20% – but you can earn up to the personal allowance tax-free.

- Don't get household insurance unless you need it. About 80% of home insurance policies cover student belongings so you're probably covered under your parent's home policy.

- When buying broadband, remember you probably won't be there over the summer. Virgin Media offers a nine-month student deal; Plusnet has a rolling monthly contract.

- Don't buy new books if you can avoid it. Sites such as sellstudentstuff.com and studentbooks.co.uk sell secondhand textbooks for a fraction of the cover price.

- Cut down on travelling costs by sharing a car with other students. Sites such as studentcarshare.com are free and safe.

- Take advantage of student deals. Sites such as studentbeans.com are free to sign up and have plenty of cheap deals."

The Week.

***

"Learn these by heart: **tips from current students**:

- Share as much as possible. Cooking together, splitting stationery and buying household utilities as a group makes sense.

- Always look at reduced sections and from now on ignore brands. They are too expensive and the supermarket's own brands are often the same quality. Cook as much as possible. Fruit and veg are cheaper than processed ready meals.

- Set yourself a weekly budget. Best thing to do is take out cash at the start of the week and don't take your cards out.

- The best thing that helped me the most was probably having a part-time job. Having two bank accounts also helps – I keep my loan in one and don't touch it other than my rent, and I have another where I have my wages, or money that I have available to spend.

- Voucher websites are a great way to save money. My favourite is quidco.com.

- Cook food in batches. Make loads of bolognaise sauce, freeze it and microwave it later.
- When you go shopping, write a list and stick to it."

The Times.

***

Contents

Contents

yes is a pleasant country
if's wintry
(my lovely)
let's open the year

both is the very weather
(not either)
my treasure,
when violets appear

e e cummings

Acknowledgements

First I would like to thank Christine Frank who three years ago proposed working on a set of non-competitive games for language teaching. You will have to forgive me Section I in this book, Christine!

Next I would like to thank Paul Davis who tested games, improved games and came up with solutions to what seemed insoluble problems, to me. He gave me courage when I had doubts about the venture. Paul also read through and criticised the manuscript.

My son, Martin, likes games and invents new ones. His liking this book has helped a lot. Thanks.

John Morgan reacted to the Pilgrims pilot edition of this book by saying that it was OK but slender. He was right. I would like to thank him for a friendly and useful kick in the pants.

Finally a thank you to the students who made the testing of the games a pleasure.

Acknowledgements for individual games come at the end of each game.

The author and publishers would like to thank the following authors and publishers who have given permission for the use of copyright material identified in the text. It has not been possible to identify the sources of all the material used and in such cases the publishers would welcome information from copyright owners.

Granada Publishing Ltd and Harcourt Brace Jovanovich, Inc. for 'yes is a pleasant country' on p. v from *Complete Poems 1913 – 1962* by e.e. cummings; Jonathan Cape Ltd and Adrian Mitchell for 'Old age report' on p. 63 from *Ride the Nightmare*; Alan Maley for 'Walking Tall' on p. 79; University of Queensland Press for 'Collected speeches of P. Arthur Truscott travelling by rail between Vladivostok and Grand Rapid Falls' on p. 82, from *Believed Dangerous: Fifty-eight Poems* by Robin Thurston; Alfred A. Knopf, Inc. for 'Cross' on p. 90, from *Selected Poems of Langston Hughes*, © 1926 by Alfred A. Knopf, Inc., renewed 1954 by Langston Hughes.

Artwork by The Dunmow Design Group and Wenham Arts. Drawings on page 93 by Mick Loates.

Grammar Games was originally published in pilot form by Pilgrims Publications, Canterbury, England. This Cambridge University Press edition has been extensively revised and expanded and contains double the number of exercises in the original Pilgrim edition.

Introduction

To teachers of languages other than English

I happen to be a teacher of English and so this book is aimed initially at teachers of English and works on English structures.

The exercises and games could act as adequate frames for the teaching of any grammar under the sun. If you want to use the games in this book for teaching *your* language you will find them extremely easy to adapt. Good luck!

What's in the book?

Section I presents traditional games like 'Noughts and crosses', 'Snap', 'Monopoly' and 'Snakes and ladders', modified to allow students to work in small groups and show themselves and you how much or how little grammar they know. Less traditional game frames in this section include 'Auction', 'Double or quits' and 'The money game'.

I use the word 'game frame' because, though each game in this section is offered as working on a particular grammar area you can fill each frame with whatever grammar content you want. The particular grammar content proposed in the section is only there by way of exemplification.

This section has the students working cognitively on grammar: they are asked to think consciously about what is correct and what is incorrect.

Section II is a collection of Silent Way, or Silent Way inspired exercises in which students build sentences and paragraphs in warm cooperation with each other rather than in competition. Your role is to give silent feedback to individuals and to the class, but only when absolutely necessary. II.14, 'With your back to the class', has you sitting with your back to the class giving them four signals, two with your head and two with your hands! Work from this section will allow you to enjoy being productively quiet in the group, while observing the students in full activity.

The average teacher in Europe today notches up a score of about 60–70% teacher-talking time in his or her classes. Just 35% or less is left to the students! The exercises in Section II could bring your teacher-talking time down to less than 5% of the overall exercise time.

Section III moves right away from cognitive work on grammar. In these exercises the students are asked to write and say things about themselves and people who are significant to them within a set of structures prescribed by the teacher. The students' focus is on *what* they are saying not on the form they are using. *They* control the content, *you* control the structures.

These exercises have the students practise given grammar points while thinking and feeling about human relationships. If you find this work relevant to the way you teach you will find more activities of this sort in *Grammar in action,* C. Frank and M. Rinvolucri (Pergamon, 1983).

Section IV, Grammar through drama, has the students off their chairs practising grammar through movement, shouting, and writing on each others' backs. Excellent for jaded classes or for groups with lots of unspent energy that needs to be channelled.

Section V is a ragbag of useful grammar-practising activities which I find it hard to classify properly.

Level?

Each exercise is proposed for a given level ranging from beginner to advanced. This refers simply to the grammar content of that particular activity. By changing the grammar content you can, in many cases, use the game or exercise frame offered at a higher or lower level. If you look at I.6 you will see that the level stated is intermediate and the grammar worked on present perfect + for/since. The game proposed in I.6 is 'Snakes and ladders'. By putting appropriate sentences of your own choice on the boards the students play on, you could use the game at post-beginner or advanced level.

Choice of structures

If you glance through the table of contents you will notice that a great many of the exercises work on the present simple and past simple. In most course books these two tenses are given the same amount of space as less used tenses like the past perfect, past continuous and present continuous. In some textbooks more time and effort is budgeted for the present continuous than for the present simple, despite the fact that the latter is used about eight times more frequently in English than the former.

I decided to give more exercise space to the most frequent tenses in the English verb system.

If you think I am wrong, all you have to do is delete these two tenses from the exercises they occur in and fill the frames with the structures you want to work on with your students.

Where do these games fit into a teaching programme?

Hard to answer because I don't know how you teach. In my own teaching I have used this sort of game in three ways:

a) diagnostically *before* presenting a given structure area to find out how much knowledge of the area is already disjointedly present in the group;
b) after a grammar presentation to see how much the group have grasped;
c) as revision of a grammar area.

I do not use grammar games as a Friday afternoon 'reward' activity – I use them as a central part of the students' learning process.

Grammar is serious!

Grammar is perhaps so serious and central in learning another language that all ways should be searched for which will focus student energy on the task of mastering and internalising it. One way of focusing this energy is through the release offered by games.

Teenagers are delighted to be asked to do something that feels like an out-of-class activity and in which they control what is going on in the classroom – they become subjects, while for a lot of the 15,000 hours they spend in school between 6 and 16 they are the *objects* of teaching. The Belgian businessman who came out to coffee after a grammar game saying 'Ce n'est pas bête du tout', was expressing his surprise that a game could be fun and serious at the same time. The point is that the fun generates energy for the achievement of the serious goal.

Can I let my students see wrong sentences?

In Sections I and II students have to decide, in the course of a game, if a sentence is grammatically correct or incorrect. This means that they are presented with quite a number of incorrect sentences.

Some teachers feel this is pedagogically bad – the argument goes that students will imprint the wrong sentences they see. I would suggest that this does not in fact happen in grammar games because the students are wary of each sentence they see and make very conscious judgements about which are correct and which incorrect. You don't willy-nilly imprint what you are highly wary of. There is more to the human mind learning a foreign language than Skinner conditioning his pigeons' responses.

3

Do these games require a lot of preparation?

For the games in Section I you have to master the rules and do a certain amount of copying of material. Once you have done the physical preparation you can re-use a game without further work in subsequent classes.

If you want to use the game frames I have suggested for structure work of your own choice, you will have more work to do, but if you decide to do this you will be the sort of person who likes this kind of extra work!

The games in Section II mostly require no physical preparation at all but you may find trying to be silent in class an experience you need to prepare yourself for internally.

Section III activities will take up almost none of your out-of-class time and will afford you a view of your students that you are unlikely to get through most traditional exercises. You will have a chance to observe the students discovering more about each other as people but *through* the target language.

The only preparation you need for Section IV, apart from making a few cards for one of the activities, is to warn the colleagues teaching either side of your classroom that they may hear a bit of noise during the period. Here I am making the serious point that, as language teachers, we have as much right to get our classes producing a volume of sound as do music teachers. There would be a strong case for sound-proofing our classrooms so that our work does not disturb that of other colleagues. How can we teach language in decorous silence?

To use Section V you simply need to do a spot of copying.

Four advantages of *Grammar Games*

1 The students have to take individual responsibility for what they think the grammar is about.
2 The teacher is free to find out what the students actually know, without being the focus of their attention.
3 Serious work is taking place in the context of a game. The dice-throwing and arguing lightens and enlivens the classroom atmosphere in a way that most people do not associate with the grammar part of a course. The 'game' locomotive pulls the grammar train along.
4 Everybody is working at once – the 15–30 minutes the average game lasts is a period of intense involvement.

Feelings about grammar

Meeting and interiorising the grammar of a foreign language is not simply an intelligent, cognitive act. It is a highly affective one too. Little work seems to have been done by psychologists or linguists on learner feelings towards specific ligaments of the target grammar and the change in these feelings as the learner moves from one level of language command to the next.

I am only at the beginning of the exploration of this field but I have found it helps to make students more conscious of what is going on inside them if you ask them to introspect from time to time during a course as to which structures they like in the target language and which they dislike, and why.

I simply ask students to write down three grammar structures and three exponent sentences they like and three they don't. Students then come to the board and put their sentences up under two headings:

NICE   UGH

They then explain why their sentences are 'nice' or 'ugh'.

Examples

A native speaker of French who had reached intermediate level in Spanish said she really liked the *ando* verb endings in Spanish, as in 'estaba caminando', because they gave a strong feeling of the progressive, of on-goingness, of continuation.

The same person said she strongly disliked Spanish first person singular preterite endings, as in 'recibí'; they seemed ridiculous to her and she regularly got them wrong.

A native speaker of German who had reached near native competence in English said many German speakers reject:

What does he look like?

not only because in German you say 'Wie (*How*) sieht er aus?', but also because as children learning their own language they were taught that 'Was' (*What*) is rude and should not be used.

A native speaker of Italian learning English at post-beginner level strongly objected to the construction:

How old are you?

He found it particularly ridiculous that English speakers even say this to a very *young* baby.

A post-beginner Portuguese speaker was unhappy about the mutual irregu-
larity of:

drINK – drANK
thINK – thOUGHT

She felt it should either be: dRINK – dROUGHT
                                            (rhyming with ought)
                                or: tHINK – tHANK

This chimes with 5 year-old native speakers of English who often give *brang*
as the past of *bring*.

An Italian post-beginner learner of English reported that these sentences
used to annoy him a lot.

You'll remember to close the door, won't you?
Yes, I will.

He said he used to dislike the auxiliary verbs being made to carry the
meaning of the main verb. This was his feeling a month previously. He said
he now found the English way of using auxiliary verbs in place of the main
verb elegant and acceptable. You couldn't do this in Italian.

   This student's evidence suggests an evolution of feeling towards the target
language structures. Was all his emotion centred on grammar structure? He
told us the sentence about closing the door was said to him by his landlady.
Maybe the month had given him time to adjust to her as a person, and thus
to her utterances, and thus to their form? What I am suggesting is that the
socio-linguistic aspect of attitudes to grammar structures can't be ignored.

A native speaker of German with a post-beginner's grasp of English disliked:

What's your mother like?

because the answer to the question should be *my mother likes chocolates*.

A French speaker at post-beginner level in English disliked:

This is the book you're looking for.

because he felt the omission of *that* is barbaric. The omission made the
sentence almost meaningless to him.

A Brazilian disliked the expression:

I'm sorry.

because it is routine, falsely polite, insincere.

A post-beginner Italian loved:

Lovely day, isn't it?

because of the music and spring of the intonation.

A post-beginner French learner liked:

I'm going to take my dictionary.

because it was really clear, as in French.

A German speaking post-beginner learner from Switzerland very much liked:
What was it like?
as she found it neat and rounded.

An intermediate learner from Italy liked:
Official notices
because adjective-noun order in English is different from Italian and, he found, much better.

An intermediate German speaker liked:
I wrote a letter with a beautiful pen.
He gave instant comprehension as his reason for liking the sentence – he said that when there is a *did* in the sentence he had to think before he could extract the meaning.

An intermediate Italian learner was unhappy with:
Does she need anything?
because she always leaves out the *es*.

A German intermediate speaker of English liked:
Do you like England?
Yes, I do.
because in German the answer would simply be *Yes*. She felt the English way is stronger and more definite.

Another German intermediate student liked:
I didn't get it.
because in German you would have to say *understand it* – she felt *get* was quicker, more direct, less pompous.

A lower-intermediate Spanish student disliked:
I wonder if you would mind opening the door?
In her own words: 'I don't like this sentence because I think it is not very usual and when I had tried (*sic*) to use it I never can because I think I will be ridiculous.'

A post-beginner Turk disliked sentences with **must/mustn't**. As far as I could gather he disliked the concept of obligation.

Whom does it belong to? sounded bad to a post-beginner German learner who strongly wanted to transfer the *to* to the front of the sentence.

To most students it comes as a new dimension that they have, and that others round them have feelings about constructions in the target language. It helps them to realise that the process of learning a new language besides being cognitive is deeply affecting. It makes the learning process a good deal more interesting.

If you run grammar-feelings-sharing sessions at intervals through a course students are able to see how their feelings change as they move through different stages in their command of the language. II.19 and II.20 are exercises that may help in this context.

Application of these ideas to lexis teaching

See *Learning English words*, J. Morgan and M. Rinvolucri (Oxford University Press, 1986).

Section 1   Competitive games

1.1   Headless sentences

GRAMMAR: Present simple passive
LEVEL: Upper-intermediate
TIME: 15 minutes
MATERIALS: One copy per three students of both the **sentence bodies** and the **sentence heads**

In class

1 Organise your class in threes and tell them they are going to compete in finding appropriate 'heads' for 14 'headless' sentences. Give out the sentence bodies. Set them a 7 minute time limit. Tell them to write in the sentence beginnings they think are correct.
2 When time is up pick one person from each triad and give them the sentence heads. Ask them to go back to a triad that is not their own and score that group's sentences.
3 Ask the scorers to tell their scores to the class and adjudicate on any points of doubt.

Note

This is a type of exercise in which the student is internalising the target structure, in this case the passive, by silently reading it, mumbling it, reading it aloud and thinking about it. This kind of exercise facilitates production of the structure at a later stage in the learning process.

Acknowledgement

I learnt this exercise type from Mike Lavery, the author of *Active viewing plus* (Modern English Publications, 1984).

Sentence bodies   (You need 1 per three students.)

....is played by two or four people, often on grass.

.... is played with big men in parks in Germany.

.... is watched by millions more than play it.

.... a try can be converted into a goal.

.... is dominated by the Chinese.

.... is an event often won in the Olympics by black competitors.

.... is enjoyed in countries that used to be directly oppressed by Britain.

.... is/are played mainly by men in pubs.

.... tends to be played by rich people with a small, pitted ball.

.... are betted on by all sorts of people.

.... is played with nothing but a simple board and small round counters.

.... a man may not be hit below the belt.

.... is banned in China, but the Chinese love to play it.

.... the big balls have to end up as close as possible to the little ball.

Sentence heads   (You need 1 per three students.)

Tennis...	Darts...
Chess...	Golf
Soccer...	Horses
In rugby...	The Japanese game 'Go'...
Table tennis...	In boxing...
The 100 metres...	Mah-jong...
Cricket...	In bowls....

Variation: Tailless sentences

This exercise continues work on the passive, bringing in the past, present and future.

Sentence bodies – Punishments   (You need 1 per three students.)

In Europe witches used to be ....

One punishment for an adulterer is to be ....

Students in French schools who misbehave are never ....

English school children are often ....

In the 19th century English criminals were often deported to ....

In a few Muslim countries thieves have their hands ....

Enemies of the French Revolution were ....

Slaves who tried to escape often got ....

The only English king to be executed was ....

Until a few years ago murderers in England were ....

Murderers in the USA are still sometimes ....

If you are caught without a TV licence in the UK you may be ....

If you park in the wrong place your car may be ....

If the police think you have been drinking and driving you will be ....

Sentence tails — Punishments   (You need 1 per three students.)

... burnt.
... stoned to death/divorced.
... caned/beaten.
... given detention.
... Australia.
... cut off.
... guillotined.
... flogged/caught.
... beheaded.
... hanged.
... electrocuted.
... fined.
... towed away/wheel-clamped.
... breathalysed/arrested/prosecuted.

I.2   Noughts and crosses

GRAMMAR: Determiners: some, any, much, many, etc.
LEVEL: Post-beginner to lower-intermediate
TIME: 15 minutes
MATERIALS: None

In class

1 Divide the class into team A and team B. Put a noughts and crosses grid (9
   squares) up on the board and make sure that everybody knows the rules
   of the game.

Someone from team A comes and puts a cross in one of the squares. Then
someone from team B comes and puts a nought in another square. The
aim of the game is to get a row of three noughts or crosses in any direction.

2 Now draw this grid on the board:

SOME	A FEW	ANY
MUCH	A LOT OF	TOO MUCH
MANY	SEVERAL	A PAIR OF

»»→

3 Tell team A they have 20 seconds to choose a particular square and produce a correct sentence using the word on that square. If they take longer than 20 seconds they lose their turn. If they produce a sentence, ask team B to say whether it is correct or not. If team B's judgement is correct accept it and if it is wrong correct it. If team A's sentence is correct, give them a cross in the corresponding square.

4 Team B then plays in the same way, with team A judging their sentence and you the correctness of team A's judgement. As the game develops the teams are forced to try and make sentences with the more difficult words in the grid.

Note

This game frame can also be used successfully with the following language areas:
'false friends' e.g. sensible/sensitive
become/receive
large/long
phrasal verbs
irregular past participles
irregular past simple

Acknowledgement

I first heard of this exercise from Julian Quail, a Pilgrims colleague.

I.3　The dice and grid game

GRAMMAR: Irregular verb parts
LEVEL: Post-beginner to upper-intermediate
TIME: 30 minutes
MATERIALS: One copy per two students of the **verb grid**
One die per student

In class

1 Give each pair of students two dice and a verb grid.

2 Explain that student A rolls the two dice. Say a SIX and a THREE are
thrown, he or she has to try and find verb correspondences between
horizontal SIX and vertical THREE. The correspondence is STEAL–
STOLE. He or she then looks at vertical SIX and horizontal THREE and
finds SWEPT–SWEEP. The player writes down (on another piece of
paper) the verb pairs found on the appropriate square. The player marks
the square(s) on the grid with his or her initial.
The aim of the game is to find more correspondences than one's opponent.
If a player throws the dice and finds no correspondences the turn passes to
the other player.
During the game, go round helping with the pronunciation of the verb
forms.

3 After 8–10 mins play, stop the students and ask them to write a *five*
sentence story about anything they like as long as they incorporate the
following past tense forms:　BIT
FORBADE
SWEPT

Verb grid   (You need 1 per two students.)

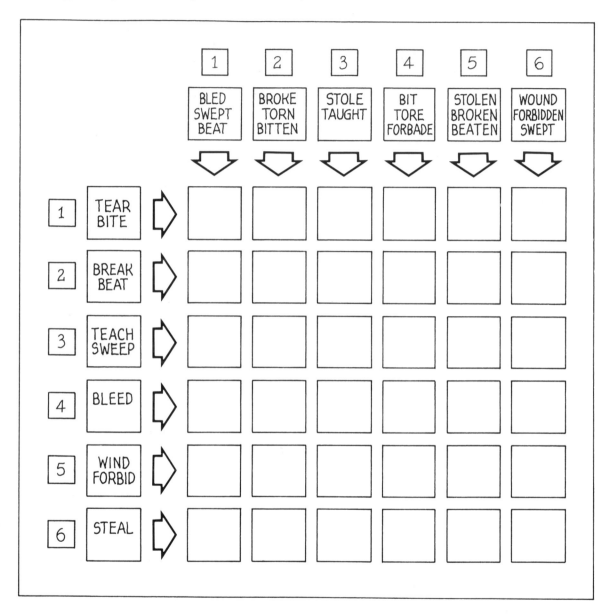

Note

'The dice and grid game' is also very useful for getting students word-building in preparation for exams such as the Cambridge First Certificate in English. The next grid is based on the kind of word-building students have to do in FCE.

Word-building grid (You need 1 per two students.)

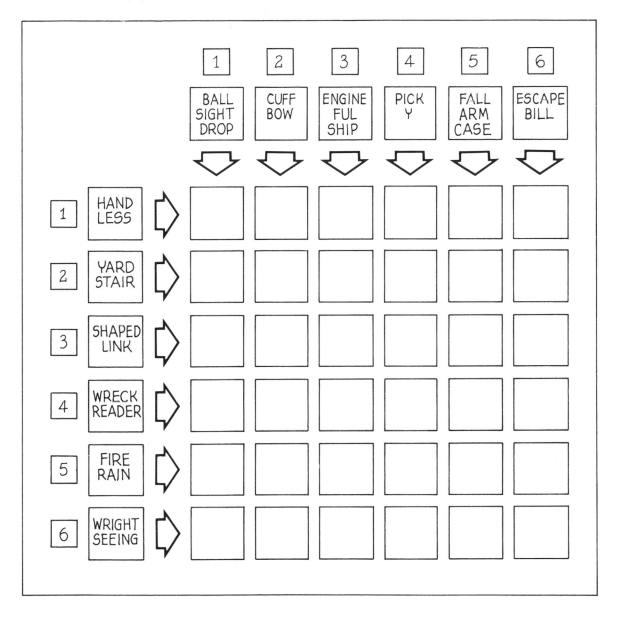

I.4 Auction

GRAMMAR:	Mixed structures
LEVEL:	Lower-intermediate
TIME:	50 minutes
MATERIALS:	One mallet or hammer
	One **auction sheet** per two students

In class

1 Ask students if any of them have been to an auction. Ask questions of those who have. Introduce necessary words like *to bid, auctioneer, a bid, What am I bid? hammer, Going, going, gone!*

2 Pair the students off and give each pair an auction sheet. Tell them that some of the sentences on the sheet are correct and some incorrect. They are to read through and decide which sentences are correct and which incorrect. In the auction that is to follow they are going to have to bid for sentences, the aim being to buy only correct sentences. Tell them each pair has £5,000 for buying sentences and ask them to note down in the *budget* column of their auction sheets how much they are willing to bid for a given sentence. They may not spend more than £5,000 in the auction. The winners of the auction are the pair with the most correct sentences *and* the most money left.

As the students work on the sentences and discuss their budgeting in pairs deny them all language help – it is up to them to take responsibility for what they think they know.

3 Before starting the auction tell them you will not accept bids of less than £200.
   START THE AUCTION:
   a) Read out the first sentence in a lively, persuasive way, even if it happens to be wrong, and then ask for bids.
   b) Keep the bidding moving fast, keep up a fast patter to convey the excitement of an auction room.
   c) When you come to the 'going, going, gone' stage, be ready to accept last minute bids. When a sentence has been auctioned off make sure students keep a note of the buyer and the amount in their *bought* columns.

d) After each sale tell the group if the sentence is correct or not and in the latter case give the correct version. Do this fast, so as not to break the 'auction' mood! *Postpone explanation of the grammar involved until after the game.*

e) Start the auction with the first sentence but then auction the rest of the sentences in *random order* – this heightens the feeling of expectancy.

4 Follow-up the grammar points the students did not understand during the auction.

Variation 1

Once you have led an auction session yourself, have a student or students as auctioneers the next time. With a class of 30 you might have three groups of nine students bidding in three separate auctions, with three separate auctioneers. You will need different auction sheets for each auction and each auctioneer must be given a key. If you don't have different auction sheets people in group A will be listening to what is going on in groups B and C! With nine or ten people per group, budgeting and bidding should be done individually, not in pairs.

Variation 2

You can auction grammar problems that come up in written homework. Don't mark the homework. Take out 12–15 mistaken sentences, re-write half of them correctly and mix them up with the uncorrected sentences so you have a fully student centred auction sheet. Do the auction in the normal way. Then give back the uncorrected homework and ask them to find each other's mistakes.

Acknowledgement

The idea of applying the auction frame to grammar work came to me after having led a values clarification auction as suggested in *A practical guide to values clarification*, Maury Smith (University Associates, La Jolla, Cal., 1977).

Auction sheet   (You need 1 per two students.)

		Budget	*Bought*
1	I wanted that you should know what happened.	_____	_____
2	What did you want to tell me?	_____	_____
3	What happened to your sister last night?	_____	_____
4	I always've wanted to visit Spain.	_____	_____
5	What killed whom and when?	_____	_____
6	Was you pleased to see your mother again?	_____	_____
7	Usually I live in a large town in Switzerland.	_____	_____
8	Oh dear, I must have catched a cold!	_____	_____
9	Nice to see you both – did you meet yourselves yesterday in town?	_____	_____
10	What'd your father say if he heard about it?	_____	_____
11	I'm have a nice warm bath every day.	_____	_____
12	Yes, it's true, I am agreed with you.	_____	_____
13	Excuse me, is there a possibility to have a meal?	_____	_____
14	If I want to learn the language, I must go to French.	_____	_____
15	She was shot while trying to escape.	_____	_____

Auction sheet—key

Sentences 2,3,5,7, 10 and 15 are correct.

The other sentences should be:

1 I wanted you to know what *was happening/had happened.*
4 *I've always* wanted to visit Spain.
6 *Were* you pleased to see your mother again?
8 Oh dear, I must have *caught* a cold!
9 Nice to see you both – did you *meet/meet each other* yesterday in town?
11 *I have* a nice warm bath every day.
12 Yes, it's true, *I agree* with you.
13 Excuse me, *can I/could I* have a meal?
14 If I want to learn the language, I must go to *France.*

I.5 Snap

GRAMMAR: Question tags
LEVEL: Lower-intermediate
TIME: 20–40 minutes
MATERIALS: One set of 72 **cards** per three students, which can be made by the students the first time you play.

In class

1 Divide your class into groups of three.

2 Give each group three sheets of A4 sized paper. Ask them to fold and tear each sheet into 24 small squares. Each group of three students should end up with 72 small squares.

3 Copy the 72 sentences and tags on pages 25, 26 and 27 onto the board as fast as you can. Ask the students to copy each sentence and each tag onto a separate small square. Ask each student to help with the copying. When they have finished, each triad should have 72 sentences and tags on 72 different squares of paper.
(If you have enough scissors, you could copy pages 25, 26 and 27 and let the triads simply cut out their squares.)
You only have to involve the students in this 'game-making' activity the first time you play 'Snap'. After the game you can collect in the sets of 72 squares, store them in separate envelopes, and have them ready for the next group you want to play the game with.

4 Demonstrate the game to the class by playing it with one student while the others watch:
a) Ask the student to sit *next to you* at a table, facing the class.
b) Give the student a set of snap cards; ask him or her to shuffle them well.
c) Draw two boxes on a piece of paper in front of you both and mark one box SENTENCE and the other TAG.
d) Ask the student to give you half the cards and to keep the other half (you each get about 36).
Each put your cards *face downwards* on the table.
e) The student turns one of his or her cards over and puts it in the relevant box, *face upwards*. You do the same; the student does the same and so on.

f) As soon as either of you sees that the *sentence* and the *tag* in the boxes fit together grammatically, you shout 'SNAP'. The first one to shout 'SNAP' gets all the cards in both boxes.

g) The aim of the game is to get all the cards in your own pile.

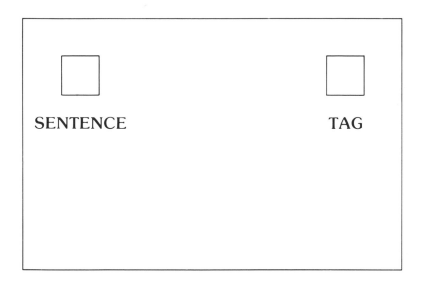

5 The students play in threes. Two players must sit side by side. The third student is to note down all the SNAP sentences in writing. The players organise themselves with a sheet of paper with two boxes marked on it. They play the game while you go round helping those who have not yet fully understood the rules and disallowing wrong SNAP sentences like: 'You divorced him, haven't you?'

6 When the game has run for 10 to 15 minutes, stop everybody and ask the 'secretaries' from each triad to write up a few of their SNAP sentences on the board. Get the students to read these sentences out fast, making sure they don't include a wrong pause between the first part of the sentence and the second.

Grammar note

The game as set out here deals with tags for sentences in the future, present simple, past simple and present perfect. At this stage you may well not want to deal with sentences where the tag and the main clause carry the same polarity, e.g. 'You've been here a long time, have you?'
The game has examples of the will/would tags for imperative sentences and of *nobody* taking the plural in the tag part of the sentence as in 'Nobody's coming, are they?'
The irregular tag: 'aren't I?' occurs.

Advantages of grammar 'Snap'

'Snap' allows students to work on *recognising* what goes with what, without having to embark immediately on oral production. The nature of the game forces them to speed up their recognition.

What structures can you use 'Snap' for?

Any structures where students have to recognise quickly whether two or three parts fit together. If you teach German you could use 'Snap' for agreement of article, adjective and noun. If you teach Spanish you could use 'Snap' with split sentences working on *ser* and *estar*. In English you could use it to make students aware of which nouns take *a* and which take *an*.

Variation

Prepare sets of 40 cards that have the *correct completion on the back*. If you are working on question tags you would have the sentence on the front of the card in large letters and the tag on the back in small ones.

Pair the students off and give each pair a set of cards. Each student takes half the set. Student A holds up his or her card and B has to supply the completion. If B completes to the satisfaction of A (who has the 'model'), then B gets the card. A holds up two more cards one after the other and again B tries to complete. Then they switch and B holds up three cards (not simultaneously) for A to try to complete. The aim of each student is to get all the cards in his or her pile.

While the first game gets the students working on recognition, this variation challenges them to produce.

Acknowledgement

Lesley Randles, writing in *Take five,* Centre for British Teachers, Colchester (subsequently published as *Take 5* by Mike Carrier, Harrap, 1981), describes lexical 'Snap' in which half the cards have words on them and half the pictures that correspond to the words. She also proposes sets of cards with synonyms, opposites and homonyms.

The variation above is an idea I learnt from Julian Quail.

Cards (1)   (You need 1 set of 72 cards per three students.)

LEND ME A BIRO,	WOULD YOU?	YOU'RE A GENIUS,	AREN'T YOU?	HAVEN'T YOU?	ARE YOU?
HAVEN'T YOU?	ARE YOU?	YOU BORROWED MY BIKE,	DIDN'T YOU?	THEY WORK HARDER THAN US,	DON'T THEY?
I'M RIGHT,	AREN'T I?	I'M WRONG,	AREN'T I?	YOU DON'T LIKE HIM,	DO YOU?
NOBODY LOVES ME,	DO THEY?	WOULD YOU PLEASE?	HAVE YOU?	HAVE YOU?	AREN'T YOU?

Cards (2)

GIVE ME A FAG,	WOULD YOU?	YOU KNOW,	DON'T YOU?	I'M STUPID,	AREN'T I?
NOBODY KNOWS,	DO THEY?	WOULD YOU?	WOULD YOU?	DIDN'T YOU?	DID THEY?
YOU'RE NEW,	AREN'T YOU?	YOU LOST THE GAME,	DIDN'T YOU?	YOU PASSED,	DIDN'T YOU?
PISS OFF,	WILL YOU?	NOBODY CAME,	DID THEY?	NOBODY RANG,	DID THEY?

Cards (3)

I'M LATE,	AREN'T I?	YOU DIVORCED HIM,	DIDN'T YOU?	AREN'T YOU?	AREN'T I?
DO YOU?	AREN'T YOU?	YOU'RE NICE,	AREN'T YOU?	YOU'VE FELT HOMESICK,	HAVEN'T YOU?
HAVEN'T YOU?	HAVE YOU?	WILL YOU?	DID THEY?	YOU HAVEN'T SLEPT WITH MY HUSBAND,	HAVE YOU?
YOU'RE LATE,	AREN'T YOU?	YOU'VE BEEN HERE A MONTH,	HAVEN'T YOU?	YOU'RE NOT SWISS,	ARE YOU?

I.6 Snakes and ladders

GRAMMAR: Present perfect + for/since
LEVEL: Intermediate
TIME: 30–40 minutes
MATERIALS: One **board** per four students
One die per four students

In class

1 Divide the class into fours and give each group a board and a die. Ask the students to sit so they can all see the board properly:

Ask each student to choose a coin to represent him or herself and to place the coin on START.

2 Explain that the aim of the game is to get from START to FINISH. Some of the sentences on the board are correct and some are incorrect. Explain/ demonstrate how you play:

a) The first player throws the die and advances to the square indicated. If there is a sentence on that square the player says whether it is correct or incorrect and, in the latter case, tries to correct it.
The other three students act as jury and have to decide if the player is right or wrong in his or her judgement. If all three, or two out of three, agree with the player, then he or she *goes forward three squares*. If they disagree with the player, the player *moves back three squares*. If the player lands on an empty square then none of the above happens and he or she stays there. It is then the next person's turn.
A player who lands on a square at the foot of a ladder must go *up* it. A player who lands on the mouth of a snake must go *down* it.

b) The winner is the first person whose score takes him or her to or beyond FINISH.

c) If a player lands on a sentence that has already been discussed, he or she automatically goes on to the next *unworked-on* sentence.

d) If a person in the group feels that the others are wrong about a grammar point, he or she should note down the number of its square and ask the teacher at the end of the game.

3 Ask the groups to start playing. At first your time will be taken up with answering queries about how to play. Once they settle down to play watch carefully for situations where both the player and the others in the group *agree* on a *wrong* verdict. Don't say anything to them and don't interrupt the game but make a note for after the game. Students will certainly ask your advice when they can't agree on a given sentence. Tell them you will deal with the point *after* the game. Ask them to play on according to the rules. It is vital that you *withhold your knowledge* during the game or you will kill it. The real pleasure and value of the game lies in the students realising and defending their own grammar criteria.

4 When most groups have finished, stop everybody and ask if there are disagreements over any of the sentences. If a student in Group A comes up with a disagreement do *not* give him or her an authoritative answer. Refer the problem to the other groups – very often they will give Group A the answer – only give the answer yourself as a last resort. This way the students teach each other.

This is also the time to bring up any sentences where everybody in a group was wrong.

Variation 1

Give pairs of students a blank board and invite them to choose 16 bits of grammar they find hard and to write 16 sentences round these structure areas, half of them correct and half incorrect. Ask them to write their sentences onto the board, leaving every second square blank. They can then add *a few* snakes and ladders. Go round helping the students.

In later classes, students play each other's games.

Variation 2

Don't mark the students' homework. Just read through it carefully and pick out 16 mistaken sentences, choosing the mistakes you want the whole group to focus on. Turn 8 of the 16 sentences into correct equivalents. Mix up the correct and incorrect sentences and fit them onto the board. Copy the resultant board so that there will be one copy per four students.

29

Don't give back the homework – ask them to play the game. In the usual way go through any doubts after the game is over. Then give back the unmarked homework and ask them to read it through. This way they find their mistakes, or some of them, for themselves. The second board, on page 32, is an example of a lower-intermediate class's homework mistakes transposed to a 'Snakes and ladders' board.

Grammar note for board on p.31

6 is correct, though many students are unhappy about the *for* in final position.
8 is correct *and* clearly refers to the future.
24 is correct and refers to the future.

Acknowledgement

My thanks to Chris Sion, the editor of the Pilgrims *Recipe book for tired teachers*, 1980 (Addison Wesley, 1984) where the grammar 'Snakes and ladders' idea was first published, for his help with improving the rules.

Board – Present perfect + for/since (You need 1 per four students.)

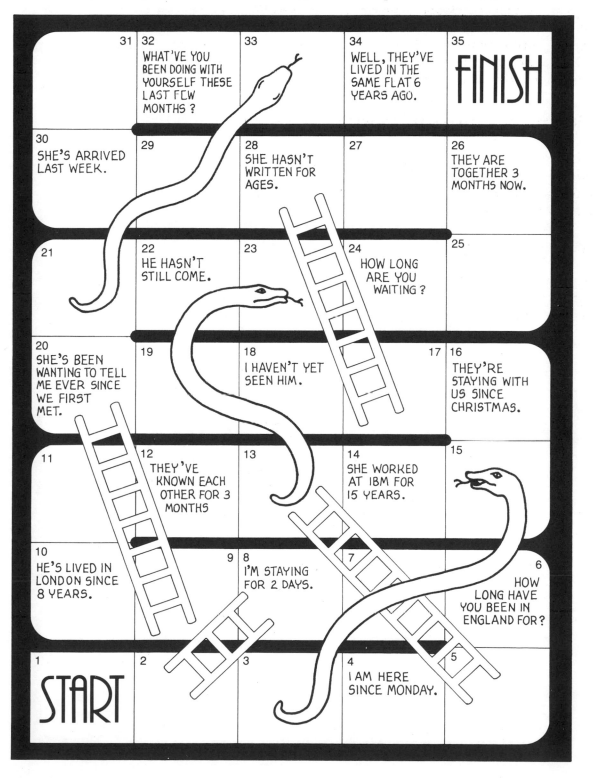

31

32 WHAT'VE YOU BEEN DOING WITH YOURSELF THESE LAST FEW MONTHS?

33

34 WELL, THEY'VE LIVED IN THE SAME FLAT 6 YEARS AGO.

35 FINISH

30 SHE'S ARRIVED LAST WEEK.

29

28 SHE HASN'T WRITTEN FOR AGES.

27

26 THEY ARE TOGETHER 3 MONTHS NOW.

21

22 HE HASN'T STILL COME.

23

24 HOW LONG ARE YOU WAITING?

25

20 SHE'S BEEN WANTING TO TELL ME EVER SINCE WE FIRST MET.

19

18 I HAVEN'T YET SEEN HIM.

17 16 THEY'RE STAYING WITH US SINCE CHRISTMAS.

11

12 THEY'VE KNOWN EACH OTHER FOR 3 MONTHS

13

14 SHE WORKED AT IBM FOR 15 YEARS.

15

10 HE'S LIVED IN LONDON SINCE 8 YEARS.

9 8 I'M STAYING FOR 2 DAYS.

7

6 HOW LONG HAVE YOU BEEN IN ENGLAND FOR?

1 START

2

3

4 I AM HERE SINCE MONDAY.

5

Board — Homework correction (You need 1 per four students.)

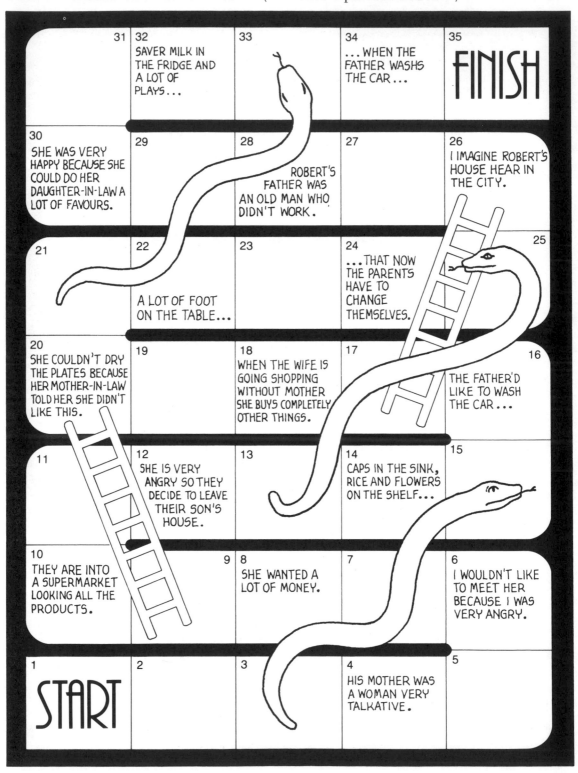

31	**32** SAVER MILK IN THE FRIDGE AND A LOT OF PLAYS...	**33**	**34** ...WHEN THE FATHER WASHS THE CAR...	**35** FINISH
30 SHE WAS VERY HAPPY BECAUSE SHE COULD DO HER DAUGHTER-IN-LAW A LOT OF FAVOURS.	**29**	**28** ROBERT'S FATHER WAS AN OLD MAN WHO DIDN'T WORK.	**27**	**26** I IMAGINE ROBERT'S HOUSE HEAR IN THE CITY.
21	**22** A LOT OF FOOT ON THE TABLE...	**23**	**24** ...THAT NOW THE PARENTS HAVE TO CHANGE THEMSELVES.	**25**
20 SHE COULDN'T DRY THE PLATES BECAUSE HER MOTHER-IN-LAW TOLD HER SHE DIDN'T LIKE THIS.	**19**	**18** WHEN THE WIFE IS GOING SHOPPING WITHOUT MOTHER SHE BUYS COMPLETELY OTHER THINGS.	**17**	**16** THE FATHER'D LIKE TO WASH THE CAR...
11	**12** SHE IS VERY ANGRY SO THEY DECIDE TO LEAVE THEIR SON'S HOUSE.	**13**	**14** CAPS IN THE SINK, RICE AND FLOWERS ON THE SHELF...	**15**
10 THEY ARE INTO A SUPERMARKET LOOKING ALL THE PRODUCTS.	**9** **8** SHE WANTED A LOT OF MONEY.		**7**	**6** I WOULDN'T LIKE TO MEET HER BECAUSE I WAS VERY ANGRY.
1 START	**2**	**3**	**4** HIS MOTHER WAS A WOMAN VERY TALKATIVE.	**5**

I.7 Double or quits

GRAMMAR:	Usage problems with like, pay, can, listen, want, be, born, die, etc.
LEVEL:	Intermediate
TIME:	20 minutes
MATERIALS:	A bag of coins: kopeks, dimes, centimes, yen, pennies or whatever is handy
	One **quiz sheet** (for your use only)

In class

1 Divide the students into between six and eight teams, groups of four if there are 28 people in the class, pairs if you have 14 students or less.

2 Explain that the teams are going to compete in an oral grammar quiz. The aim of each team is to get as much money as possible – shake your bag of coins!

3 Start the quiz by reading the first sentence from your quiz sheet – if this sentence is incorrect make sure you can read it convincingly; you must not give away by your tone of voice or look that it is incorrect. Pick a team and ask: 'correct or incorrect?' Give them time for a quick consultation (up to 20 seconds). If their answer is right, give them *two coins*.
If they think the sentence is incorrect and they are right say: 'Please correct the sentence.' If they do this successfully give them *five coins*.
Now offer them the chance of *double or quits* in the shape of another sentence. If they choose to *double* they risk losing the money already won – the prize money for the second sentence is the same as for the first, two coins and five coins. If they choose to *quit,* you move on and offer the second sentence to another team.
You may of course offer *double or quits* if a team has rightly said their first sentence is correct.
Do not offer *double or quits* again when a team has successfully got through their second question – turn to another team. Go round the teams in turn.

4 Work through the 16 sentences at a fast pace – enforce the 20 second rule by having a watch in front of you.

5 Work on any grammar points that people in the class were not happy with during the quiz.

Variation

You can make more quiz sheets by using errors that come up in students' written homework. Don't mark the homework. Lift out 16 mistaken sentences, re-write half of them correctly and mix them up with the uncorrected sentences, so you have a fully student-centred grammar quiz sheet. Do the quiz in the normal way. Then give back the unmarked homework and ask them to find each other's mistakes.

Acknowledgement

The format of this quiz is an adaptation of the format used in the British TV programme 'Mr and Mrs'.

Quiz sheet on verb usage

1   Do you like something to drink now?
2   Let me pay your dinner.
3   The general dead yesterday.
4   Would you like to come through, please?
5   I really like cycling in the rain.
6   We want you to feel at home here.
7   Are you born in 1965?
8   I can to help you, I think.
9   Did you listen the concert?
10 I like very much reading.
11 I am born in Cardiff.
12 They listened the radio.
13 We can probably do it for you.
14 She wants that you understand.
15 Did you pay the car in cash?
16 Would you like coming to the cinema?

I.8 Find who

GRAMMAR:	Past simple active/passive
LEVEL:	Lower-intermediate
TIME:	20 minutes
MATERIALS:	One **completion sheet** per student

In class

1 Go through any vocabulary from the completion sheet that the group may find hard.

2 Give each student a completion sheet. Tell them the object of the game is to find people in the group who had done to them or did the various things on the completion sheet. So student A might ask student B 'Were you conceived in December?' If B says 'yes', then A can write down B's name on his or her sheet next to:

.... was conceived in December

3 Tell the students that the winner is the person who gets *most names soonest*.

4 Get the students standing up and milling – encourage a cocktail party atmosphere with quick changes of partner – impose a fast rhythm by yourself darting round asking questions to fill in your own completion sheet. The game forces speed and the courage to be rude in the target language.

5 Finish the game off by putting the students in a circle and asking:
Who did you find who was conceived in December?
Who did you find who was born at home?
etc.

What structures can you use 'Find who' for?

I have successfully used it for practice of future tenses, present simple (habits), present perfect (achievements/failures), mixed tense practice and practice of the simple past of irregular verbs, e.g.:

Find a person who, when aged between 3 and 10...
> rode a bike
> bit his or her father
> broke his or her leg
> had mumps
> clung to his or her mother on the first day of school
> fought other children a lot
> slept in the afternoon, etc.

In constructing your own completion sheets round a given structure for a group you know, make sure that most of the sentences will have a person from the group attachable to them. Don't put in sentences that require no search at all, e.g. in the week after your national football cup final do not give a group of 14 year-old boys a completion like '...who has recently watched a football match'.
Avoid competitions that stress embarrassing socio-economic differences between students.

Acknowledgement

I was first taught this exercise by Jim Brims and later found it suggested in Gertrude Moskowitz's *Caring and sharing in the foreign language class* (Newbury House, 1978). Both Brims and Moskowitz propose the exercise principally as an ice-breaker – here I am suggesting it for rapid, speed practice of a given pattern.

Completion sheet: Past simple active and passive   (You need 1 per student.)

Name(s)   **Find a person who...**

.... was conceived in December

.... was born at home

.... was born in June

.... was breast-fed

.... liked carrots as a child

.... was looked after for three months by a grandmother or an aunt

.... was sent to kindergarten at the age of 2

.... was an only child

.... was sent to school at 5½

.... was forced to eat fish

.... was made to clean his/her teeth

.... had more than 15 cousins

.... was dressed-up for Sundays/feast days

.... was spanked for stealing apples/yams/grapes

.... disliked birthdays

.... was given a bike at the age of 6

.... was often made to stand in the corner

.... was caught smoking at 7

.... was sent away for holidays

I.9   Grammar tennis

GRAMMAR: Parts of irregular verbs
LEVEL: Post-beginner
TIME: 10 minutes
MATERIALS: None

In class

1 Bring two students out to the front of the class – they sit facing each other.
   You are by the board and have the role of umpire and secretary.

2 To start the game student A 'serves' by saying the *past participle* of an
   irregular verb he or she knows, e.g. hidden.
   If A gets the past participle wrong, e.g. hidded, you give him or her a
   second chance (like the second service in tennis). If A still gets the past
   participle wrong then B gets a point and you tell the players and the class
   what the correct form is, writing it up on the board.
   It is now B's turn to respond to the 'service' and give the *simple past* form
   of the same verb. B only gets one chance. If B is right then A has to give
   the *infinitive* of the same verb. If B is wrong then you give the correct form
   and write it up on the board, following which A gives the infinitive.

3 Now B serves, choosing a new irregular verb he or she knows. The
   'service' is always the past participle, etc.

4 The first person to get five points is the winner.

5 Repeat the process with a new pair. Keep the games short and snappy.
   Write up the parts of the verbs on the board as they are got right or as you
   have to correct them. Insist that the 'spectators' at the grammar tennis
   game refrain from helping the players.

Other language you can teach with this game

I have had students practising:

language / nationality / country
Turkish   Turk   Turkey

adjective / comparative / superlative
good   better   best

Acknowledgement

The game frame comes from *100 + ideas for drama*, Anna Scher and C. Verrall (Heinemann, 1975).

I.10   The best sentence

GRAMMAR: Phrasal verbs
LEVEL: Upper-intermediate to advanced
TIME: 30–40 minutes
MATERIALS: None

In first class

1 Divide the students into four groups.

2 Give each group four phrasal verbs e.g.:

Group A	*Group B*	*Group C*	*Group D*
put off	catch on	walk out on	draw up
bring about	come up with	put up with	get down to
hint at	cut down on	back up	face up to
put across	part with	enlarge on	turn out for

3 For homework ask each student to write one illustrative sentence to bring
   out clearly the meaning of each of the verbs allotted to his or her group.
   Tell the students that in the next class they will be voting, within their
   groups, on which sentences best illustrate the meanings of the four verbs.

In second class

1 Ask the students to sit in the same groups as in the first class.

2 Ask them to take the first verb allotted to their group: each person is to
   read out his or her sentence illustrating that verb. Within each group they
   then vote on which is the best sentence in terms of making clear the
   meaning of the verb. They do this for the other three verbs. At this stage
   there may be disagreements as some verbs have more than one possible
   meaning. Go from group to group correcting inadequate sentences.

3 Rearrange the students into new groups so that each has people from A,
   B, C, and D in it. Ask the students to teach each other their set of verbs
   using their own illustrative sentences and the one(s) judged best in their
   original group.

Other language you could teach with this game

Difference in meaning between remember to + infinitive/remember + ing. Similar differences with forget/regret/stop/go on.

Acknowledgement

Beverley Sedley taught this exercise in a seminar at the Department of Linguistics, Cambridge.

I.11   Dominoes

GRAMMAR: Word-building: prefixes and suffixes
LEVEL: Intermediate
TIME: 15–20 minutes
MATERIALS: One set of 56 **dominoes** per three to six students

---

Before class

Copy as many sets of dominoes as you have groups of three to six in your class.

In class

1 Put the students in circles of three to six round a flat surface. Give each group the two pages of dominoes and ask them to carefully fold and tear the pages to create dominoes. Ask someone in each group to shuffle them and deal them out. People should not show their dominoes to other players.

2 Player A in each group starts by laying down a domino. The player to his or her right then lays down a domino one end of which matches one end of A's domino. If the left side of A's domino is SANE and the next player lays down a domino with IN on its right side this is a correct match.

3 Play continues round the circle – if a player can't lay down a domino he or she misses that turn. The winner is the first person to get rid of most of his or her dominoes.

4 You should go from group to group and be available to help when people want to know if a particular match is correct. Give them immediate feedback.

5 Keep the domino sets in envelopes for later use with another group.

Acknowledgement

The domino set given here was devised and tested by Paul Davis. I had tried to use the domino frame for practising parts of irregular verbs but this had proved a mess. Paul discovered that the multiple matchings in word-building neatly fit the domino frame.

Dominoes (1) (You will need 1 set per three to six students.)

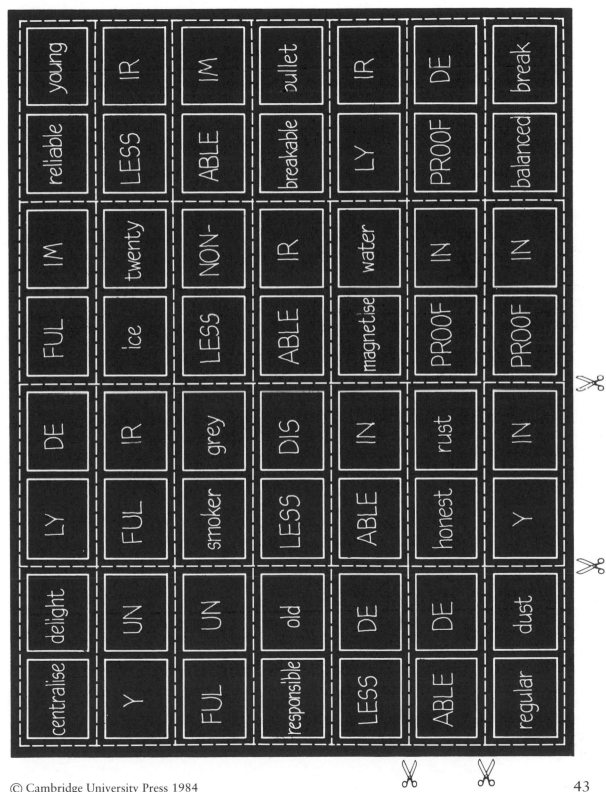

Dominoes (2)

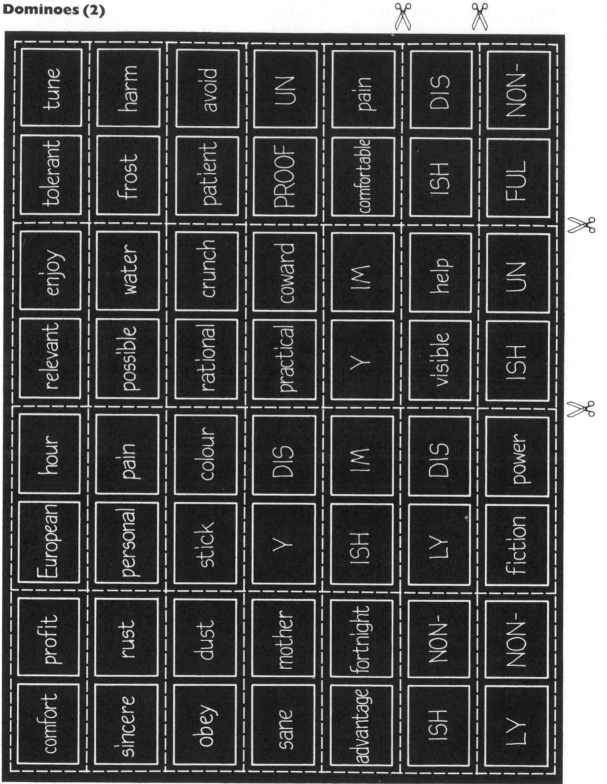

tune	harm	avoid	UN	pain	DIS	NON-
tolerant	frost	patient	PROOF	comfortable	ISH	FUL
enjoy	water	crunch	coward	IM	help	UN
relevant	possible	rational	practical	Y	visible	ISH
hour	pain	colour	DIS	IM	DIS	power
European	personal	stick	Y	ISH	LY	fiction
profit	rust	dust	mother	fortnight	NON-	NON-
comfort	sincere	obey	sane	advantage	ISH	LY

I.12   The money game

GRAMMAR: Peer correction of spontaneous speech
LEVEL: Post-beginner to advanced
TIME: 15–30 minutes
MATERIALS: 80–120 coins (10 each for one group of 8–12 students)
           One sheet of paper marked 'The speaker is right'
           One sheet of paper marked 'The challenger is right'

In class

1 Ask 8–12 students to form a central 'players' group round a flat surface,
  be it a table or the floor. Get the other students to space themselves round
  the ring of players so they can watch what's going on. (If the class is small,
  e.g. 10 students, there will be no spectators.)

2 Give each player 10 coins and lay down the two sheets of paper in the
  middle of the ring of players.

3 Explain the rules:
   a) Player A gives player B a topic to speak on e.g. 'houseplants'.
   b) B starts to speak on the topic. Anybody in the group who hears B
      make a *grammar mistake,* or who thinks he or she hears a grammar
      mistake can stop the speaker and say:
      'You said:"......................". It's wrong.'
      At this stage the challenger must *not* propose a correction.
   c) The members of the group vote by placing *one* coin on either 'The
      speaker is right' or 'The challenger is right' sheets. No fence-sitting!
   d) The teacher then gives his or her verdict. If the speaker is right he or
      she takes all the money from 'The speaker is right' sheet. If the
      challenger is right, he or she takes all the money from 'The challenger
      is right' sheet. The money from the other sheet is withdrawn from
      circulation by the teacher. This money is now out of the game.
   e) If the teacher declares the challenger right, the latter must attempt a
      correction. If this is right the challenger *takes* two coins from the
      speaker. If it is wrong the challenger *gives* the speaker two coins.
   f) Whether the challenge was right or wrong B goes on talking on his or
      her topic. After a second challenge B must stop talking and pick
      another student and another topic so the game can carry on.

g) The winner is the group member with most coins after an allotted time, say 15 mins.

Acknowledgement

This exercise owes something to the BBC radio programme 'Just a Minute'. For a full description of how this can be used for grammar work see *Learning English words,* J. Morgan and M. Rinvolucri (Oxford University Press, 1986). The exercise also owes a lot to a psychodrama exercise I learnt from Bernard Dufeu, University of Mainz.

I.13 Grammar monopoly

GRAMMAR: Past simple interrogative, conditionals, present tenses, present perfect
LEVEL: Intermediate
TIME: 30–40 minutes
MATERIALS: One **board** per four students
One die per four students
One **hotelier grammar sheet** per student (there are four grammar sheets)

In class

1 Divide the class into fours and give each group a board and a die.

2 To each group give out four hotelier grammar sheets, an *A* sheet, a *B* sheet, a *C* sheet and a *D* sheet. Each student takes one and becomes the owner of the corresponding hotels on the board. Tell the players to keep their sheets to themselves.

3 Ask the students to choose coins to represent themselves and place these on START.

4 Explain to the groups:
a) Each hotelier starts off with £10,000 marked in his or her *accounts box*. No 'money' is provided with the game so the player must keep a note of all transactions in his or her *accounts box*. A player may well find that he or she is noting down negative figures – a player may go into the red (i.e. may be in debt) to the tune of £10,000. If a player goes lower than minus £10,000, they are bankrupt and must leave the game.
b) The aim of the game is to get as much money as possible and to bankrupt the other players.
c) To start the game player X throws the die and moves his or her coin from START to the square indicated. If X lands on a blank nothing happens and the next player throws the die. If player X lands on one of his or her own hotels nothing happens.
If X lands on someone else's hotel, say a *present perfect hotel*, then the hotelier will read out one of the present perfect sentences to X. X has to say whether the sentence is correct or not. The hotelier then tells X if X's judgement was right or wrong. If X was right, he or she can stay at the hotel free of charge. If X was wrong, he or she must pay the hotelier the amount shown on the square.

⟫→

If X has rightly said the sentence is incorrect he or she *may* offer a correction. If the correction is accurate the hotelier must pay X half the sum shown on the square.

d) Every time a player passes START he or she receives £500.

You should circulate to help with the understanding of the rules. Since the hoteliers have the grammar information they need, you should keep out of arguments between guests and hoteliers over grammar points. The students can ask your advice over contentious points at the end of the game. This is an excellent diagnostic time for you to really find out what notions *they* have of the grammar.

Note

The *'ll* in Hotelier grammar sheet C's last sentence is not pure future but expresses intention.

Other language you can work on with this game

The hotelier grammar sheets can cover any area of grammar structure, usage, collocation, lexical appropriateness, etc. that you wish to include in them. The game can be used at any level from post-beginner to advanced. Psychologically the game stresses appropriating and *owning* the target language grammar.

Variation: Personalised grammar monopoly

Possibly the best use for the monopoly frame is to fill it with the students' own expressions, taken from homework they have done.

Board   (You will need 1 per four students.)

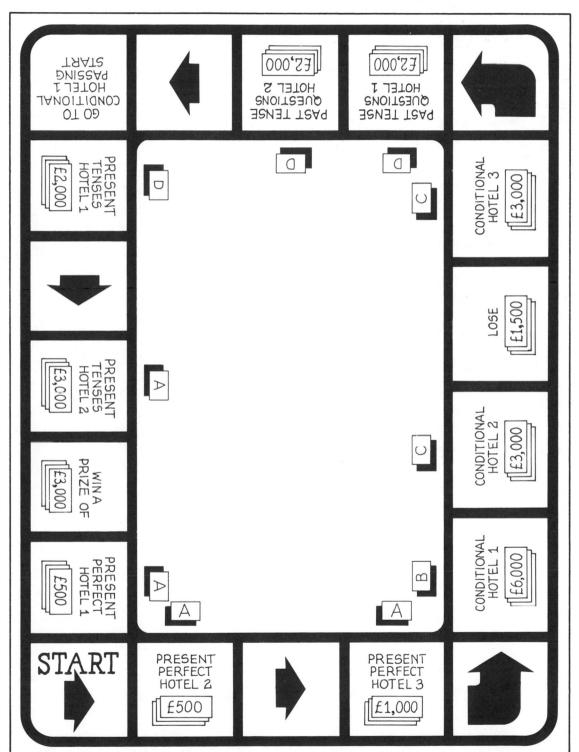

Hotelier grammar sheet *A* (You will need 1 per four students.)

Present Tenses Hotel 2

He's coming down the field, controlling the ball beautifully – now he shoots for goal!	CORRECT
Yes, true, I quite see your point of view.	CORRECT
What do you think about at this moment? *Should be:* **What are you thinking about...?**	WRONG
What do you think of the state of the Venezuelan economy?	CORRECT

Present Perfect Hotels 1, 2 and 3

I am here since Friday. *Should be:* **I have been here since Friday.**	WRONG
How long have you been learning Spanish?	CORRECT
She's been wearing black tights since 10 years. *Should be:* **...for 10 years.**	WRONG
I am a musician since I was five. *Should be:* **I've been a musician since...**	WRONG
I have lived in Rome last year. *Should be:* **I lived in Rome last year.**	WRONG
How long have you been waiting for me last night? *Should be:* **How long did you wait...**	WRONG
Since when are you knowing her? *Should be:* **Since when have you known her?**	WRONG
I've always loved Mozart.	CORRECT

ACCOUNTS BOX

+ £10,000

Hotelier grammar sheet *B*   (You will need 1 per four students.)

Conditional Hotel 1

Wouldn't he respond if you loved him?	CORRECT
I'd've come if you would have told me.	WRONG

Should be: **I'd've come if you'd/had told me.**

In a case like that, what'd you have done?	CORRECT
If he paid you the money, it's clear he's serious.	CORRECT
If it will rain, he won't come.	WRONG

Should be: **If it rains, he won't come.**

If I was you, I'd tell the truth.	CORRECT
Supposing he asks you, what'll you say?	CORRECT
If I were you, I'd tell the truth.	CORRECT
If it would rain, I'd take an umbrella.	WRONG

Should be: **If it rained, I'd take an umbrella.**

ACCOUNTS BOX

+ £10,000

Hotelier grammar sheet *C*   (You will need 1 per four students.)

Conditional Hotel 2

If you musted to join the army, how'd you feel?	WRONG
Should be: **If you had to join...**	
What'd you have done in her shoes?	CORRECT
If you'd let him know, he'd be here now.	CORRECT
Had she told you, would you have be angry?	WRONG
Should be: **... would you have *been* angry?**	

Conditional Hotel 3

Sorry, but if he comes, I go.	CORRECT
It would be better that we insure the luggage.	WRONG
Should be: **We'd (had) better insure the luggage.**	
What would have been done to him if he'd arrived late?	CORRECT
I won't go and see him, unless he'll give me an interview.	CORRECT

ACCOUNTS BOX

+ £10,000

Hotelier grammar sheet *D*   (You will need 1 per four students.)

Present Tenses Hotel 1

I hate my husband, he's always going on at me.	CORRECT
How does he earns his living? *Should be:* **How does he earn his living?**	WRONG
Are you believing in God? *Should be:* **Do you believe in God?**	WRONG
I am a Frenchman, I am coming from France. *Should be:* **I come from…**	WRONG
I live in London and I use to go to the park every day. *Should be:* **…and I go to the park every day.**	WRONG

Past Tense Questions Hotel 1

What wanted you to say? *Should be:* **What did you want to say?**	WRONG
What made them leave so fast?	CORRECT
Who gave these stupid orders?	CORRECT
Who *did* give these stupid orders?	CORRECT

Past Tense Questions Hotel 2

Did you were happy in your new job? *Should be:* **Were you happy…?**	WRONG.
Did you must get married to him? *Should be:* **Did you have to get…**	WRONG
Why didn't they dislike her?	CORRECT
He fell in the river; was he able to swim?	CORRECT

ACCOUNTS BOX

+ £10,000

I.14 Grammar draughts

GRAMMAR: Present simple, pronoun agreement
LEVEL: Post-beginner
TIME: 30–40 minutes
MATERIALS: One **draughts board** per two students
One **pronoun/noun sheet** per two students *(white)*
One **verb sheet** per two students *(black)*

In class

1 Pair the students and give each pair a draughts board, a pronoun/noun sheet and a verb sheet.
2 Ask the pairs to fold and tear the verb and pronoun/noun sheets so as to produce grammar draughts counters. (If you collect these in at the end of your class and store them in envelopes you will have them ready for future use.)
3 Tell the students to place the pronoun/noun counters on the black squares one side of the draughts board and the verb counters on the black squares the other side.
4 Now ask someone who knows the rules of draughts to explain them to the whole class.
5 Add this rule: a pronoun/noun counter may only take or 'eat' a verb counter or vice versa when there is grammatical agreement between them. So, for example, the *GOES* counter is in no way threatened

Verb sheet
(You will need 1 per two students.)

WONDER	STOP	BUY	REFUSE
WONDER	STOP	BUY	REFUSE
SELLS	WANT	DRINK	GOES
SELLS	WANT	DRINK	GOES
THINKS	LIVES	ASKS	HITS
THINKS	LIVES	ASKS	HITS

Pronoun/noun sheet
(You will need 1 per two students.)

JOHN	THE POLICE	THE MEN	YOU
JOHN	THE POLICE	THE MEN	YOU
WE	MY FRIEND	PEOPLE	I
WE	MY FRIEND	PEOPLE	I
THEY	SHE	HE	HER HUSBAND
THEY	SHE	HE	HER HUSBAND

by the *I* counter but would be in mortal danger from a *SHE* or *HE* counter.

6 Invite the students to start play. There may be some who don't know the rules of draughts – if this is the case have a couple of students who do moving round the room and helping.

7 If a verb reaches the pronoun/noun back line it becomes a Queen – get the student to simply mark Q on this counter. Ditto if a noun or pronoun counter reaches the verb back line.

8 Give immediate feedback if people ask you grammar questions during the game.

Draughts board (You will need 1 per two students.)

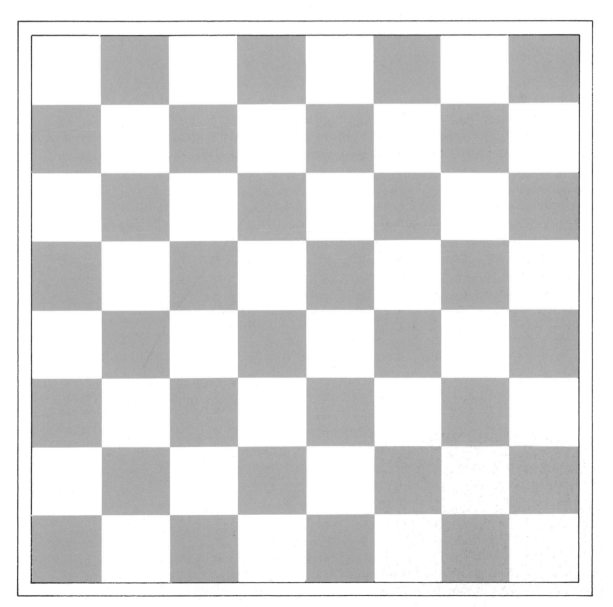

Section II Collaborative sentence-making games

II.1   Rub out and replace

GRAMMAR: 'First' and 'second'* conditionals
LEVEL: Lower-intermediate
TIME: 5–15 minutes
MATERIALS: None

In class

1 Ask someone to create a picture on the board of a man, a woman and a
   volcano. Be no more specific than that. Don't draw the picture yourself.

2 Ask a student secretary to write up this sentence (which presumes the
   class need practice on *if* sentences) in a speech balloon coming out of the
   mouth of the man or the woman:
   If the volcano goes on erupting, we'd really better move away.

3 From now on you, the teacher, can work completely *silently*. Rub out one
   of the words or phrases in the sentence and mime the need for a replacement word. As soon as a student volunteers one, write it in, *even if it
   doesn't fit*. Get the student to read the sentence with the new word in to
   see how it sounds to him or her. *Silently* enquire if (a) the volunteer, (b)
   the group is/are happy with the new word. If they are not, and they are
   right not to be, rub the new word out and get someone to volunteer
   another word. If everybody is happy with the word then rub out another
   word/phrase elsewhere in the sentence and so on. The aim is to end up
   with a completely new sentence. Through all this process you can enjoy
   your own silence which creates a vacuum for the students to fill; it will
   also afford you time to observe students in a way you can't if you are
   chatting away.

*Note**

You will notice that the terms 'first', 'second' and 'third' conditional are
always written in quotation marks in this book. This is because they are
misleading terms, resulting from pedagogically motivated simplification of

descriptive grammar. In real-life English native speakers use all kinds of conditional combinations which go way beyond the neat, mendacious packaging of the so-called three conditional patterns.
For example:

'If Giovanni Basta got through my road blocks last night, then we in the police force can only be called incompetent fools.'
(If + past simple, present simple)

'If you are going to persist in refusing medication, Mr Jones, then my first diagnosis was clearly spot on.'·
(If + going to, past simple)

'If I'd've known, I'd've told you.'
(If I would have + past participle, I would have)

'Had the Prime Minister known in time, we wouldn't be in this mess now.'
(Mixture of so-called third and so-called second conditional)

'If you decided to join the club, I'll certainly let you know all our fixtures.'
(Here the speaker is very doubtful about the likelihood of the addressee joining the club.)
(Mixture of so-called second with so-called first conditional)

For a descriptive grammar treatment of the conditional area see *A grammar of contemporary English*, R. Quirk et al (Longman, 1972). For exercise material on the reality of the conditional structures in English see *Well said*, J. Dixey and M. Rinvolucri (Pilgrims Publications, 1977).

One lower-intermediate group transformed this volcano sentence in the following stages (there were also some abortive replacements I have not included):

1   **run**
  If the volcano goes on erupting, we'd really better ~~move~~ away.

2   **maybe**   run
  If the volcano goes on erupting, we'd ~~really~~ better ~~move~~ away.

3   **boss**   maybe   run
  If the ~~volcano~~ goes on erupting, we'd ~~really~~ better ~~move~~ away.

4   boss   **under-paying** maybe   run
  If the ~~volcano~~ goes on ~~erupting~~, we'd ~~really~~ better ~~move~~ away.

5   boss   under-paying, **he'd** maybe   run
  If the ~~volcano~~ goes on ~~erupting, we'd~~   ~~really~~ better ~~move~~ away.   ⟫→

6   boss   **stops** under-paying, he'd maybe **hope to** run
   If the ~~volcano goes on erupting, we'd~~   ~~really better move~~ away.

7 **When**   boss stops under-paying, he'd   maybe hope to run
      If the ~~volcano goes on erupting, we'd really better move~~ away.

8 When   boss   stops under-paying, he'd maybe **make a profit.**
      ~~If the~~ ~~volcano goes on erupting, we'd~~   ~~really better move away~~.

9 When **a** boss stops under-paying, he'd   maybe hope to make a profit.
      ~~If the volcano goes on erupting, we'd really better move away.~~

Acknowledgement

I learnt this technique at Pilgrims in the summer of 1980 from John Pint, a strong Silent Way practitioner. I do not know if the technique originated with Gattegno.

II.2   Silent sentence

GRAMMAR: Past simple
LEVEL: Elementary to intermediate
TIME: 20 minutes
MATERIALS: None

In class

1) Ask a student to come to the board and draw a woman looking at a window ledge three storeys up – her son is crawling along the ledge.

2) Write up the following sentence:
   'Anne came down the stairs and crossed the courtyard when suddenly she looked up and saw her tiny son in his brown dungarees crawling along the kitchen window ledge: she was just in time to catch him when he fell.'

3) Tell the class they are going to reduce this sentence to one word. In any one go they may take out up to and including three consecutive words. They may not add words – they may not change any endings or re-arrange words. This is how the game works:
   a) Student A: Take out 'brown'.
   b) Teacher silently rubs out 'brown'.
   c) Student A reads the whole sentence aloud, minus 'brown'. As the sentence is correct the teacher silently invites another deletion.
   d) Student B: Take out 'kitchen window ledge'.
   e) The teacher *immediately* rubs out 'kitchen window ledge'. *The teacher makes no language judgement at this stage.*
   f) Student B tries to read the sentence without 'kitchen window ledge' and realises it isn't possible because of the trailing 'the'.
   g) The teacher silently writes 'kitchen window ledge' back into the sentence and invites other deletions.

It is vital in this exercise that you make no judgement about the rightness of a deletion before the deleting student has had a chance to read the sentence aloud to check their own language feeling. Obey the deleting student, however wrong they may be. If, after reading, they fail to realise the deletion is wrong then you should silently ask the opinion of the rest of the class. If the class fails to see the problem all you have to do is to write the deleted part back into the sentence.

This is *not* a precis exercise. As the students reduce the sentence further and further the meaning often changes quite radically. The students may at first be surprised at this, feeling it must be a form of precis exercise.

4 Once the students have reduced the sentence to one word, reverse the deletion process and tell them they are going to build a sentence by adding up to and including three words consecutively. The students may want to try and re-find the original sentence, or they may want to invent a quite new one. Up to them. Each addition must leave a grammatically correct and meaningful sentence, though the meaning will change with new additions.

Note

Given the sentence proposed above the students will do a lot of work on the past tense forms of the verbs *come, cross, look, see, be* and *fall* as they work on the reduction. During the expansion phase in step 4 they will almost certainly also work on the past tense forms of other verbs they feel they need. This much can be predicted from the 'mother sentence' the teacher provides. But much of the most important grammar work provoked by this technique is unpredictable and depends on the sequence of deletions the students actually propose. This unpredictability keeps both teacher and students on their toes and makes this one of the most beautiful exercises I know.

Acknowledgement

I learnt the reduction idea from teachers steeped in the Silent Way tradition. The re-expansion comes from Piagetian thinking. A complete example of a sentence reduction process, mapped step by step, comes on pages 98–101 of *Once upon a time,* J. Morgan and M Rinvolucri (Cambridge University Press, 1983).

II.3　The Marienbad game

GRAMMAR:	Present simple, 'first' conditional
LEVEL:	Post-beginner to lower-intermediate
TIME:	10–15 minutes
MATERIALS:	None

In class

1　Write this text up on the board as it is printed here, in four separate lines:

> Darling
> I love you so much
> You must never leave me
> If you go, I fear I will kill myself.

2　Divide the class into two teams. Tell them they are going to reduce the 'poem' on the board. Team A starts and may take out a whole line or any number of words within a line. After they have told you what to rub out get someone in team A to read out what's left. It must still be grammatically correct in English; it must also have a meaning, but the meaning will change. If team A tells you to rub out something that cannot be rubbed out, do as you are asked. At the reading stage they will realise that it is an impossible deletion. If they don't, ask team B what they think. Only impose your own criteria in the last resort. Team B now proposes a further deletion of a whole line or any number of words within one line. The aim of the game is to force the other team to take the *last word*.

3　The first time you play, the students are really just getting the hang of the rules; now play the game again with this extract from a poem by Adrian Mitchell:

> When a man's too ill or old to work
> We punish him.
> Half his income is taken away
> Or all of it vanishes and he gets pocket-money.

Note

I first saw this game played in a film called 'L'Année Dernière à Marienbad'. In the film it was played with matchsticks, which unlike words, have no grammatical or syntactic restrictions on them. The main grammatical work done by the students is when they realise they cannot take out this or that word or group of words.

The students may be interested to hear the whole of the poem by Adrian Mitchell. (For copyright reasons this may not be photocopied.)

OLD AGE REPORT

When a man's too ill or old to work
We punish him.
Half his income is taken away
Or all of it vanishes and he gets pocket-money.

We should reward these tough old humans for surviving,
Not with a manager's soggy handshake
Or a medal shaped like an alarm clock –
No, make them a bit rich,
Give the freedom they always heard about
When the bloody chips were down
And the blitz or the desert
Swallowed their friends.

Retire, retire into a fungus basement
Where nothing moves except the draught
And the light and dark grey figures
Doubling their money on the screen;
Where the cabbages taste like the mummy's hand
And the meat tastes of feet;
Where there is nothing to say except:
'Remember?' or 'Your turn to dust the cat'.

To hell with retiring. Let them advance.
Give them the money they've always earned
Or more – and let them choose.
If Mr Burley wants to be a miser,
Great, let the moneybags sway and clink for him,
Pay him a pillowful of best doubloons.
So Mrs Wells has always longed to travel?
Print her a season ticket to the universe,
Let her slum-white skin
Be tanned by a dozen different planets.
We could wipe away some of their worry,
Some of their pain – what I mean
Is so bloody simple:
The old people are being robbed
And punished and we ought
To be letting them out of their cages
Into green spaces of enchanting light.

II.4 Expand

GRAMMAR: Word order
LEVEL: Beginners
TIME: 5–30 minutes
MATERIALS: None

In class

1 Ask a student to draw Eve, Adam, the Tree and the Apple on the board.

2 Write a minimal sentence about the picture like this:

SHE   GIVES   HIM   AN   APPLE

Tell the students you want them to add one word where you indicate:

SHE   GIVES   HIM   AN   ∧   APPLE

Write in whatever word a student volunteers and then have him or her read the new sentence. You should stay completely *silent*. If the word proposed is wrong, mime-ask the other students what they think. In the final resort you disallow the word by rubbing it out again.
Continue this process putting in 'carets' (∧) *everywhere*, even in places you know no word will fit – it is important for students to discover where they *can't* put words as well as where they can.

One beginner group transformed the sentence above in the following stages; I have included unsuccessful proposals, as much of the learning lies in these:

	SHE	GIVES	HIM	AN		∧	APPLE.
	SHE	GIVES	HIM	AN		RED	APPLE.
	SHE	GIVES	HIM	AN	∧		APPLE.
	SHE	GIVES	HIM	AN	OLD		APPLE.
	SHE	GIVES	HIM	AN	OLD	∧	APPLE.
	SHE	GIVES	HIM	AN	OLD	RED	APPLE.
∧	SHE	GIVES	HIM	AN	OLD	RED	APPLE.
IS	SHE	GIVES	HIM	AN	OLD	RED	APPLE?
∧	SHE	GIVES	HIM	AN	OLD	RED	APPLE.
YES,	SHE	GIVES	HIM	AN	OLD	RED	APPLE.
YES,	SHE	GIVES ∧	HIM	AN	OLD	RED	APPLE.
YES,	SHE	GIVES TO	HIM	AN	OLD	RED	APPLE.
YES,	SHE ∧	GIVES	HIM	AN	OLD	RED	APPLE.
YES,	SHE **ALWAYS**	GIVES	HIM	AN	OLD	RED	APPLE.

Variation 1

At higher levels than beginners, you can ask the students to add *one word*, or *two words together* in the space you indicate. You can ban *one word* and *two words together*, and only allow phrases with *three words together*. Each of these changes of rule dramatically alters the type of sentence produced.

Variation 2

In the exercise described above you retain very strict control. A livelier expansion activity is as follows:

1 Give the students a minimal sentence *orally*.
2 Tell them they can add *two words together* anywhere in the sentence they want by simply repeating the sentence with their words in. It goes like this:

Teacher: 'Sports cars are expensive.'
Student A: 'Sports cars are *really very* expensive.'
Student B: '*Our pink* sports cars are really very expensive.'
            etc.

Make sure that each student faithfully reproduces the sentence handed on by the last student as well as adding his or her new words.
Disallow impossible additions. Do this silently – you talking stops them talking.

Acknowledgement

I learnt the above exercises, which come from the Silent Way tradition, from Lou Spaventa.

II.5   Contract and expand

GRAMMAR: 'First' conditional
LEVEL: Intermediate
TIME: 10–20 minutes
MATERIALS: None

In class

1 Ask a student to draw on the board a Japanese girl in a kimono looking questioning by the side of a lake.

2 In a speech bubble, coming from her mouth, write:

I wonder what I'll do if he doesn't come to see me by this strange lake tonight.

3 Tell the students the aim of the exercise is to transform the sentence completely. To do this they may take out either *one word* or *two words together,* but each time they must replace them with *a phrase of three words.*
   When the first student suggests a deletion and addition, rub out the word or two words, and add in the three words proposed. Ask the volunteer student to read the new sentence to see whether it works for him or her and the group. You don't need to speak at all – if the students can't make up their minds about a substitution, and if it is wrong, all you have to do is rub out the three words and put back the original one or two. When a student proposes something that is wrong, avoid commenting with your face and body – you can be silent and still very unneutral.

One intermediate class transformed the above sentence through the following stages. Wrong sentences have been omitted.

I *really don't know* what I'll do if he doesn't come to see me by this strange lake tonight.

I really don't know what I'll do if he doesn't come to see me by this strange *sea of tears* tonight.

I really don't know what I'll do if he doesn't come to see me by this strange sea of tears *some enchanted evening.*

I really don't know what I'll do if he doesn't come to see me by this *marvellous and incredible* sea of tears some enchanted evening.

I really don't know what I'll do if he doesn't come and see me *close to that* marvellous and incredible sea of tears some enchanted evening.

I really don't know what I'll do if he doesn't come to *die in agony* close to that marvellous and incredible sea of tears some enchanted evening.

I really don't know *just how well* I'll do if he doesn't come to die in agony close to that marvellous and incredible sea of tears some enchanted evening.

I really don't know just how well I'll do if he *isn't actually able* to die in agony close to that marvellous and incredible sea of tears some enchanted evening.

I really don't know just how well *my old grandfather*'ll do if he isn't actually able to die in agony close to that marvellous and incredible sea of tears some enchanted evening.

I really don't know just how well my old grandfather'll *get to heaven* if he isn't actually able to die in agony close to that marvellous and incredible sea of tears some enchanted evening.

Some of us really don't know just how well my old grandfather'll get to heaven if he isn't actually able to die in agony close to that marvellous and incredible sea of tears some enchanted evening.

Some of us really don't know just how well my old grandfather'll get to heaven, *though his wife* isn't actually able to die in agony close to that marvellous and incredible sea of tears some enchanted evening.

II.6　Sentence collage

GRAMMAR:　Let/have something done
LEVEL:　　　Lower-intermediate
TIME:　　　5–15 minutes
MATERIALS: Strips of paper and Blu-Tack

Before class

Take a sentence with the structure you want to work on built into it, e.g.

Listen mum, if you let me have my hair cut the way I want, I'll have it done by your hairdresser.

Copy each word of the sentence onto separate strips of paper, using a felt pen and writing in capitals. Put a blob of Blu-Tack on the back of each strip of paper.
You will need a set of the words that make the sentence for every five to seven students in your class.

In class

1　Ask a 'Picasso' from the class to draw a picture of a girl of 13 talking seriously to her mother.

2　Split the class into groups of five to seven – have one group at the blackboard and the other groups round the walls of the classroom.
Give each group a set of the words in the sentence (shuffled), two to four words to each student, and ask them to find *a* sentence into which *all* the words fit grammatically and intelligibly.

3　Do not interfere or help – let the students argue among themselves where the words should go. They may well end up with sentences that are different from your original one, which is fine.

The sentence above might well turn out:

Listen hairdresser, if you let me have my hair done the way I want, I'll have it done by your mum.

or:

Listen mum, if you let me have my hair cut, I'll have it done by your hair-dresser the way I want.

or:

I'll listen: mum, if you let me have my hair cut by your hairdresser, have it done the way I want.

Sentence collage is quite a neat form of initial presentation of a new structure. The work of creating the collage focuses everybody's attention very powerfully.

Variation

Once students get used to sentence collages you can give them word sets with certain key words left out, say three in a sentence set of 20 words. In place of the three missing words you give the students three blank slips of paper. They decide what the words should be.

II.7   Your words – my grammar

GRAMMAR: Present perfect continuous
LEVEL: Lower-intermediate
TIME: 15–20 minutes
MATERIALS: None

In class

1 Write a sentence in the target structure on the board, e.g.

Who's | *been* | eating my porridge?

Explain to the students that you want them to write sentences that have exactly the same grammar as the above sentence, but all the words apart from the one in the box, *been,* must be different and must be their own words. So the first word must be an interrogative pronoun, the second an auxiliary verb, the third no change, the fourth a main verb + ing, etc. From the above sentence students produce sentences like:

What's been killing her flowers?

Which ones have been chasing our cat?

2 Ask the students to write their sentences on the board – do not correct their sentences before they get them up on the board. Now ask the class to decide which sentences are right and which wrong – allow the students as much room as possible in this discussion.

The first time you do this exercise with a class there may be some confusion in the students' minds as to what exactly you are after. It is therefore important to start with a short, simple sentence.

Acknowledgement

I learnt this exercise from the Silent Way tradition in the person of Lou Spaventa.

II.8 Give a meaning

GRAMMAR: Varied structures
LEVEL: Lower-intermediate
TIME: 5–15 minutes
MATERIALS: None

In class

1 Write on the board:

I am a hotel.

Tell the students they can change the meaning of the sentence by *adding one word only*. Write up their suggestions. One class gave me the following:

I am not a hotel.
I am a hotel manager.
I am a hotel porter.
I am a hotel failure.
I am never a hotel.
I am running a hotel.
Only *I* am a hotel!
I am selling a hotel.
I am a hotel receptionist.

2 Now give them the sentence:

He told the dustbin.

Tell the students they can add *two words*, either separately or together. Ask them to work on their own and write as many different sentences as they can. Do *not* correct them as they write.

3 Get the students to write up some of their sentences on the board and to decide as a class which are right and which wrong. You should obviously allow sentences like:

He told Mary the dustbin story.

as here the students have realised that *tell* often takes an animate object.

⫸→

You should also allow sentences like:

He told the dustbin bedtime stories.

as long as everybody understands that here the dustbin is being thought of as animate.

Clearly, depending on your grammatical aims, you will vary the rule of how many words are to be added.

Acknowledgement

This exercise was invented by John Morgan when he was presented with the expansion and contraction techniques described in II.2, II.3 and II.4.

II.9   My sentences – your paragraph

GRAMMAR: Linking words
LEVEL: Intermediate
TIME: 20–30 minutes
MATERIALS: None

In class

1 Ask the class to tell you all the linking words they know. You might start them off by suggesting *and, but*. Build up a list on the board. There will be some you will have to explain/translate for people who do not know them, or are not sure they know them.

2 Write up on the board five open, general sentences around a theme, e.g.

Teenagers have never been pensioners.

In old age you may want to be close to your relatives.

I don't like thinking about ageing.

Some young people feel guilty about old people.

At times old people want to be independent.

Ask the students to work on their own and put the above sentences in any order they want, linking them into a two or three sentence paragraph. They may add linking words and further linking clauses or sentences to make a full paragraph. While this is going on, go round and help students who are getting linking words wrong.

3 Ask the students to stick their paragraphs up on the walls of the classroom; they then go round and read each other's.

Acknowledgement

I learnt this technique from Lou Spaventa. An excellent source of suitable 'empty', 'open' sentences round a theme is Caleb Gattegno's *1000 sentences* (Educational Solutions, New York, 1974).

II.10   Complete cloze

GRAMMAR: Could be, must be, might equally well be
LEVEL: Intermediate
TIME: 20 minutes
MATERIALS: A large piece of cardboard or an overhead transparency
             Masking cards
             One copy of the **picture** per two students.

Preparation

If you have no overhead projector write the sentence you want the students to work with in large letters on the piece of cardboard. Number the words. Over each word stick a masking card and number it. At the bottom of the masking card write the word it covers in very small letters which you will be able to read but which the students won't.

If any words occur more than once in the sentence, mark the numbers of the re-occurrences on the first masking card. In the sentence which follows, *a* occurs five times so the masking card covering the first occurrence of *a* will look like this:

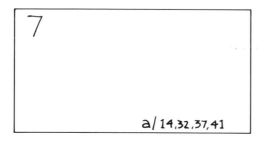

These numbers allow you to quickly find the other four occurrences of *a* later in the sentence. The first few words of your masked sentence should look like this:

If you have an overhead projector write your sentence on a transparency and prepare masking cards as above.

Picture   (You will need 1 per two students.)

In class

1 Give out the picture without comment.
2 Project or put up the masked sentence and tell them it refers to the picture.
   Explain that they will 'discover' the sentence by guessing each masked
   word. Tell them they can work on whichever word they like by simply
   referring to its number. Also tell them that each time they hit on a word
   that occurs more than once in the sentence you will uncover all the
   instances of the word.
3 If you are working with the sentence on card, stand *with your back to the
   class* and keep looking up at the masked sentence. Try to react to class's
   guesses as fast and *neutrally* as possible.

The complete cloze sentence

1   2   3   4   5   6 7   8   9   10   11
IT SEEMS LIKE THIS MUST BE A TRICK PICTURE: IT COULD

 12   13 14   15   16   17   18   19   20   21
EITHER BE A NAKED WOMAN SITTING WITH HER LEG BENT

 22   23 24   25   26   27   28   29   30   31 32
ROUND OR IT MIGHT EQUALLY WELL BE THE FACE OF A

33   34   35   36 37 38   39   40 41   42
FAT, MIDDLE-AGED MAN WITH A BIG NOSE AND A LOPSIDED

   43
MOUTH

Note

The complete cloze is an excellent exercise for introducing a new structure or set of structures to a class.

Acknowledgement

I first met the complete cloze idea in Graham Davies and Christoper Jones's micro-computer programme *Storyboard* (Wida Software, 1982), based on ideas by John Higgins. There is certainly an added attraction in doing the exercise on the little screen with green letters but the method set out above allows you to do essentially the same thing but without having to spend around £3,000 to get a class of 30 students round six micro-computers. Complete cloze is one of several exercises that can be reclaimed from the computer by the blackboard-only teacher.

II.11   Cloze dictogloss

GRAMMAR: Present simple/past simple
LEVEL: Intermediate
TIME: 20 minutes
MATERIALS: One copy of the **poem** per student
           One **verbs in the poem** per two students
           One **nouns and pronouns in the poem** per two students
           One **other words in the poem** per two students

In class

1 Tell the students that you are going to read them a short poem. Ask them to note down all the key words they catch as they listen. After the reading their task will be to re-construct the poem as closely and accurately as possible. Tell the students you will read them the poem *once only*.

2 Allow a couple of minutes for the writing down of key words following the reading.
   Then offer the students either all the verbs in the poem, all the nouns and pronouns in the poem or all the other words in the poem. Have all the people who choose verbs sit together, etc. Give out the cloze version chosen.

3 When you do 'Cloze dictogloss' for the first time, break the rule on reading the text once only, as students never realise how closely they *must* listen in the exercise until they have experienced the blankness of not having listened well. So give them a second reading, with the cloze version they have chosen in front of them.

4 Give time for the students to 'marry' the key words they have written with the cloze version chosen. Many more words will come to mind in doing this.

5 Allow people from the three different groups to work together in pairs or threes. In this way they fill out their texts further.

6 Have a student come to the board and write out a complete version, with the help of the class.

7 Give everybody a copy of the poem.

Note

The cloze dictogloss technique can be applied to any short passage. For useful grammar work it is sensible to choose an authentic piece of writing that happens to be loaded with the structure you are after and poems are especially useful as their structure loading is often backed by the full weight of the message, as with the contrast between present and past in 'Walking Tall'.

Acknowledgement

Teachers at Pilgrims were taught the dictogloss idea in 1980 by Jane Lockwood, who had learnt it in her work in Australia. The idea was mentioned in a 1963 edition of *ELTJ*. A further use of dictogloss is suggested in *Once upon a time,* J. Morgan and M. Rinvolucri (Cambridge University Press, 1983).

Poem   (You will need 1 per student.)

Walking Tall

Whenever I see
A new block go up,
I think of us as kids,
Impatient to grow;
How slow it seemed at first,
The others so far ahead,
Above –
Almost out of sight.
(Would we ever reach your height)
Then, overnight,
There we were
Up there among the best of them,
And there we remain –
Stuck on the top
Of our separate buildings.

Alan Maley

© Cambridge University Press 1984

Verbs in the poem   (You will need 1 per two students.)

Walking Tall

see
go up,
think of   ,
to grow;
seemed   ,

–

.

(Would   reach   )
,   ,
were

remain –

Stuck

Nouns and pronouns in the poem   (You will need 1 per two students.)

Walking Tall

```
            I
         block        ,
I          us    kids,
                   ;
            it                  ,
      others                ,
         –
               sight.
   (      we          your height)
      ,         ,
        we
                              them,
         we          –
               top
    our          buildings.
```

Other words in the poem   (You will need 1 per two students.)

Walking Tall

```
Whenever
A new              ,
            as     ,
Impatient        ;
How slow          at first,
         so far ahead,
Above –
Almost out of      .
(        ever                  )
Then, overnight,
There
Up there among the best of     ,
And there          –
        on the
Of     separate            .
```

II.12　Present perfect poem

GRAMMAR:　Present perfect simple
LEVEL:　Elementary to intermediate
TIME:　20–30 minutes
MATERIALS:　None

In class

1　Give the students this list of words (on the board, dictated, etc.):

we/us/our
see/saw/seen
have/has
work/s/ed
face/s/d
enemy/ies
and
the
of
to
it
the
to
an

2　Tell them to write as many different sentences as they can, working in pairs and using *only* the words given above. Their sentences can include some of the words given or all of them.
3　Put the pairs together in fours to read their sentences to each other.
4　Put the fours together in eights.
5　Read the Arthur Truscott poem to the students or write it on the board.

The beauty of this exercise is that the group partially writes Thurston's poem by following the same restrictions as he imposed on himself. The reading of the poem comes as a big boost to a group of non-native learners.

Acknowledgement

Alan Maley's work from *La litterature potentielle* by Oulipo (Gallimard, 1973) set me thinking in the direction of the above exercise.

Poem   (For copyright reasons this may not be photocopied.)

COLLECTED SPEECHES OF P. ARTHUR TRUSCOTT
TRAVELLING BY RAIL
BETWEEN VLADIVOSTOK AND GRAND RAPID FALLS

We have seen the face of the enemy and it works.
We have worked to see the face of the enemy.
We have enemy work to be seen and faced.
We have faced the enemy work and seen.
We have to face the enemy and work.
We have to face the enemy to see.
We and the enemy have to face.
We face the enemy to have work.
We work to have an enemy to face.
We have to have an enemy to face work.
We have faced the enemy work and it's a have.
We have faced the work of HAVE and it's the enemy.
We have the face of the enemy.
Have the enemy – will face work.

Robin Thurston

II.13   From pattern sentence to poem

GRAMMAR: Revision of structures recently learnt
LEVEL: All levels except beginners
TIME: 30 minutes
MATERIALS: None

Preparation

Choose six representative pattern sentences from the textbook you are using
– try and choose the ones that are most suggestive. In testing we used the
following taken from the textbook being used (Robert O'Neill's *Kernel
lessons plus*, Longman, 1973):

We've been doing this for years.
Her friend told her what to do.
It's getting harder and harder.
I haven't broken it, have I?
If I told my fiancé, he'd be angry.
It's supposed to give satisfaction.

In class

1 Dictate or write up on the board the six pattern sentences you have
   chosen.
2 Tell the class you want them to write a poem, a letter, a story or a
   dialogue in which they use at least three of the given sentences. They may
   incorporate the sentences into longer ones but the pattern sentences must
   not be internally altered. They can work individually or in pairs.
3 Have the students stick their writing up round the walls and go and read
   each other's.

Acknowledgement

La litterature potentielle by Oulipo (Gallimard, 1973), offered me the
original idea that you could create a poem out of sentences as bizarre as
pattern ones. John Morgan then told me that he has frequently used this
technique in his classes.

II.14   With your back to the class

GRAMMAR: Interrogatives: present simple, past simple, past continuous
LEVEL: Elementary to intermediate
TIME: 20 minutes
MATERIALS: None

In class

1 Write three words at the top of the Board e.g. *explosion, manager, roof.*
   Tell the students these are three key words in a story you have in your
   head. They are to ask YES/NO questions to try and discover what
   happened in the story. They are to come up and *write* these questions on
   the board, as the exercise is going to be entirely silent.
2 Sit with *your back to the class.* Explain that as soon as a student has
   written a question on the board you will give a THUMBS UP signal if it is
   grammatically correct and a THUMBS DOWN signal if it is wrong. If the
   signal is THUMBS DOWN then the writer of the question and the class
   have to try and correct the mistake.
   Once the sentence on the board is correct, you will either nod your head
   vigorously to indicate YES to the question, or shake it from side to side to
   indicate NO to the question.
3 During the silent, written questioning you may want to give the class
   another clue – write an extra key word on the board.

The story

The manager of a Sports Centre woke up one morning to find there had
been a very heavy fall of snow. He realised that the flat roof of the Centre
was in danger of collapsing.
He got on the roof to shovel off some of the snow. His extra weight made
the roof cave in causing the air inside the hall to compress and blow the
doors out, hence the explosion.

Note

When you first do this exercise with students they are somewhat shocked at
working only with your back. They soon get used to it, though, and your
back allows you to be much more neutral than you would otherwise be. You
interfere less with their learning process.

This is a fiercely grammatically focused exercise and initial interest in the story soon shifts to getting the questions correct.

Acknowledgement

This exercise derives from a marriage of Gattegno's Silent Way with the idea of puzzle stories. For other uses of puzzle stories, see *Once upon a time*, J. Morgan and M. Rinvolucri (Cambridge University Press, 1983) and *Challenge to think*, C. Frank, M. Rinvolucri and M. Berer (Oxford University Press, 1982).

II.15   Correcting homework

GRAMMAR: Mistakes from homework
LEVEL: All levels above beginners
TIME: 30–40 minutes
MATERIALS: One **team A worksheet** per two or three students
             One **team B worksheet** per two or three students
             A large piece of card per six to eight students

Preparation

Select 12 representative mistakes from your students' homework. Put half of them on the team A worksheet and half on the team B worksheet. Write correct versions of the mistakes on team A's worksheet onto the team B worksheet and vice-versa. Wrong sentences and corrected sentences should be mixed together on each worksheet. Do not mark the students' homework.

In class

1 Do not give back the students' homework yet. Divide the class up into groups of six to eight. Split each group up into an A team and a B team. Give out the appropriate worksheets and ask the students to work in their A or B teams deciding which sentences are correct and which wrong. Tell the A and B teams to work quite separately.

2 During this phase your task is to walk round and listen to the thinking and discussion. Students will ask your opinion – at this stage refuse all help. If you intervene you will kill the exercise.

3 When most of the groups have worked through their sheets give each pair of A and B teams a large piece of card to stick up on the wall in their part of the classroom. One person from each pair of teams acts as secretary, writing on the card.
   Tell all the A teams to read out their first sentence. The B teams then have to read out their corresponding sentence. Working cooperatively the two teams decide which is the right version; the secretary writes this up on the card.

4 Now ask the secretaries to read out the sentences their group consider to be correct. Allow discussion before giving your authoritative feedback. It is not until this stage of the lesson that you actually do any overt teaching.

5 Give back the homework and ask the students to mark each other's. There will be plenty more mistakes than the ones you put on the work-sheets. These may or may not get worked on. Don't worry – you can't usefully correct everything.

Note

You will find that the students do not confine themselves to working on what to you are the 'obvious' grammar points in the sentences. They often end up expressing doubts about areas of grammar that were not in question at all when you prepared the worksheets.

The worksheets given here, to illustrate the activity, were based on the mistakes made by a group of lower-intermediate students whose mother tongues were Spanish, Portuguese, German, French and Italian.

Team A worksheet   (You will need 1 per two or three students.)

My friend is 25 old.
They didn't have modern machines.
My uncle likes too much good meals.
How are you? Have you had a good day? (UK)
I like the ski.
I hope you will enjoy yourself.
How are you? Did you have a good day? (US)
My brother wants to do good exam results.
We walked slowly to Trafalgar Square.
The cupboard of the bathroom.
The first time in my life.
I have been in London 4 years ago.
People could not travel as fast as today.
They had no modern machines.

© Cambridge University Press 1984

Team B worksheet   (You will need 1 per two or three students.)

I like skiing.
They had not modern machines.
My friend is 25 years old.
My brother wants to get good exam results.
The bathroom cupboard.
I like to ski.
How are you. Do you have a good day?
My friend is 25.
We walked slowly to the Trafalgar Square.
My uncle likes good meals very much.
The first time in my live.
People could not travel so fast than today.
The cupboard in the bathroom.
I was in London 4 years ago.
I hope you will enjoy.

© Cambridge University Press 1984

II.16   Mistakes dictation

GRAMMAR:	Mistakes from homework
LEVEL:	Intermediate
TIME:	30 minutes
MATERIALS:	One copy of the correct version of all the sentences dictated for each pair of students

Preparation

Extract 14 or so sentences from the homework with representative mistakes in them. Prepare and copy a sheet on which all the sentences are corrected. Prepare a dictation in which half the sentences are corrected and half are left as they were written. Mix the right and wrong sentences together. Do not correct the homework.

In class

1 Tell the class that you are going to give them a dictation in which half the sentences are mistaken and half arc right. The sentences are from their homework. Their task is to take down the correct sentences as they hear them and to correct the sentences they know to be wrong immediately.
2 Give the dictation at a slow, steady, deliberate pace. Read the wrong sentences exactly the same as you read the correct ones.
3 Allow the class time to work over the dictations in pairs. Circulate and listen but do *not* help at this stage.
4 Give each pair the correct version you have prepared.
5 Give back the homework and ask the students to mark each other's. They may miss mistakes. This does not matter, since the main thing is to get students to really work on *some* of the mistakes.

Rationale

The dictation format is useful in this correction exercise as it forces the students to make quick right/wrong decisions and, in the dictation phase, does not leave time for a great deal of agonising. Sometimes, with some people, the quick decisions are the best ones.

II.17   Memorising structures

GRAMMAR: 'Mixed' conditionals
LEVEL: Intermediate
TIME: 15 minutes
MATERIALS: None

In class

1 Write the first two verses of the poem (by Langston Hughes) on the board:

> CROSS
>
> My old man's a white man
> And my old mother's black.
> If I ever cursed my white old man
> I take my curses back.
>
> If I ever cursed my black old mother
> And wished she were in hell,
> I'm sorry for that evil wish
> And now I wish her well.

2 Read the poem to the class and explain any unknown words.

3 Rub out a couple of words from any of the eight lines and ask a student to read the two verses as if the words were still there.
   Rub out one or two more words, and after each rubbing out ask someone to read the full eight lines. Little by little the students are 'reading' more and more words that aren't there, in other words committing the poem and the structures to memory.
   If a word is forgotten, point to the exact place where it was before – this spatial cueing often brings it back to mind.
   Finally the students should be able to 'read' the two verses from a completely blank board.

4 Now write up the last verse, *below* the space where the first two no longer are:

My old man died in a fine big house,
My ma died in a shack.

I wonder where I'm gonna die,
Being neither white nor black?

Ask someone to 'read' the whole poem.

Acknowledgement

I learnt this technique from Dorothy Brown on a teacher training seminar in Sydney, but am fairly sure that it was one of the earliest techniques used in EFL, dating back to the fifties or earlier. The technique can be used with any memorable piece of writing.

II.18   Defining birds and brothers

GRAMMAR: Indefinite article, present simple third person singular and plural
LEVEL: Post-beginner
TIME: 30 minutes in first class and 30 minutes in second class
MATERIALS: One copy of **the bird page** per pair of students

In the first class

1 Ask all the students to write seven sentences starting:
     A bird...   Birds...
   Tell them the sentences should describe characteristics common to *all*
   birds. The sentences should lead towards a definition of what a bird is. As
   they write, go round helping with words and correcting.
2 Pair the students and ask them to read each other's sentences and see how
   many of them apply to *all* birds. Give out the bird page.
3 Ask one student to come and write on the board. Each pair of students
   proposes their best definitional sentences and the 'secretary' student writes
   them on the board. If a sentence is wrong in grammar or spelling ask the
   class to correct it. Don't pre-empt them by correcting the error yourself.

In the second class

1 Ask all the female students to write seven sentences starting:
     A brother...   Brothers...
   Ask all the male students to write seven sentences starting:
     A sister...   Sisters...
   Emphasise that they are to write about siblings in general, not about their
   own particular brother or sister. Since this is hard and people tend to
   think of their own experience, the concept of *indefiniteness* is made very
   clear. This is especially useful for students from languages like Chinese,
   Turkish and Japanese where the grammar concept does not exist.
2 Ask a male and female secretary to come to the board and build up a
   series of parallel statements about sisters and brothers.

Acknowledgement

The stimulus for creating the activity came from *Your memory,* by Alan
Baddeley (Penguin, 1982).

The bird page   (You will need 1 per two students.)

Pelican

Sparrow

Chaffinch

Penguin

Ostrich

II.19 Rating wrongness

GRAMMAR: Mistakes in written work
LEVEL: Post-beginner and beyond
TIME: 30–40 minutes
MATERIALS: A sheet of mistakes drawn from the students' uncorrected homework; one sheet per two students

In class

1 Write half a dozen language mistakes in the students' mother tongue(s) up on the board. Ask them to work in pairs and grade the sentences' 'wrongness' on a scale of 0–5.
   Ask for their judgement on each sentence. Allow their criteria to emerge without imposing your own. Refuse to comment if they ask you to.

2 Give out the mistakes sheet. Ask them to rate these sentences on a 0–5 'wrongness' scale, as they have just done for the mother tongue sentences. Help pairs who are not sure what is wrong with a given sentence.

3 Pick five or six of the target language sentences and ask for the pairs' ratings. Allow discussion – don't impose your own criteria.

4 Now ask the students to read through each other's homework and correct it, adding a 0–5 rating for each error.

Acknowledgement

I learnt this exercise from John Morgan.

II.20 Right that seems wrong and wrong that seems right

GRAMMAR:	Patterns proposed by the students
LEVEL:	Post-beginner and beyond
TIME:	20 minutes
MATERIALS:	None

In class

1 Ask the students to work on their own and write down five sentences they *know* are wrong but that feel right to them.

2 Now ask them to write five sentences they know are correct English but which all the same *feel* wrong to them.

3 Ask the students to read out some of the sentences from both categories and explain why they feel the way they do. For many people this is a novel and curious linguistic awareness activity.

4 To help students deepen their awareness of feelings of grammatical rightness and wrongness in the target language, have two envelopes pinned up in your classroom, one marked:
Right that feel(s) wrong
and the other marked:
Wrong that feel(s) right
Invite students to put new sentences they find that fit either category into the appropriate envelope.
Every now and then ask the class to look at the sentences so collected and discuss them.

Note

The activity described above may seem strange to some people . Here are some sentences that students I have worked with produced:

Wrong that feel(s) right
French: I like very much the drums.
French: I go always to the cinema.
Italian: I have been to London last week.
German: I am here since last week.

Right that feel(s) wrong
French: I have a button missing.
French: I beg your pardon. (She had aurally interpreted *beg* as *big,* and so
                      the phrase seemed monstrous.)
German: I have to have a bath. (Makes nonsense if you transpose it to
                      German.)
Greek: Much money (ridiculous, as money is clearly countable)
French: I am used to living in Cambridge. (a confusing construction)

As you can see, the feelings of the students are partly based on features
where there is a clear contrast between the mother tongue and the target
language grammar – in other cases the reasons for their feelings are more
complex and intriguing. To help students become conscious of these feelings
is already a big step forward. (See Feelings about grammar, page 5.)

Acknowlegement

I learnt this exercise from Paul Davis.

Section III   Awareness activities

III.1   Times of day

GRAMMAR: Present continuous to express habitual action
LEVEL: Intermediate
TIME: 30 minutes
MATERIALS: One **time grid** per four students
One die per four students

In class

1 Give every four students a time grid and a die. Explain that the numbers
on the grid are times, starting at the bottom lefthand corner with 6.00 am.
Ask each student to find a coin to represent him or herself and to place it
on the time he or she gets up on a normal working day.

2 Ask the first player in each foursome to roll the die and move forward the
number of squares shown on the die. He or she should then tell the others
what *he or she is usually doing* at this time. Insist that the student starts
with the time, e.g.
'At 7.15 I am usually having a shower.'
If the action mentioned is very vague like 'I am starting work', the other
students in the foursome should question the speaker. Then the next
student in the foursome rolls the die, etc.

3 Once most people have reached the time when they have got to work and
started work it is best to ask the whole class to move their coins forward
to around half an hour before they finish work in the afternoon or
evening. The periods of transition seem to be the most interesting ones in
this game. An incidental aim of the game is to reach Finish.

If you are teaching secondary school students ask them to do the whole
game not about themselves but about a member of their family who works.

Grammar note

Many teachers associate the present simple with habitual action. When the
above game has been tested with native speakers of English they have always

used the present continuous. This is because (a) a time is mentioned, and (b) the speaker is visualising and describing a scene.

Acknowledgement

A similar exercise, focusing on the years in a person's life, comes in *Grammar in action*, C. Frank and M. Rinvolucri (Pergamon, 1983).

Time grid (You will need 1 per four students.)

9.30	9.45	10.00	10.15	10.30	11.00 P.M.	FINISH
9.15	9.00	8.45	8.30	8.00	7.45	
6.15	6.30	6.45	7.00	7.15	7.30	
6.00	5.45	5.30	5.15	5.00	4.45	
3.00	3.15	3.30	3.45	4.00	4.30	
2.45	2.30	2.15	2.00	1.45	1.30	
12.00	12.15	12.30	12.45	1.00	1.15	
11.45	11.30	11.15	11.00	10.45	10.30	
9.00	9.15	9.30	9.45	10.00	10.15	
8.45	8.30	8.15	8.00	7.45	7.30	
START 6.00 A.M.	6.15	6.30	6.45	7.00	7.15	

III.2   Animal habits

GRAMMAR: Present simple to express habitual action
LEVEL: Post-beginner to lower-intermediate
TIME: 30–40 minutes
MATERIALS: One **completion sheet** for each student

In class

1 Ask one student to come to the board to be the class's secretary. He or she writes down all the animal, bird or fish names the students can think of. The words should be written all over the board in disorder.

2 Ask each student to choose an animal, bird or fish that he or she can associate with. Tell them to avoid cats, dogs and other pets. Ask each student to draw his or her animal. Ask them to hold up the drawing and make the noise this animal/bird/fish makes.

3 Give out the completion sheets. The students work on the completions individually – they are writing as their animal *in the first person*.

4 Ask the students to get up and mill around. Tell them to find a *suitable* partner and read their completions to each other. It might be dangerous for a spider to pair with a hen.

5 Then ask the students to find the most *dangerous* partner they can and read their sentences again to them.

Completion sheet   (You will need 1 per student.)

I normally eat ....

At night I ....

I am afraid of ....

When I have to move I usually ....

If I want to find a mate, I ....

I don't eat ....

.... is/are afraid of me.

During the day I ....

I live in ....

My mother taught me to ....

My young usually live in/on/under ....

I normally live for ....

III.3   My view of you

GRAMMAR:	When, as soon as, just before, just after, the moment, etc., whenever + present simple
LEVEL:	Elementary
TIME:	30 minutes
MATERIALS:	One **sentence stem sheet** per student

In class

1 Give out the sentence stem sheets and ask the students to complete them as accurately as possible, working individually.

2 Put the students in threes. Don't let them show their sheets to each other. It is best to mix students who have not sat next to each other during the writing phase.
Ask students B and C to guess the first thing student A does when he or she gets up. They should guess as many times as necessary to get close to the truth. Student A then reads out the relevant sentence. Then A and C guess about B and so on.

Acknowledgement

I learnt this projective technique from Helen Green who used to work at the Marble Arch Cooperative, London.

Sentence stem sheet   (You will need 1 per student.)

The first thing I do when I get up in the morning is ....

Just before guests arrive I ....

Just before I go to sleep, ...

When something scares me, I ....

Whenever I forget something, ...

The moment I hear the phone ring, ...

As soon as I get home in the evenings, ...

The last thing I do before going off to sleep at night is ....

Just after having a bath/shower, I ....

As soon as I realise another person is angry with me, I ....

© Cambridge University Press 1984

103

III.4 Brain storming structures

GRAMMAR: Present perfect, let/make
               (in Variation 1, future, present simple, conditional)
               (in Variation 2, modals)
LEVEL: Elementary to intermediate
TIME: 30–40 minutes
MATERIALS: None

In class

1 Write up on one half of the board:
   Good experiences I have never had
   and on the other:
   Bad experiences I have never had

2 Get two students with small handwriting to stand ready at either half of
   the board. Ask the rest of the students to propose experiences of either
   sort they have *never* had:
   I haven't ...
   I have never ...
   I haven't ... yet.
   The appropriate secretary writes the sentences up. Let this brain storming
   go on until both halves of the board are completely covered with present
   perfect sentences. Maybe 20–30 sentences on each side.

3 Ask the students to pair off and choose, for them, the five best experiences
   never had and the five worst experiences never had.

4 Group the students in fours or eights depending on the size of the class, so
   the pairs can report to each other on their five best and five worst
   experiences.

Variation 1

1 On one side of the board write up:
   Things my parents made me do at ... (+ age)
   On the other:
   Things my parents let me do at ... (+ age)

2 As above, with two secretaries. In each case make sure the student giving the sentence explains the situation sufficiently for everybody to understand its significance. So, for example:
'They let me play basketball at eight'
became quite dramatic when the student explained that this meant her having to travel a long way and walk quite a distance alone in the dark in a fairly dangerous part of suburban Rome.

3 Now ask the students to write four sentences with *make* and four with *let* about their children or their possible future children.
Tell them to use the present simple or the future if they are already parents.
Tell them to use the 'second' conditional (If I had children aged ..., I'd ...) if they are early teenagers.
If they are childless young adults ask them to use the 'mixed' conditional (If I have children aged ..., / 'd...).
Ask them to mention the *age* of the child in each sentence.

4 Group them in fours to discuss their sentences.

Variation 2

Other structures that could be practised by grammar brain storming:
Things I can do
Things I ought to be able to do
Things I must do
Things I need to do

Acknowledgement

Paul Davis suggested the structures in Variations 1 and 2.

III.5   From puzzle to punishment

GRAMMAR: Past perfect, past simple passive
LEVEL: Intermediate
TIME: 45–60 minutes
MATERIALS: None

In class

1 Dictate the following:

Crime and punishment

A man got on the train and sat down in a compartment which was empty except for one lady. She took her gloves off. A few hours later the man was arrested by the police. They held him for 24 hours and were then logically forced to let him go free.

GARDEN
LOVER
30 YEARS
VANISH
JAIL

---

2 Tell the students that the two paragraphs above and the key words all come from a mystery story and they have to act the detective and question you. You only answer YES or NO.

Solution

Thirty years before, the gloved lady had been married to the man on the train. She and her lover had disappeared and left the country. Before vanishing they had cut off the two middle fingers of her left hand and buried them in the garden. The police found the fingers while investigating her disappearance and accused the man of murdering his wife and burying the rest of her elsewhere. He was jailed for 30 years for a crime he had not committed.
He did not recognise her at first on the train. When she took off her gloves he did. He killed her. The police had to release him as he had served his life sentence before committing the crime it was for.

If the students need help in their questioning give them more clues. Once they establish the root of the problem as 30 years before the moment in the train it will be natural for them to need to ask questions in the past perfect.

3 Give the students a couple of instances of times you were punished as a child, using this kind of pattern:
'I was beaten by my father for pulling the hearts out of young cabbages when I was six.'
Give real personal examples.
Ask them to write four or five sentences on the same model, describing things they got punished for as children. Ask them to include the agent and their age at the time.
Now tell them of a time you were punished for something you did not do. Ask them to write a paragraph describing when this happened to them. Finally ask them to write a few lines about a time when they were not punished for something they should have been punished for.

4 Put the students in small groups to read out their sentences and paragraphs. Encourage them to say more.

III.6　Time

GRAMMAR: Verbs that don't take the present continuous
LEVEL: Elementary to intermediate
TIME: 30–45 minutes
MATERIALS: None

In class

1　Write up on the board ten roles you play in your life, e.g.
　　teacher　　sister　　friend　　aunt　　etc.
　　Ask each student to write down ten roles he or she plays.

2　Draw a clock face with the hands pointing to the time at the moment you draw it. If the class is an international one ask round the group what time it is in their home towns right now.

3　Put up on the board the following patterns:

　A　Right now my ... is probably ... ing　　　B　He or she wants ...
　　　　　　　　　　　is possibly ... ing　　　　　　　needs ...
　　　　　　　　　　　　　　　　　　　　　　　　　　doesn't want ...

　　Ask the students to write two true sentences about each of the people they are in role to, one sentence using pattern A and one using pattern B:
　　e.g.　Right now my son is practising for a table tennis match. He wants to get back the wallet he lost on Monday in Liverpool.

4　Pair the students. Ask each student to describe the person they are in role to and then to read out their sentences about this person and explain any necessary background.

Note

If you have 30 students in the room at the beginning of the activity you end up with 300 'absent people' by the end of the session, and all of them relevant in a way 'characters' in a textbook never could be. This kind of exercise is especially useful if you happen to be teaching very small groups or if you are working in a one-to-one situation, when you desperately need to bring more people into the room.

III.7 Exchanging routines

GRAMMAR: Habitual use of the present simple
LEVEL: Elementary
TIME: 30 minutes
MATERIALS: None

In class

1 Ask each student to write down ten things he or she normally does on a
  Sunday, or the normal free day in the week in your country.
  e.g. I get up at ...
       I have ... for breakfast.
       At 10 o'clock I go to ...
       I usually sleep in till 10.

2 Pair the students. Tell them not to write anything but to try and memorise
  what they hear as accurately as possible.
  A reads routine to B.
  B reads routine to A.
  (Hamid: I usually sleep in till 10.)

3 Ask the students to move round the room and form new pairs.
  B takes A's identity and tells routine to C.
  A takes B's identity and tells routine to D.
  (I'm Hamid and I usually sleep in till 10.)

4 The students change partners again. They take on the identity of the
  person whose routine they have just heard, memorising the sentences as
  well as they can.
  C takes A's identity and tells routine to E.
  D takes B's identity and tells routine to F.
  (I'm Hamid and I usually sleep in till 10.)

5 Ask each student to go to the person whose mangled routine he or she has
  just heard. He or she assumes their identity and itemises the routine.
  E tells A his or her routine.
  F tells B his or her routine.
  (I'm Hamid and I usually sleep in till 10.)
  The person in question then reads out the original ten sentences.
  There is often a big gap between the two versions.

Acknowledgement

A group of Bavarian Volkshochschule teachers were shown the principle of role reversal in a seminar at Buchenried in November 1983 and asked to invent activities incorporating the idea. Exchanging routines was one of several exciting exercises to come out of this session.

III.8   It reminds me of ...

GRAMMAR:	It reminds me of + noun/gerund, I remember + noun/gerund,
	It makes me think of ...
LEVEL:	Elementary to lower-intermediate
TIME:	15 minutes
MATERIALS:	A very large collection of snapshots, preferably family ones, in which you yourself don't appear. If you have a class of 30, you need over 100 snapshots. The snapshots need to be loose, so they can be spread on a table

In class

1 Spread out the photographs and ask all the students to choose one that reminds them of some scene, incident or time in their lives.

2 Write up on the board:
It reminds me of ...
I remember ...
It makes me think of ...

3 Ask them to write three sentences about their picture, expressing a different memory idea in each one.

4 Group the students and ask them to show each other their pictures and read out their sentences, enlarging on their memories where possible.

Acknowledgement

An elder sister exercise to this one is to be found in *Once upon a time*, J. Morgan and M. Rinvolucri (Cambridge University Press, 1983).

III.9 Things I wish I'd known at 18

GRAMMAR: I do wish I'd ... , If only I'd ... , I wish I'd ...
LEVEL: Intermediate
TIME: 15–20 minutes
MATERIALS: None

In class

1 Write up these sentences written by the best-selling novelist, Catherine Cookson, about her teens:
I do wish I'd known more about sex – at that age I still thought that babies came through kissing.
I wish I'd known in those early days that I had the ability to draw.
Oh, if only I'd had an education at that age!

2 Ask the students to pick an age in their past and write five sentences expressing their regrets about that time:
I wish ...
If only ...
I do wish ...

3 Put the students in threes to compare regrets.

III.10 Gripes auction

GRAMMAR:	I wish + present or timeless verb
LEVEL:	Intermediate
TIME:	30–40 minutes
MATERIALS:	None

In class

1 Ask one student to come to the board. Ask the other students to express their complaints about their relatives using these patterns:

I wish X + past tense
+ would
+ could, etc.

Each time a student shouts out a sentence the person at the board writes it down. In this way you build up a pool of 20–30 complaints about relatives.

2 Pair the students and allot each pair 1,000 dollars. Tell them they are going to an auction where they can pay to get rid of their complaints. They have to work as a pair and decide which relative-directed complaints they want to spend money on getting rid of. They then have to budget how much they feel like spending on each complaint.

3 When the pairs have had enough budgeting time, start the auction. Do this in style. Abandon your teacher role and become an auctioneer:

'Ladies and Gentlemen, welcome to this complaints auction. For a little money you can get rid of really serious problems with your families. How much am I bid for complaint number 1? 50 dollars from the lady in the corner? 50 dollars, 50 dollars, any increase on 50?' etc.

Don't accept bids of less than 20 dollars. Keep up a fast rhythm. Don't auction the complaints in order. Make sure no pair spends over their 1,000 dollar allocation. Don't auction all the complaints if the pace begins to flag.

Note

I chose relatives for the example in the exercise above, but you could choose any group it feels acceptable to complain about. Working with foreign students studying in the UK, I suggested they voice their gripes about their landladies. Sentences like these came tumbling out:

I wish she'd change my sheets more often.
I wish the house wasn't so horribly cold.
If only my landlady would learn to cook.
I wish her son would stop kicking me, etc.

Acknowledgement

The idea of a values auction comes from Maury Smith's book, *A practical guide to values clarification* (University Associates, La Jolla, Cal., 1977). Application of this frame for getting rid of things you don't want is a reversal I learnt from Denny Packard.

III.11   Our lives

GRAMMAR: Past simple
LEVEL: Post-beginner
TIME: 30–40 minutes
MATERIALS: Ten small sticky labels per student
           One die per three students
           One large sheet of paper per three students

In first class

Give each student ten labels. For homework ask the students to write one
sentence on each label about important things that have happened to them
in the past. On each label they should also write the month and year in
which the thing happened, e.g.

```
September 1970
I spent my first
day at school.
```

```
July  1975
I went by plane
for the first time.
```

```
March  1978
My aunt died in
hospital – she was
34.
```

In second class

1 Ask the students to work in threes. They are to read the sentences on the
   other two people's labels and correct their grammar. You go round and
   help.

2 Give each threesome a large sheet of paper and a die. Ask the students to stick the 30 labels on the sheet of paper in chronological order.

3 Now student A in each threesome throws the die and moves to the label the number from the chronological beginning that his or her throw indicates. The person *whose label it is* speaks for one minute about the event described by the sentence on the label.

Next B throws the die and moves to the label indicated. Again the owner of the label describes the event, etc.

If a player lands on a label already discussed, he or she moves on to the next undiscussed one.

4 The activity ends when all the players have completed the course. At this point some students insist on going back to one of their undiscussed labels and speaking about it. Great.

During the speaking you go round helping with words they need and doing some discreet correction.

Acknowledgement

This is a variation of an exercise in *Grammar in action* by C. Frank and M. Rinvolucri (Pergamon, 1983).

Section IV   Grammar through drama

IV.1   The shout in the circle

GRAMMAR: Present simple, third person singular
LEVEL: Beginner to elementary
TIME: 10 minutes
MATERIALS: None

In class

1 Form the class into a standing circle and ask one student to stand in the middle of the circle. Ask the student in the centre to tell the others the daily routine of someone he or she knows well, e.g.
'My father gets up at 7.00', etc.
Every time the teller uses a verb the whole group must shout out the verb, e.g. 'GETS'. If the teller says the verb incorrectly the circle must try to chorus the right form.
When the first teller's turn has finished, get the circle to clap him or her vigorously – this raises the energy level.

2 Before he or she leaves the centre of the ring get the first teller to designate the next person to come into the centre and repeat the exercise, etc.

Note

This exercise can be used with any area of grammar you want the students to highlight for themselves. You can ask the protagonist student to describe his or her living room and have the circle shout out the spatial prepositional phrases. You can ask the protagonist student to compare him or herself to each other person in the group; the group shout out all the comparative adjectives they hear. Instead of shouting people can whisper, croak or say the verb, etc., romantically, thoughtfully or sadly.

Acknowledgement

In the original drama technique that I learnt from Mike Gradwell, the participants have to shout out the last word or two words of what the circle centre person has said, which pushes the protagonist to say some more.

IV.2   Same and different

GRAMMAR:	I'd like you to + infinitive, comparatives: as ... as ..., ... er than ..., more ... than ..., less ... than ..., the same as ..., different from ..., similar to ..., we both ...
LEVEL:	Elementary to intermediate
TIME:	25 minutes
MATERIALS:	None

In class

1 Get the whole class sitting in a big circle. You should also be in the circle, sitting with an empty chair beside you. Start the game off like this:
'Patricia, I'd like you to sit next to me because you're younger than me.'
The student crosses the circle and sits down next to you, leaving an empty chair the other side of the circle. One of the students either side of the empty chair invites someone to sit next to them, adding a reason couched in the comparative form.

2 You may want to stop the game at some point and do some blackboard work on the different patterns they find they need to use.
You may also want to change the rules of the game so that someone opposite the empty chair says to someone next to it:
'I'd like to sit next to you because ...'

Note

Another use of this exercise as an ice-breaker and name learning device is put forward in *Grammar in action* by C. Frank and M. Rinvolucri (Pergamon, 1983).

IV.3 From word to story

GRAMMAR:	I want you to, past simple
LEVEL:	Post-beginner
TIME:	20–30 minutes
MATERIALS:	A full set of word cards per ten students
	One pin per student

Preparation

Using a thick marker pen prepare word cards for the following story. These cards will be pinned to the students' clothing. If you have 30 in your class, you will need three sets of word cards.

Store your word cards for each of the six sentences in the story in separate envelopes.

Here is the story:

1 [A WOMAN] [VERY] [MUCH] [WANTED] [TO] [HAVE] [A] [BABY] [BUT SHE] [COULDN'T.]

2 [SHE] [WENT] [TO SEE] [ALL] [THE DOCTORS] [SHE] [COULD] [FIND –] [NO] [GOOD.]

3 [SHE] [WENT] [TO] [A HYPNOTIST] [WHO] [SAID] ['I WANT] [YOU] [TO] [RELAX.']

4 ['I DON'T] [WANT] [YOU] [TO] [WORRY. I WANT] [YOU] [TO] [GO] [TO] [SLEEP.']

5 ['I WANT] [YOU] [TO] [BECOME] [A] [HEN] [AND] [LAY] [AN] [EGG.']

6 [SHE] [LAID] [AN] [EGG!] [LATER] [ON] [SHE] [HAD] [A] [BABY.]

In class

1 Divide your class into standing circles of ten. Give each student in the circle a pin and a word card from the first sentence. Ask the students to pin the word cards to their fronts.

119

2 Ask the students to re-arrange themselves in their circles until they have put together a sentence that makes sense.

3 As soon as a circle has got a correct sentence, ask them to lay it out in order on a table or desk top near them. Give them the second sentence, and so on.

Note

You may well not have a class of 10 or 20 or 30. When you put the words on to cards you can alter the number of words you put on each card and so make the sentences fit your particular class size.

Alternatively, you can, supposing you have 27 people in your class, organise them into three circles of nine, and have the tenth card in each circle on the floor where everybody can see it.

This technique can be used with any structure–loaded story – it is an excellent way of introducing a structure for the first time.

Acknowledgement

I first learnt the idea of people as words in a sentence in an *All's well* (by Sagot et al, Didier, 1974) class in the Adult Migrant Education Service centre in Bankstown, Sydney, Australia.

IV.4   Back-writing

GRAMMAR: Irregular plurals
LEVEL: Intermediate
TIME: 10 minutes
MATERIALS: Cards with irregular singulars and plurals on them

In class

1   Have the students stand up and take a partner. Tell them to imagine that their partner's back is one of those white boards that someone has written on with an indelible pen. They must try and rub it clean. A rubs B's back. Ask them to change round. B rubs A's back.

2   Ask A to write any irregular plurals he or she can remember on B's back. B then writes the singular form on A's back.
   e.g. A writes OXEN
        B writes OX
   Tell the students to write slowly and to write in capitals (with their fingers).

3   Start handing students cards with nouns on, some in the plural, some in the singular. In this way you feed new material into the exercise and the back-writing becomes a learning as well as a revision process.
   The cards could have words like these on them:

LOAF	GENII	GENIUSES
SCARF	TEETH	SCARVES
MANSERVANT	HYPOTHESIS	FORMULA
SCARFS	LICE	BROTHERS
LOUSE	MEMORANDUM	MEMORANDA
BROTHER	MENSERVANTS	BRETHREN
FORMULAS	LOAVES	ANALYSES
TROUT	FISH	CORPUSES
LEBANESE	CORPUS	HYPOTHESES
GENIUS	FORMULAE	TROUT
CORPORA	MEMORANDUMS	TOOTH
ANALYSIS	FISH	

4 Finish the exercise by asking a student to come to the board and, with the help of the others, list all the singulars and plurals that have been worked on round the room.

Grammar note

English is in a state of flux at the moment over the plurals of many words of Latin and Greek origin. Many nouns that used to take Latin-sounding plurals, e.g. corpus – corpora are now being regularised and given English plurals, e.g. corpus – corpuses. For a full analysis of this area, see Quirk's *A grammar of contemporary English* (Longman, 1972).
Back-writing is useful for vocabulary revision and for work on any language elements that match each other, e.g.
infinitive – past participle
names of countries – names of languages
and for work on collocation, e.g.
one student back-writes SEA and the other replies with DEEP BLUE.

Acknowledgement

I learnt back-writing from colleagues in France who had learnt the technique in seminars run by Eve Ogonowski.

IV.5 Experiences

GRAMMAR: Present perfect interrogative, *they* used as unisex singular pronoun
LEVEL: Elementary
TIME: 15 minutes
MATERIALS: None

In class

1 Ask one person to go out of the room.

2 The group designates another student as 'it'.

3 The person outside comes back into the classroom and has to ask present perfect questions about the designated person's experiences. The class may answer only YES or NO. The outsider has to guess who 'it' is from the answers. This sort of question will be used:
Have they ever been to ... ?
Have they been in this class since September?

Note

For the game to work efficiently people need to know each other fairly well. This game structure can be adapted to practising other verb structures, e.g. past simple
    future
    'second' conditional, etc.

V.1   Verb search

GRAMMAR: Irregular verbs
LEVEL: Post-beginner
TIME: 10–20 minutes
MATERIALS: One **verb search sheet** per two students

In class

1 Give each pair a verb search sheet. Tell the students there are a large
   number of irregular verbs buried in the sheet – they will find infinitives,
   pasts and past participles. Their task is to unearth as many verb parts as
   they can as fast as they can. Every time they unearth a verb part they are
   to jot it down and also jot down the other two parts and its meaning in
   their own language.
   Warn them they may find verb parts going horizontally, vertically, and
   diagonally, as well as backwards.

2 After about 5 minutes' search ask the students to change pairs. Do this a
   couple of times during the exercise.
   While this is going on go round and check that they are trying to jot down
   the other parts of the verb – help especially with pronunciation – get them
   to say the parts of each verb they have written down. You will have to go
   fast to get round the whole class – your speed will help to heighten their
   sense of urgency in the search.

Note

The search idea can be used for getting students to focus on different sets of
words which they have to commit to memory,
e.g. Irregular comparatives and superlatives and those that require a spelling
      change like *happy/happier*
      Verbs that only take the infinitive
      Verbs that only take the gerund

If you are teaching Spanish you can use this technique for focusing on root
changing verbs, e.g. *rogar/ruego*, etc.

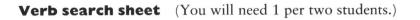

Verb search sheet   (You will need 1 per two students.)

```
K E P T Q D E R T D R E A M T
Y U I U O P R A S D F G H E W
H K L C Z X C I V B M E E T I
I D A B G E I D V O R H V Y S
D A E O R R P K T E W X O W L
D M A N B V E C X Z N A S D E
E A T U F E T W Q W E R T U P
N Y E O P P A S D F S P E N T
Z O K H S F U O P W A P H E Y
M N V B W C X G H J B U Y O W
C A E T O U S G K G O T A T F
T A G O N E Y T N O U G A T T
W H T G R S T H O U G H T O F
T E M C B O T I Q E H E Y O N
Z M X C H V N N O U T N E J K
H I H R H A N K S O U D T O T
O I R I V U S W I T P F Z K I
Q W D E D R R Y P A E G V E L
E M E Y T E A T F D F I N D A
C O T T Y A G I E O K I M P U
J O Z A T U N E U X U P W I E
C A T A L U T N P D O N O R T
F F A L L O D T U I Q M U N D
W E R T L A S Y N E M A N U T
F O F A L L E N Y W I N D L Y
```

Verb search sheet: Teacher's master

```
K E P T     D           D R E A M T
                R           M E E T   E
H               I                       S
I           G           V                 L
D           R     K     E                 E
D     A     E           N                 P
E A   T     E     W           S P E N T   T
N     E     P                 P
                              U
            W           B     Y
C           O     G     O     T
  A         N     T H O U G H T         J
    T           T H I N K     G         O
      C         H I             T       K
H   H   H     U   N                     E
  I   I   D   R   K                     D
    D   D   E   T           F I N D
                      O
                U       W
              N       O
  F A L L   D         U
                       N
  F A L L E N   W I N D
```

V.2 Translation 'Call my bluff'

GRAMMAR: Mixed structures
LEVEL: Intermediate
TIME: 15–30 minutes
MATERIALS: One **translation sheet** per two students

This frame can only be used for classes where the students all share the same mother tongue. The example given here is for French speakers learning English.

In class

1 Pair the students and give each pair a translation sheet. Tell the students that they have to decide which of the translations into English are correct. Sometimes one translation is right, sometimes more than one. Sometimes none of the translations are right – when this is the case they are to write in the correct translation themselves.

2 Ask the students to change pairs two or three times during the course of the exercise.
Go round observing but *do not help* the students, even if they ask you. In this exercise they are checking their own criteria about the grammar of the two languages.

3 Ask a student to write up on the board the six correct translations he or she has decided on. Allow discussion of contentious points – only come in yourself in the last resort. What they teach themselves will stick much longer than what you dictate to them.

Translation sheet   (You will need 1 per two students.)

1 *J'y suis allé la semaine dernière.*
   a) I am gone there last week.
   b) I am last week gone there.
   c) I went there last week.

2 *J'ai toujours voulu la voir.*
   a) I wanted always to see her.
   b) I always wanted to see her.
   c) I have always been wanting to see her.
   d) I've always wanted to have it.

3 *Est-ce qu'il est toujours chez vous?*
   a) He is still at you?
   b) Is he always with you?
   c) Is he with you yet?
   d) Is he still at your house?
   e) Is he still with you ?

4 *Qu'est-ce-que vous avez fait hier soir?*
   a) What were you doing yesterday evening?
   b) What have you done yesterday evening?
   c) What did you yesterday evening?
   d) Yesterday evening, what've you done?

5 *On est là depuis samedi soir.*
   a) We have been tired since Saturday evening.
   b) One has been here since last Saturday evening.
   c) We've been here since last Saturday evening.
   d) We are here since Saturday evening.

6 *Elle habite Grenoble depuis au moins 5 ans.*
   a) She inhabits Grenoble for at least 5 years.
   b) She's lived in Grenoble at least 5 years.
   c) She lives Grenoble since at least 5 years.
   d) She has lived in Grenoble for at less 5 years.
   e) She has been living in Grenoble for at least 5 years.

V.3   Verbs to story

GRAMMAR:	Regular and irregular past simple
LEVEL:	Post-beginner
TIME:	30–40 minutes
MATERIALS:	None

In class

1 Write these words up on the board or dictate them:

PUT	RAN	SAW
PUT ON	WENT IN	SAID
WENT OUT	ATE UP	JUMPED OUT
WALKED	PUT ON	ATE UP
STOPPED	LAY DOWN	HEARD
PICKED	CAME	CAME IN
SAW	KNOCKED	KILLED
ASKED	SAID	LIVED
ANSWERED	WENT IN	

2 Check the students understand all the verbs – explain unknown ones.

3 Put the students in pairs. Tell them all the verbs come from a very well
known children's story. Ask them to work together to decide which story
it is and to tell the story to each other in English.
Different students may decide on different stories – this is fine, allow
stories other than Little Red Riding Hood, from which the verbs were
taken. Go round helping, especially with the pronunciation of the past
tenses.

4 Get the students to change partners and to tell the story as they have
re-constructed it to a new partner. Before this stage rub the words off the
board and get them to turn their verb lists over (if they have them) so that
the telling is more flowing and natural, even if things get left out.

Note

This technique works much better with stories that are likely to be
well-known to the group than with completely unknown stories.

Acknowledgement

I learnt this technique from Christine Frank who tells me she heard it from Pat McEldowney.

V.4   We are furniture

GRAMMAR: Past and present simple passive, spatial prepositions
LEVEL: Intermediate
TIME: 30–40 minutes
MATERIALS: Furniture cards

The furniture cards provided here are designed for groups of 14 (28,42) students. If you have 14 students you will need one card for each of them. If you have 28 students you will need two sets of cards, if you have 42, three sets of cards.

For different class sizes you will have to add or take away cards. Always add if you can, as taking away cards reduces the connectedness of the remaining cards in the set.

In class

1 Pick out any difficult vocabulary from the cards and pre-teach it. Find new contexts – do *not* use the contexts given on the cards.

2 If you have a class of 26–30 divide them into two groups. Give one set of cards to one group and one set to the other group. Each student should have a card. You may have to write an extra card or two for your particular class size.

3 Tell the students to *learn by heart* the information on their cards. Give them time to do this. Check that they have by going up to a student, taking away his or her card and getting him or her to whisper the contents of the card into your ear.

4 When the students have memorised the information, remove the cards. By now some students will be bored and others will be mystified. Tell the two groups, who are to work separately in two parts of the room:

   'You are 14 parts of a room or pieces of furniture in this room. I want you to get up and talk to each other, *using only the information on your cards.* Your aim will be to organise yourselves into the room, with all the furniture in the right place.'

   Before they start, quickly draw the following plan of the room:

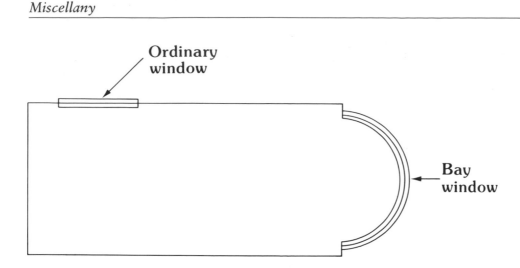

5 The students now mill around and exchange information – check that they are only using the information from their cards. Let them get on with the job of positioning themselves. The confusion this entails will force plenty of practice of spatial prepositions.

6 When everybody is in position get them to say the contents of their card.

Acknowledgement

I learnt this exercise type from Lou Spaventa. The exercise he used was called 'Cocktail Party' and the student cards had on them family relationships, not spatial relationships. The students discovered that they were all members of one family.

Furniture cards (1)   (You will need 1 set per fourteen students.)

I'm a grand piano and I stand in the bay window.
I was built in 1850.
I was last tuned 6 months ago.
I don't like my modern piano stool.

I know the piano doesn't like me.
I was given to the family by a friend.
I am made of pine wood.

I am full of music scores.
I stand with my back to the wall, at one end of the bay window.
I don't like pine wood stools.

I was re-painted last year.
I am the big bay window at the end of the room.
At the opposite end of the room I can see something big, made of mahogany.

I was built at the same time as the piano.
I am a big bookcase of dark wood.
Opposite me is the bay window – to my right is the china cabinet.

I am full of china.
Opposite me is the ordinary window.
To my right is the door.

I am made of wood and glass.
To my left is the china cabinet.
Opposite me is a writing desk.
I swing on my hinges.

I am an elegant writing desk.
There is a pile of dust between me and the bookcase.
There is a vulgar ping-pong table between me and the music cupboard.

Furniture cards (2)

I am a little pile of dust.
I am between the desk and the bookcase.
I was forgotten here three months ago.
I am very sad.

I can be folded up and put away easily.
I am used a lot by the children.
I stand opposite the door and between the ordinary window and the music cupboard.

I am the sofa.
I have my back to the ping-pong table.
I face the mantelpiece.

I lie on the floor between the sofa and the mantelpiece.
I was made in Iran 40 years ago.
I was last shaken out 2 weeks ago.

I am not much used.
I am near the Persian carpet.
I am an armchair and I have my back to the bay window.
I was inherited from a great aunt, just like the sofa.

I am the mantelpiece.
I was installed at the same time as the bay window, which is on my right. I am opposite the ordinary window.
The glass and wood door is to my left.

V.5   Memory tricks

GRAMMAR: Past simple
LEVEL: Lower-intermediate
TIME: 30 minutes
MATERIALS: **Story** (for your use only)

In class

1 Send four of your better students out of the room with an exercise they
   can do outside in about 15 minutes.

2 Dictate a story to the others. The story should be fairly easy for the
   language level of the class, e.g. at lower-intermediate level:

Story

The time: about 200 years ago in Paris. The streets were full of people.
They were angry. They broke shop windows, they burned down
houses, they were rioting.
    A colonel came to clear a square. His soldiers raised their guns.
There was silence.
    The colonel stood on a wall.
    'Ladies and Gentlemen,' he shouted, 'I have orders to fire on the
mob. I can see only good, honest people. I want all the good, honest
people to leave the square, because I want to fire on the mob!'
    Two minutes later the square was empty.

---

3 Make sure they understand all the words in the story.

4 Explain that one student in the group is to prepare to read the story aloud
   to one of the four who have gone out. Then this student will be allowed to
   ask two questions about the story.
   The second 'outside' student will be brought back in, and the first one will
   tell the story he or she heard to the second one. During this telling the
   group are to note down how the story gets changed using these three
   categories:

Things added   *Things left out*   *Things changed*

⟫→

5 'Outside' student A comes back in. A group member reads him or her the story *twice*. He or she has the right to ask two questions about the story. 'Outside' student B comes back in and A tells the story as he or she understands it. B can ask A two questions. C is brought in and B tells the story. C can ask two questions. D comes in and C tells the story to him or her. D can ask two questions. D then tells his or her by now much modified story to the group. Finally someone in the group reads out the original story. Meanwhile the people in the group have been taking notes.

6 Put the three categories up on the board and ask people to volunteer what was added, left out or completely changed/distorted.

Acknowledgement

I learnt this technique from Patty Farrands and Helen Green in the course of a seminar at Marble Arch Cooperative, London. I believe the idea originated with Bartlett's memory experiments in Cambridge in the 1930s.

V.6   Exchanging socks

GRAMMAR: So as to, to, in order to, although, because, as a
LEVEL: Intermediate
TIME: 20 minutes
MATERIALS: None

In class

1 Tell your students how you were sitting in a bus/tube/train and there were two young men sitting opposite you. One of them was wearing white socks and another was wearing black socks. These two suddenly exchanged one of their socks. They got off the train wearing a black sock and a white sock each.

2 Tell the students to write sentences giving as many different reasons as they can for this odd behaviour using these words/phrases:
The men exchanged socks so as to ...
                                   to ...
                                   in order to ...
                                   although ...
                                   because ...
                                   as a ...

3 When most students have written between eight and 12 different reasons, ask them to get together in fours and decide on the three best hypotheses the group has come up with.

4 Ask each foursome to write its three best sentences on the board.

Bibliography

Baddeley, Alan. *Your memory*. Penguin, 1982

Carrier, Mike. *Take 5*. Harrap, 1981

Dixey, James and Rinvolucri, Mario. *Get up and do it*. Longman, 1978

Dixey, James and Rinvolucri, Mario. *Well said*. Pilgrims Publications, 1977

Frank, C. Rinvolucri, M. and Berer, M. *Challenge to think*. Oxford University Press, 1982

Frank, Christine and Rinvolucri, Mario. *Grammar in action*. Pergamon, 1983

Gattegno, Caleb. *1000 sentences*. Educational Solutions, New York, 1974

Gattegno, Caleb. *Common sense in language teaching*. Educational Solutions, New York, 1976

Lavery, Mike et al. *Active viewing plus*. Modern English Publications, 1984

Melville et al. *Towards the creative teaching of English*. Heinemann, 1980

Morgan, John and Rinvolucri, Mario. *Learning English words*. Oxford University Press, 1986

Morgan, John and Rinvolucri, Mario. *Once upon a time*. Cambridge University Press, 1983

Morgan, John and Rinvolucri, Mario. *The Q book*. Pilgrims Publications, 1984

Moskowitz, Gertrude. *Caring and sharing in the foreign language class*. Newbury House, 1978

Oulipo. *La litterature potentielle*. Gallimard, 1973

Quirk, R. et al. *A grammar of contemporary English*. Longman, 1972

Sagot et al. *All's well*. Didier, 1974

Scher, Anna and Verrall, C. *100+ ideas for drama*. Heinemann, 1975

Sion, Chris, ed. *Recipe book for tired teachers*. Pilgrims Publications, 1980, Addison Wesley, 1984

Smith, Maury. *A practical guide to values clarification*. University Associates, La Jolla, Cal., 1977

Grammar Games

Cognitive, affective and drama activities for EFL students

Mario Rinvolucri

CAMBRIDGE
UNIVERSITY PRESS

CAMBRIDGE UNIVERSITY PRESS
Cambridge, New York, Melbourne, Madrid, Cape Town, Singapore, São Paulo

Cambridge University Press
The Edinburgh Building, Cambridge CB2 2RU, UK

www.cambridge.org
Information on this title: www.cambridge.org/9780521277730

First published 1984
27th printing 2006

Printed in the United Kingdom at the University Press, Cambridge

Library of Congress catalogue card number: 84–7738

British Library Cataloguing in Publication data
Rinvolucri, Mario
Grammar games.
1. English language – Study and teaching
– Foreign speakers 2. Educational games
I. Title
428.2'4'078   PE1128.A2

ISBN-13 978-0-521-27773-0 paperback
ISBN-10 0-521-27773-6 paperback